CW01666857

The Global Contemporary Art World

The Global Contemporary Art World

Jonathan Harris
Birmingham City University

WILEY Blackwell

This edition first published 2017
© 2017 John Wiley & Sons, Inc.

All rights reserved. No part of this publication may be reproduced, stored in a retrieval system, or transmitted, in any form or by any means, electronic, mechanical, photocopying, recording or otherwise, except as permitted by law. Advice on how to obtain permission to reuse material from this title is available at http://www.wiley.com/go/permissions.

The right of Jonathan Harris to be identified as the author of this work has been asserted in accordance with law.

Registered Office(s)
John Wiley & Sons, Inc., 111 River Street, Hoboken, NJ 07030, USA

Editorial Office
9600 Garsington Road, Oxford, OX4 2DQ, UK

For details of our global editorial offices, customer services, and more information about Wiley products visit us at www.wiley.com.

Wiley also publishes its books in a variety of electronic formats and by print-on-demand. Some content that appears in standard print versions of this book may not be available in other formats.

Limit of Liability/Disclaimer of Warranty
While the publisher and authors have used their best efforts in preparing this work, they make no representations or warranties with respect to the accuracy or completeness of the contents of this work and specifically disclaim all warranties, including without limitation any implied warranties of merchantability or fitness for a particular purpose. No warranty may be created or extended by sales representatives, written sales materials or promotional statements for this work.
The fact that an organization, website, or product is referred to in this work as a citation and/or potential source of further information does not mean that the publisher and authors endorse the information or services the organization, website, or product may provide or recommendations it may make. This work is sold with the understanding that the publisher is not engaged in rendering professional services. The advice and strategies contained herein may not be suitable for your situation. You should consult with a specialist where appropriate. Further, readers should be aware that websites listed in this work may have changed or disappeared between when this work was written and when it is read. Neither the publisher nor authors shall be liable for any loss of profit or any other commercial damages, including but not limited to special, incidental, consequential, or other damages.

Library of Congress Cataloging-in-Publication Data

Name: Harris, Jonathan (Jonathan P.), author.
Title: The global contemporary art world / Jonathan Harris, Birmingham City University.
Description: First edition. | Hoboken: Wiley, 2017. | Includes bibliographical references and index. |
Identifiers: LCCN 2017013717 (print) | LCCN 2017016069 (ebook) | ISBN 9781118339091 (pdf) | ISBN 9781118339084 (epub) | ISBN 9781118288917 (cloth) | ISBN 9781118338513 (pbk.)
Subjects: LCSH: Art–Economic aspects–Asia–21st century. | Art and society–Asia–History–21st century.
Classification: LCC N8600 (ebook) | LCC N8600 .H376 2017 (print) | DDC 701/.03–dc23
LC record available at https://lccn.loc.gov/2017013717

Cover Design: Wiley
Cover Image: Bashir Makhoul: *Enter Ghost, Exit Ghost* (detail; cardboard boxes, as part of installation, Yang Gallery, Beijing, 2011–12)

Set in 10/12pt Warnock by SPi Global, Pondicherry, India
Printed and bound in Malaysia by Vivar Printing Sdn Bhd

10 9 8 7 6 5 4 3 2 1

Contents

About the Author

Jonathan Harris is Head of Birmingham School of Art at Birmingham City University, UK. He is the author and editor of twenty books on modern and contemporary art, including *The New Art History: A Critical Introduction* (2001), *Globalization and Contemporary Art* (Wiley-Blackwell 2011) and *The Utopian Globalists: Artists of Worldwide Revolution*, 2013 (Wiley-Blackwell). He has taught and lectured in universities, museums and galleries throughout the world for more than thirty years.

Introduction: "Global," "Contemporary," "Art," "World"

Entering the Maze

The photograph on this book's cover illustrates an artwork made by Bashir Makhoul, a Palestinian artist based in England, exhibited at the Yang Gallery in Beijing's "798" art district in the People's Republic of China in 2012. One of the two parts of this installation work called *Enter Ghost, Exit Ghost* was made from large-scale lenticular photographic panels showing images of "old" and "new" Jerusalem joined together into a maze-like structure of paths erected in the gallery's converted factory space. Lenticular images, when seen from different angles, project alternative views apparently simultaneously present on a single surface. (This illusionistic device has been used in postcard design since the late nineteenth century.) "Lenticular" means both "shaped like a lentil" and "of the lens of the eye." In this manner, a structure of 2.4-meter-high photographic "walls" depicting Jerusalem during and after British Mandate rule (subsequently occupied by Israel since 1967) confronted viewers as they made their way through the maze. The second part of the work consisted of a cardboard box "city," built up almost to the ceiling of the gallery.

Enter Ghost, Exit Ghost, covering a floor space of more than 400 square meters, invited visitors to find and follow the right path through the maze to what looked like a makeshift model of a refugee camp. This was of the kind that millions have had to live in since the creation of the State of Israel in 1948, following what its protagonists called the "War of Independence" that forcibly displaced the Palestinian population and whose calamitous implications for local, regional and world history continue down to the present day.[1]

It would be hard to find a more appropriate example of an artwork that encapsulates my motivations and objectives in writing this book—the interconnected primary questions and concerns of which require that equal stress is placed on all the nouns and adjectives in its title: *The Global Contemporary Art World.* The last two decades have seen an extraordinary rise in the public visibility of contemporary art and of what have come to be

The Global Contemporary Art World, First Edition. Jonathan Harris.
© 2017 John Wiley & Sons, Inc. Published 2017 by John Wiley & Sons, Inc.

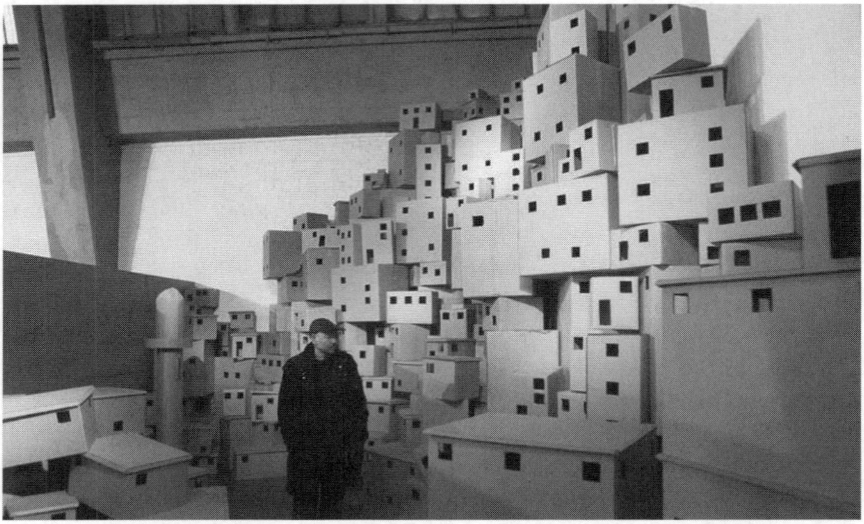

Figure 1 Bashir Makhoul *Enter Ghost, Exit Ghost* (2012, mixed media installation; detail). *Source:* © Bashir Makhoul.

recognized as its characteristic forms, museum buildings and producers. These first two categories remain relatively straightforward to exemplify. The installation form—instanced here by *Enter Ghost, Exit Ghost*—is typically made from combined or "mixed materials" and constructed on a site either inside an already existing building (though this is by no means always an art gallery) or outside, in a wide range of settings. The Yang Gallery, which opened in 2010, is an example of a recent contemporary art exhibition space hewn from a derelict industrial building. This renovation trend developed in the 1990s and so far has been most spectacularly embodied in Tate Modern, which opened in London in 2000.[2]

The category of producer, however, presents more complexity. The figure of the artist, understood either as the actual lone physical maker or at least director of a work's fabrication, certainly remains at the apex of the art world. Both the ideal of the artist and actual artists are essential to contemporary narratives of art's authenticity and quality, as well as to calculations of its financial value. Think here, for example, of the global status of Jeff Koons and Damien Hirst. But other kinds of producers in the art world have risen to almost equal public significance in the last two decades. For instance, in 2014 it was Sir Nicholas Serota, Director of the Tate galleries in London—not an artist—who was named the most influential player in the global contemporary art world by US-based *Art Review* magazine in its annual "Power 100 List."[3] Serota's greatest achievement was the opening of Tate Modern in a converted electricity power station on the south bank of the Thames in Southwark. The gallery's cavernous

"Turbine Hall" space then became the venue for the annual creation of spectacular large-scale installation works co-conceived and commissioned by Tate and supported financially by the multinational Unilever Corporation.[4]

In addition, then, to the indispensable agency of artists, the vitality and expansion of the contemporary art world has come to depend upon such productive and creative intervention by influential museum and gallery directors. These "facilitating agents" are also sometimes high-profile collectors of contemporary art, although they do not themselves necessarily own the works they purchase or the institutional spaces in which they exhibit them. This is true of others, however, such as the former advertising tycoon Charles Saatchi, who was able to use his own considerable financial wealth to buy artworks to show in his own gallery in central London. Serota, in contrast, has bought artworks with Tate's public money for its public art collections maintained by, and on behalf of, the British nation. However, a fundamental blurring of such distinctions between the spheres of state (meaning "publicly owned") and private (meaning commercial but also sometimes "non-profit") has emphatically shaped the development of the global contemporary art world and visual arts funding—along with all other kinds of "public provision"—in Western societies, especially since the 1980s.This was the decade when capitalism in the democratic countries entered its globalizing "neoliberal" era under two of its chief political representatives, President Ronald Reagan in the USA and Prime Minister Margaret Thatcher in the United Kingdom.[5]

The following chapters illustrate how the global contemporary art world is not separate from this wider world. In fact, its character has been formed through the particular ways—economically, socially, politically—in which the world has become globalized. This "world order" as a whole is steered now through immensely powerful, though shifting, alliances of state and private corporate organizations, forces and resources. "Steered," I stress, rather than "planned" and "governed." Our globalized world certainly still includes panoplies of national and international state governance agencies (such as the United Nations and the European Union) based on moral objectives and legal principles derived, in large part, from formal commitments to the ideals of democracy and human rights. But, especially since the 1990s, the most globally powerful states, acting in concert with large commercial and technology corporations, have increasingly operated transnationally, and sometimes with imperious disregard for the known wishes or interests of their own peoples and in opposition to democratically elected governments around the world.[6]

This global socioeconomic and political system is one wherein autonomous might, as much if not more than public mandate, now compete in the building and ruination of whole regions, societies, states, markets, cultures and communities. This is true throughout the world, but perhaps most evidently, as the global media shows daily, in the Middle East and Asia. Partly in response to this inveterate developmental turmoil militantly theocratic "proto-state" Islamic organizations proclaiming their "Jihadism" (Holy War) emerged in these and other regions to challenge the many embattled, corrupt or "failed states" and their Western backers in the new world order. The "War on Terror," declared by President George W. Bush following the September 11, 2001, bombings, US-led Western punitive military retaliation in Afghanistan in 2002, and the invasion and occupation of Iraq in 2003–2004 are the most salient recent events in this history. A full explanation, however, of these disasters constituting our own era—one as much, surely, of global disorder as order—requires analysis tracked back at least to the mid-twentieth century Cold War between the US and Soviet superpowers, a confrontation played out over a half-century in violent regional conflicts around the world.[7]

If our global world order/disorder does constitute a "system"—that is, a functioning totality that is organizing and productive, though manifestly also chaotic and destructive, as the 2008 Global Financial Crisis demonstrated—then the contemporary art world comprises a part of this wider world. This is my central contention and I set out to demonstrate here the contemporary art world's own systemic yet volatile character, understood as a sector of the globalized world as a whole. But this global art world also has its own distinct and relatively autonomous connecting parts, functions, agents and products. Each chapter here will examine some of these elements and their interrelations. These include, as I've noted, its typical art forms and exhibiting institutions, along with a wider cast of significant "producers" besides its artists—agents who, individually and collectively, are active and necessary to the art world's making and remaking.[8] The purpose of my book is to elucidate through a series of complementary case studies what I shall argue are the key facets in the working of the global contemporary art world.

Focus in these case studies will be on five Asian centers, three of which are nation-states. I shall explain why and how in the next few pages. But it is their imbrication and significance within a globalized system as part of the global contemporary art world that concerns me. The rise of Asia economically, within neoliberal global capitalism, has certainly been a condition of the emergence of these centers as places where contemporary art, and local contemporary art worlds, have flourished. But definitions of Asia are complex and contested, and the specificities of these five locations—whatever features they may have in common—must be recognized. The chapters concern territories in the region of "greater Asia": Hong Kong, South Korea, India, the People's Republic of China (PRC) and the State of Palestine.[9] These places, vastly different from each other in many ways but with a shared postcolonial past, have all become incorporated quite rapidly and recently—in differing ways and to differing degrees—into the global contemporary art world dominated by Western (predominantly Western European and North American) institutions, networks and discourses historically created for art's production, sale, collection, curation, exhibition and validation.

The intertwined concepts of "contemporary" and "contemporary art" are particularly significant within this account. They will feature in terms of understanding, firstly, how the global world order/disorder operates now in any and all spheres of human activity, and, secondly, in differentiating art made since the 1990s (usually called "contemporary art") from the preceding era of modern art within which the key Western art museums and galleries, such as the Museum of Modern Art and the Solomon R. Guggenheim Museum, both in New York, were created.[10] It will become clear that the terms "historical art," "modern art" and "contemporary art" all pull into their orbits of habitual use critically important related senses of local, national, regional and global developments that have helped to shape the present world. It should also be or become obvious that these sets of terms name evaluative and ideologically freighted ideas that are both indispensable to the following analyses and yet in some ways also impede insightful movement beyond the conceptual frameworks of received disciplinary practice in art-historical and theoretical discourse. In this sense the global art world profoundly challenges existing explanatory paradigms formed in the era of the rise of nation-states in the late 19th and early 20th centuries.[11]

The Global Contemporary Art World is the final book in my trilogy exploring the character, history and meaning of art made in the 20th and 21st centuries' "core" or "developed" Western countries, principally Western Europe and North America, and in the "peripheral" or "emergent" regions of greater Asia, as well as in South America and Africa (sometimes called the "global South"). It is my view that there is no decisive single point—historically, societally or aesthetically—at which "modern art" became or gave way to "contemporary art." The distinction remains, however factual and firm it may seem, the product and purpose of contrasting perceptions, emphases and interests. Critics and theorists have variously asserted, for example, that contemporary art "began" after 1945, or after 1960, or after 1989, in arguments linking these chosen points of genesis to a wide range of sociocultural conditions, events and historical processes. All these accounts have both strengths and weaknesses.[12] The second book in my series, *The Utopian Globalists: Artists of Worldwide Revolution, 1919–2009* (2013), traced the development of installation art made in the recent past—since 2000, and therefore "contemporary" according to virtually all definitions—back to the 1917 Russian Revolution and the huge tower that the Bolshevik artist Vladimir Tatlin planned to erect to commemorate it, known as the *Monument to the Third International.* Though never built, Tatlin's 1919 scale model in iron and glass became an inspiration for a considerable lineage of artists whose diverse artworks carried Tatlin's utopian-Left modernist radicalism down to the present day.

The Utopian Globalists concluded with a discussion of the large installations commissioned for Tate Modern's Turbine Hall, works paid for in part with funding from the Unilever Corporation. The book closed with a skeptical questioning of the radicalism possible under such corporate-patronal circumstances—for several of the artists who received these commissions had drawn, directly or indirectly, on Tatlin's political and aesthetic avant-garde legacy. *The Utopian Globalists* offers an historical (or "diachronic") context for *The Global Contemporary Art World.* My chief motivation in writing the earlier book had been to provide such an interpretative grounding, robust though certainly to a degree speculative, for those trying to understand the sometimes mystifying forms of contemporary art—part "sculpture," part "architecture," as many installations are—made since the 1990s.[13] My argument remains that in art and broad sociocultural terms the contemporary, and the contemporary in art, necessarily contains the historical, and that contemporary art itself emerged historically—from and out of the historical process—however profoundly its forms may appear alien to the historical and modern pasts of art, and even to disown or reject them.[14]

Books are always selective and can only offer partial perspectives. In studies dealing with all aspects of "the global" in contemporary art, acknowledgement of this necessity is particularly required. No single author could "master" this terrain of inquiry, and these two metaphors indicate the geopolitical as well as intellectual stakes in attempting to make sense of culture and social change in an increasingly integrated but increasingly unequal world. The first text in my trilogy recognized this reality by offering a substantial collection of mostly newly commissioned essays on contemporary art written by thirty different authors. Within the main and section introductions to *Globalization and Contemporary Art* (2011) I set out a theoretical framework based on seven thematic parts through which to make sense of the art world and its products seen as a systemic whole—and to understand it, systematically, through a series of interlinked concepts and analytic modes. Though various narratives and theoretical positions are traceable across the essays in the anthology, including the one I presented in the book's introductory discussions, the totality was heterogeneous and even at times contradictory. Most of these essays dealt with art and the art world created since the 1990s. The critical framework they comprised, in contrast with *The Utopian Globalists*, was largely "synchronic"—that is, a kind of analytic slice through the recent contemporary art world looked at from different though interrelated perspectives.[15] The chief focus was on artists, art forms and organizations outside of the Western countries, but understood in relation to the control or influence of Western global "gatekeeper" art institutions. By this term I mean the main art auction companies (i.e., Sotheby's and Christie's), leading art fair businesses (e.g., Art Basel and Frieze) and powerful museums and galleries (e.g., the Tate, the Museum of Modern Art in New York, the Guggenheim Museum, White Cube, Gagosian, etc.).

Globalization and Contemporary Art also offered some sets of essays on "regional" or "area" themes. These included contemporary artworks made by indigenous peoples in Australia, new formations of artists and publics in Latin

America and the development of art movements and styles in Japan and China. The anthology demonstrated that, if there is a global contemporary art world and that if this constitutes a system, then it centrally pivots around the fundamentally asymmetrical (unequal) though dynamic relationship between the "core" Western nation-states—still in the most potent ways the effective owners of modern and historical Art, a Western concept and practice that emerged during the Enlightenment—and all the other, "peripheral," parts of the world. This contemporary art world, part of the world order/disorder, is the product of a historical process inseparably bound up with the Western imperial and colonial system that dominated most of the world until the end of the Second World War in 1945, when the concluding phases of formal decolonization began.[16]

Globalization and Contemporary Art's synchronic, theoretical framework comprised complementary analyses based on a series of interconnected concepts. These were: institutions, formations, means and forces of production, identifications, forms, reproduction and organization. While it is not the purpose of *The Global Contemporary Art World* to regurgitate the detail of either of the two earlier studies, it does draw on materials and ideas from both. It is already clear, for example, that examinations of "forms" and "institutions" will feature strongly here, and therefore that these two sections of related essays in *Globalization and Contemporary Art* await the reader wishing to find out more. (Its "formations" section also includes related discussion of collective production in contemporary art, an idea closely related to the complexities of the term "producer" introduced earlier.)

The resources of intellectual and political radicalism that I drew on in these earlier texts—those based on the writings and activisms of, for instance, Raymond Williams, Edward Said, Tariq Ali, David Harvey and Mike Davis—continue to provide inspiration for this book. If the most compelling studies in global contemporary art and culture do have strong if complex genealogical connections to the Marxist, feminist and "Third World" art-historical and art-theoretical writings from the 1960s, 1970s and 1980s, then it is one based on recognition of the ever more pressing mutual necessity for critical understanding and progressive societal transformation on a global scale.[17] The following sections in this Introduction set out further explanation of the aims, structure, content and context of this continuing project as I have pursued it through the case-studies that constitute *The Global Contemporary Art World.*

Modernity, Contemporary Art and Globalization

All the following chapters explore different facets of the character of contemporary visual art. However, as the title of the book emphasizes, it situates these analyses within a broader account of the systemic cultural forms, materials, practices, networks and contexts (economic, social, political and ideological) within which this art has been made and as a component of which it is meaningful. While "contemporary art" understood as a descriptive category of modes and products now includes much that would not have been recognized as visual art at all before the 1960s—for example, those classes of objects and events deemed "performance" and "conceptual" works—its relations to architecture, graphic and environmental design; to folk, popular and mass culture; and to advertising and digital culture have become ever more integral to the circuits of its production, dissemination and consumption.

This is true in both simple and complex ways, as my case studies show. The empirically heterogeneous category of contemporary art now includes, for example, a DVD video—such as Sun Yuan and Peng Yu's 2010 *I Do Not Sleep Tonight*, exhibited at the Hayward Gallery, London in "Art of Change: New Directions from China" (2012); an installation temporarily erected at the Reichstag Parliament building in Berlin—Christo's and Jeanne-Claude's *Wrapped Reichstag* (1971–1995)—and a graffiti drawing by Banksy of a donkey and an Israeli soldier stenciled onto the "Separation Wall" erected near Ramallah in Palestinian territory across the border from the State of Israel. Contemporary art, it seems, can literally be, as one recent commentator suggests, anything, anywhere.[18]

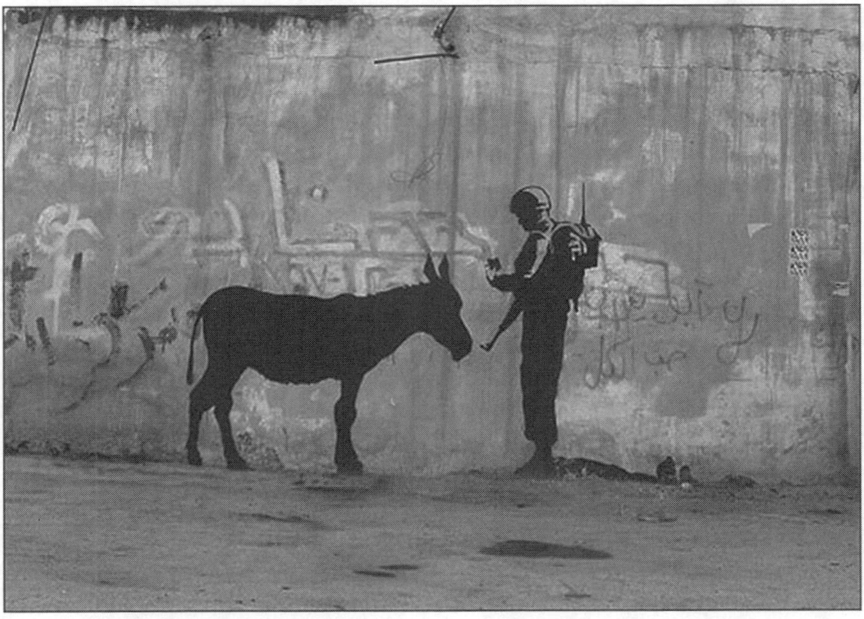

Figure 2 Banksy Graffitti image of donkey and Israeli soldier on Separation Wall near Ramallah, Palestine (2012). *Source:* © epa european pressphoto agency b.v./Alamy Stock Photo.

But in this book artworks have not been singled out as the primary, most significant objects of study against which everything else within the global contemporary art world is to be set as mere "background" or "context." My contention is that the contemporary art world—understood as a subsection of the globalized world order/disorder—is a system of interrelated and interdependent objects, producers, groups, networks, organizations and socioeconomic relationships, materials and means of production and reproduction, legal, critical and advertising discourses (and much else besides). This system as a whole is my object of study however much I may focus in on specific bits of it in these chapters. Further, the broader globalized world will remain as much my object of explanatory concern as the contemporary art world nesting within it. This perspective and objective certainly raises important questions, problems and dilemmas. Surely, for instance, one might reasonably ask, doesn't the extraordinary rise in the financial value of contemporary artworks since 2000 (especially those from Asia) indicate that these objects do actually have an overriding importance? Or, in another direction, one might plausibly argue that a focus on the contemporary art world in Asia necessarily implies that the globalized world around it must recede into at least an analytic "background," in the way that a photograph presents layers of more or less visible and highlighted detail depending on where the camera has been pointed?

While the latter may turn out to be at least partially true in terms of the sense these chapters actually make, the reader should nevertheless recognize that the foreground/background distinction remains an analytic effect generated within the process of written composition. With an effort, the reader should be able to shift focus back and forth without necessarily affirming or conceding the primacy, of any particular layer of detail within the overall interpretative "image" that my text creates. (Readers, of course, may also choose to keep their own pre-established priorities.) It is also worth stating that this book is in no way offered as a "survey," though it presents what is at least the outline of a comprehensive systemic analysis. The comparatively tiny number of artworks discussed or referred to here are, inevitably, made to bear the burden of a range of explanatory tasks—including that of representing, or typifying, an idea of "global art" and the global contemporary art world system. But their significance as such is heuristic. I am "trying out" how they might be interpreted within the logic of the account as a whole. Other, very different accounts of the same artworks are possible, and defensible in other terms. This dilemma, partly one of the relations between quantitative and qualitative analyses in cultural studies, has plagued the discipline of art history since its origins, and recurs frequently in the chapters ahead.[19]

Another objection might be that the deeper intellectual problems actually lie with the innocuous-looking prepositions, such as "in" and "from," that often characterize discussion of global contemporary art (in phrases such as "contemporary art from Africa," a usage discussed later in this Introduction).

I discarded an earlier title for this book because it seemed to me implicitly to prejudge the analysis: that wording was "Contemporary Art in a Globalized World." There are two sets of significant and still open questions raised by this formulation. Firstly, is, or in what ways is, contemporary art formed and meaningful before it is brought into contact with the public world of sales, exhibition and critical review? Secondly, is the globalized world itself to be conceived as formatively without contemporary art in some basic ways—to which it is then added, like sugar or salt?

Many different responses attend the negotiation of these important—though perhaps in some ways ineffable—questions in the chapters that follow here. My considered view, however, is that in the same way that we still do need to say, for example, that an artist is "from" Hong Kong or India, the prepositional formulation "in a" performs a necessary holding operation. That is, the lower-case "in a" links but also separates all the heavy-lifting capitalized nouns—"Contemporary Art"/"Globalized World." It facilitates recognition of both the difference between and interrelation of its two balancing sides. The chapters here are based on empirical studies where analytic focuses highlight, respectively, the role of art fairs (Hong Kong), new technologies (South Korea), biennials (India), visual arts higher education (PRC) and neoliberal sociopolitical intervention (Palestine). Each chapter, however, is also concerned with many other elements to do with the specific way that contemporary art, and the contemporary art world, has developed in that place, within and as part of the globalized world order/disorder as a whole. This order/disorder is—as that schismatic slash is intended to indicate—systemic, dynamic and disruptively volatile: the order/disorder is global (globalized) and globalizing still to ends we do not and may not fully understand.[20]

It has become commonplace for commentators to claim, for example, that installation and video works in particular are inherently and typically the globalized media of contemporary art. This is because, as innovative modes, they have ostensibly become available for appropriation and transformation equally by anyone from anywhere, compared, say, to the culturally loaded use of traditional "Western" art media such as oil painting or sculpting in bronze.[21] Part of this argument is based on the relative historical recentness—the "newness"—of both installation and video. (I'll come to the issue of irritating scare quotes in a while.) These were modes effectively created in the 1960s and only subsequently, and quite slowly, critically validated by museums and related institutional–critical discourse in the 1970s and since. Though I have some sympathy with this view, which is usually articulated as part of an affirmation of these practices, the grounds often given for it raise a set of troubling questions.

These concern the broader and persisting problem of sociocultural modernity, which exists at once as an objective, factual matter and as a subjective idea and ideal. It is bound up with definitions of modern and what is modern in art and culture, to processes of "modernization," and hence is a key to debate over the claimed transition from modern art to contemporary art, and from modern to contemporary societies. These now very longstanding arguments over the shift have been couched partly and necessarily in discussion of proposed world-historical transition moments and processes. They centrally include, to reiterate: "after 1945," meaning decolonization in greater Asia and Africa; "the 1960s," meaning the rise of the New Left, Anti-Stalinism, Third World movements, Environmentalism; and "after 1989"/"1991," meaning the reunification of Germany, the end of the Soviet Union and supposed triumph of global capitalism. But the combined factual and value-laden (ideological) uses of the terms "modern" and "modernity" pose particularly pressing and contentious issues for cultural analysis in our era of globalization. Given the power and predominance of the modernizing economies, societies and globally colonizing states of Europe and the United States—on both side of the Cold War—in the twentieth century, did all peoples, societies and cultures in the world really manage to become equally modern and then, since the 1990s, equally contemporary? This was a critical question in 1945, during the 1960s, in 1991, and still is in 2016. The answer remains "No."

The recent era of globalization in economic and financial terms has been driven by industries, corporations, state institutions, international networks, agreements and protocols established by US and Western European states mostly since the Second World War. These primarily included the creation of the Bank of International Settlements (founded 1919), the World Bank (1944), the International Monetary Fund (1945), the European Economic Community and European Union (1958, 1993), the North American Free Trade Association (1994), and the World Trade Organization (1995). But the rise of south Asian and East Asian economies since the 1980s has brought into question assumptions of the continuing dominance of Western power within globalization, especially as the PRC's economy grew to become the second biggest in the world by 2009 and its robustness seems to be a necessary condition for continuing global economic stability.[22]

In the contemporary art world, however, although the volume and value of sales of Asian art rocketed after 2000, the historically dominant institutions profiting from these markets remained Western, based in New York and London. Hong Kong has now become the third most important art-trading city—although the US/UK auctioneers Sotheby's and Christie's compete to run most of the high-value auction sales there, both having decided to use the territory to centralize their entire Asian operations. In 2012 MCH, the company that owns Art Basel, the most successful art fair business in the world, based in Switzerland (established in 1970), purchased a majority of shares in the ownership of the Hong Kong Art Fair and rebranded the annual event from 2013 as Art Basel Hong Kong. This was another sign, then, of the growing global significance of the contemporary art world in the PRC and Asia broadly.[23]

Sociocultural modernity and contemporaneity—the state of "being contemporary"—are centrally implicated in the development of the global contemporary art world. This process was driven in the 2000s by a lucrative and rapidly expanding world market dominated by Western auction houses and commercial galleries—whether the sales actually take place, as they have done and do, in New York, London, Hong Kong and other Asian centers. Given this predominance and the interrelated ability of powerful Western museums to validate contemporary art through purchase and exhibition of works by its global producers—many "from Asia," if not resident there—it remains the case that the global contemporary art world is fundamentally asymmetrical in its power relations.

This situation might be posed polemically in terms of the grip that Western interests continue to have over the economic exploitation of contemporary art produced in Asia and all other parts of the decolonized or postcolonial world. It might be dramatized in a statement such as "global contemporary art is essentially a Western construct," even if it is true that installation and video art modes have fundamentally superseded use of traditional Western media and materials. The latter remain bound up with philosophical definitions of Art elaborated in Europe in the Enlightenment and since: the epoch and episteme of Western modernity. From this perspective the global contemporary art world is a system that is being played and a game whose top players use some distinctly loaded dice.[24]

Amongst these players are its commentators. These include critics and theorists, who often work in universities and write for a wide range of magazines, journals and newspapers. Related to the complexities of "collective production" in the global contemporary art world is the development that some players may now occupy several roles both consecutively and simultaneously. An artist will curate their own and other artists' shows; a critic will take up a curating role in a gallery or museum; directors and curators of contemporary art biennials (which have hugely expanded in number since the 1980s) write essays and books that may both justify and auto-critique their day job of selecting works and artists for these exhibitions. Hans Ulrich Obrist, for instance, has been hovering around the top of the list of polymath game-players for several years and was named sixth most influential art world figure in the 2014 *Art Review* Power List, though he was down five places from 2013. Some of these role combinations, of course, occurred in decades well before the 1990s. The French artist Gustave Courbet curated an exhibition of his own paintings in Paris in 1855![25] (I will use "after 1989" as shorthand for my own practical sense of when contemporary art "began," or at least moved up a few gears.) All serious players, however, performing as many roles as they do or can, decide to declare or conceal their interests that are economic as much as anything else. They certainly "do it for the money," that is, but not only for that reason.

I work as an art historian in an art school that is part of a British university. As well as writing books and essays—on modernist art for twenty years and more recently on art made after 2000—I publish reviews and essays on artists and exhibitions I've seen or sometimes with which I have had some personal or professional involvement. In 2011 I helped to establish a university research center concerned with global contemporary art and culture. I was lucky enough to begin to travel to some of the "signature" events in the contemporary art world calendar—especially those in Asian countries and in one case where my university at the time had set up a campus, with a partner institution in the PRC. The chapters in this book in one sense constitute an embellished, reflective record of my visits to cities hosting contemporary art events of varying kinds. These included fairs, biennials, conferences, museum development meetings, inaugural exhibitions and "private views," parties and other "VIP" events. Though getting to these events often involved fairly uncomfortable long-haul flights because, in the main I wasn't able to travel as a VIP, I know that I've been very lucky to experience something of the texture and social life of the global contemporary art world. I can confirm that some of it is glamorous (though some aspects are squalid) and that this occasional immersion alters the way one sees and understands it.

I had thought to add a subtitle to the book: *A Rough Guide*. This term would have indicated several significant factors marking its conception, production and organization. The book has a picaresque dimension. As I've just noted, its choice of case studies is partly based on some of my trips involving fairly short if intense visits to the contemporary art world happening around me, performing itself, as it were. This world is urban, metropolitan and cosmopolitan, though these terms can mean quite different things in the diverse centers and regions I focus on.[26] Though I believe the selection and sequence of case studies is coherent intellectually, it certainly also reflects the contingencies of my life as an institutionalized academic over the last seven years. The book's first chapter investigates Hong Kong, where I attended the first "Art Basel Hong Kong" art fair in May 2013 and gave a lecture at one of the fair's "collateral events." The second chapter turns to Seoul, South Korea, where I took part in a conference on new media in contemporary art in November 2013 and attended various exhibitions. The third focuses on Kochi in southern India, when I visited the opening of the first biennial of contemporary art held there in December 2012. The fourth chapter concerns contemporary art and visual arts higher education in the PRC. It relates to numerous visits I've made to Beijing, Shanghai, and Dalian, where I worked for several years with one of the local universities on an art and design project. The final chapter concerns Palestine (and inevitably its relations with Israel), where I have taken part in conferences and seminars, in Jerusalem, Ramallah and Tel Aviv, Israel, over a longer period of years.

A Rough Guide would, however, also have signaled something about the style of argument and conclusions of my book.It contains occasional reference to these visits and my experience of and reactions to these places. All travel guide series to a degree reflect the globalization process as it developed in the last third of the twentieth century. This was when cheaper international, relatively "non-packaged," excursions became available to millions—though again differentially and unequally, as foreign holidays and travel came to form one of the linchpins of the "postindustrial" or "postmodern" Western states' economies. But these guides themselves helped to produce a kind of globalization and a kind of globalism (by which I mean a theory or ideal of global development) in their style and practicality.[27] These guides often identified and recommended cheap, or cheaper, places to stay, less known locations and aimed to give tourists the confidence and knowledge to perceive the world to be a set of expanding, reachable, livable and affordable destinations. I acknowledge, then, that I am a part of the global contemporary art world, whatever my criticisms of it may be. This has been true both when I've travelled to the art world's locations and events in Asia and elsewhere, but also when I've sat at home writing about it. Subjective experience, while travelling always limited and often rooted in ignorance and bafflement, is not to be posed against a theoretical knowledge of the contemporary art world. The two forms of response and understanding interpenetrate, inform and complement each other.

Travelling also remains a matter of actual, physical borders. Though "border" can be a capacious metaphor—one that I exploit a good deal in these chapters—I am concerned to point out here the material borders dividing states, territories and peoples. Globalization processes have not, in the main, eroded the attempted maintenance (or principle) of national borders and have, if anything, helped lead to their reinforcement. Consider, for example, European Union attempts in 2014, later abandoned and then reinstated in 2016, to prevent refugees sailing from North Africa and the Middle East to Italy and Greece; or the decision taken by the British government, following the dramatic referendum result in June 2016, to take the United Kingdom out of the European Union. Globalization and "internationalization" have thus occurred concurrently, if also asymmetrically, for decades.[28]

The former process has become dominant in economic and industrial terms, but the latter is entrenched in legal and sociopolitical spheres, especially in response to the threat of terrorism. Nevertheless, conglomerates of states such as the European Union and the conventions that now underpin the global capitalist economy have steadily worked to remove or erode individual states' abilities to control capital transfer and domestic industrial assets, contract tendering, immigration and imports.[29] Globalization in this way has certainly "opened up" Asian economies, cultures and their artists to influence from other nations and regions. Many of these have travelled to the "core" North American and Western European countries as part of their higher education, in order to produce and exhibit work and to experience the freedoms and opportunities that helped produce Western modern and contemporary art.

But these postcolonial societies, holding components of the "peripheral" global contemporary art world, remain in significant part the historical and cultural products of the actual borders and regimes imposed by the Western imperial, colonial and Cold War powers of the last century.

Five Asian Centers within the Global Contemporary Art World

Every chapter here is, amongst other things, a sketch of such an historic border zone. Hong Kong, defined by the Chinese Communist Party government as a "special administrative region" (SAR), had been, since the mid-nineteenth century, a British economic and military colony. It is now "relatively autonomous" from, though a part of, the PRC, a nation-state that became finally independent of multiple colonizers—Asian and European—in 1949 with the victory of Mao Zedong's communists. Looming within all the case studies is the active contemporary legacy of the dichotomous territorial system erected by the two chief protagonist states of the Cold War after the Second World War. This "iron curtain" divided Europe, but also most regions in Asia, the Middle East and Africa in the names of either Soviet communism or US-Western European capitalist democracy.

But the Cold War actually created another kind of totality. This was effectively a global system based on the volatile but symbiotic interdependence of two spheres of influence driven by ideological and territorial dispute that, over a 45-year period, sought to contest the interests of all those other peoples and territories that tried to avoid cooption into either bloc. The Asia-based Non-Aligned Movement, begun in Bandung, Indonesia in the mid-1950s was one such attempt, though it was of course not free of power struggles amongst its participating states.[30] My own view is that Western capitalist democracy is as tainted now as Soviet communism became in popular consciousness. Global neoliberalism's "victory" in 1991, with the end of the USSR, rapidly became a hollow one in the face of serial systemic economic crises and mounting "legitimation entropy" as ostensibly democratic political systems perceived to offer little real differences between parties became widely discredited across the whole world.

Hong Kong's SAR—a key node in financial capitalism's global network—is about 2,000 kilometers southwest of South Korea (the Republic of Korea). My second chapter touches, inevitably, on facets of South Korea's connection to and dislocation from North Korea (the Democratic People's Republic of Korea), after the peninsula was divided in an armistice agreement in 1953. The still-temporary ceasefire in this civil war begun in 1950 brought the suspension, but not the termination, of the early Cold War's hot "Korean War." This was fought directly by opposing US-led Western and Chinese military forces in a conflict estimated to have resulted in 2.8 million military and civilian deaths. Is contemporary art made in South Korea or that made by artists displaced from the two territories throughout the world inevitably to be marked by this trauma of division and unresolved conflict? Visiting North Korea wasn't possible for me. But "cultural diplomacy" of a kind has been practiced by the two states over the last few decades, its feasibility, character and significance dependent on the wildly oscillating intensities of the dispute. Beyond South Korea, the role of foreign diplomacy, trade missions and NGO (Non-Governmental Organization) aid activity across the global contemporary world, and in its Asian art worlds, will become evident in the chapters that follow.

Might North Korea's monumental public art and its vast set-piece media spectacles of mass adoration for the Leader constitute an authentic variant of contemporary art? The question might seem impertinent or outrageous but it raises some important issues. For instance: what (if any) might be the unacknowledged but necessary sociopolitical and even moral–ideological conditions for the emergence of a regional center in the global contemporary art world? It may well be that North Korea clearly fails to meet these conditions—if they exist at all. After all, the Democratic People's Republic has been subject and has subjected itself to a highly restricted version of globalization, denuded of contact with most other nation-states, peoples and cultures, though it maintains a complex relationship with its chief remaining "communist" ally to the north, the PRC, as well as with Russia and a few other countries. A broader question raised by this chapter concerns a highly significant issue for the book as a whole. Is all of Asia's contemporary art equally globalized, equally contemporary, equally marked by the asymmetrical "core–periphery" relations of dominant Western sociocultural power and emerging Asia's late entry into modernity and contemporaneity?[31]

The first Kochi–Muziris Biennale, held in 2012–2013 in Kerala state in southern India, comprises my third chapter's case study. I attended its official opening, some symposia events and visited its venues, located in the industrial, social and cultural buildings and spaces of a city—formerly known as Cochin—that had been colonized several times over, most recently by the Dutch and then the British. I offer a critical reading of the Biennale organizers claims for their exhibition, its varying contexts, meanings and significance for contemporary Indian art. Two Indian (Kerala state-born) artists, not curators, were responsible for developing and articulating the Biennale's "vision." The show was not intended simply to replicate the sundry recurrent exhibitions put on by jet-setting elite curators following the well-established "multicultural diversity" template deployed in many other cities of the world.[32] The Kochi Biennale is another example of artist-become-curator "collective production" in the global contemporary art world, although there was also the familiar concerted mix of public and private corporate involvement ("investment") in the event.

I also provide a broader analytic framework for making sense of this biennial, considering works made by artists from across another nearby border, in Pakistan. This is a state and territory sharing with India what were crudely drawn and violently contested borders created in 1947 by the British colonizers, at great human cost, as they prepared to evacuate the subcontinent. Pakistan, with its originally west and east regions divided by Indian territory, proved unsustainable and a third state, Bangladesh, was created, following more extreme violence, war and suffering, in 1971. Some of these artists (born in places that at the time were part of British India) were invited to participate in the Kochi Biennale. I consider the organizers' ambitious claims for the significance of the event and the wider development of contemporary art in India through a discussion of the country's economic, societal and cultural neoliberal modernization over the past two decades. If "rough guide" also suggests a tentative understanding and even perhaps some unreliable information, then this may prove to be an apt description, too, of at least some of the discourse produced by some central players—curators, directors, critics, artists—in the global contemporary art world. Genuine critical analysis and advertising have become more interrelated, blurred, even perhaps interchangeable modes; the ingenuous claims are serious but sometimes sit alongside excitable rhetoric. This inflated currency of terms and spin in the global contemporary art world, in which market relations are both highly determinant and have become fetishized, constitutes a form of multiple, cross-investment or speculative "hedging of bets"—another way of playing the system.

This accusation, of course, might be turned against my own account. Perhaps the hugely capacious term "Asia" is also just too rough an idea? But it should be clear by now that all the words I have been placing in scare-quotes should be interrogated carefully, their senses revised and perhaps even eventually abandoned. "Core," "periphery," "dominant," "emergent"—these have been common ideas and presuppositions in contemporary art debate based on "postcolonial" theoretical perspectives developed since the 1970s.[33] Is the world actually like this now? In what ways does Tate Modern remain one of the dominant contemporary art institutions? Are artists in Kochi or Seoul aware that they are miserably still only peripheral? These terms, I will argue, however, remain useful; they have some truth content, but also entail inadequacies in many ways.

Part of the inadequacy lies in what may be called their "performative" role. Their continued use may work, that is, to entrench a situation that is actually changing, or could be changed precisely if a different language, a different mode of understanding, were used. But their adequacy remains in them naming a reality that needs to be acknowledged before and as a condition that—along with other conditions—such change can occur at all. So these terms are, in the end, maddeningly both inadequate and yet necessary. Within discourse on Asia, for example, the term "West Asia" has been coined, with good intentions, to replace the manifestly imperialist usages "Near/Middle/Far East."

For this sequence manifestly spelt out the distance from and relations between the metropolitan centers of late-nineteenth century Empire—that of the British above all—and the colonized territories located on the edge of the eastern Mediterranean Sea and those progressively further to the east.[34] "West Asia" tries to shift the meaning from, in one sense, a concluded past (that of European colonialism) but can act as a euphemistic mystification because the power relations of European imperialism and Cold War spheres of influence manifestly still operate powerfully and destructively in this "post-Cold War" part of the world.

Along with the exploration of the use of all these terms, however, I offer a new set that I have borrowed and fashioned in order to articulate the systemic character of the global contemporary art world. This world, for example, requires what might be called a "resource infrastructure" in order to take root and develop. Central to creating this at once economic, material, institutional and knowledge-based organizational framework is the production and reproduction of a diversely skilled and professionalized art workforce. At the apex of this labor hierarchy—above curators, directors and critics, though wholly dependent upon them—stand the artists. As I noted earlier, these agents remain potent symbols and embodiments of ideals of creativity and individuality, however much collective agency and production has grown over the last two decades. This system's maintenance and self-regulation is one of the chief subjects of my fourth chapter concerned with the PRC's now highly significant place in the global contemporary art world.

The globalized visual arts higher education system, dominated by Western, English-speaking universities able to attract thousands of Asian international students to their postgraduate courses, is instrumental in helping to fashion the proto-identity and "branding" of aspirant artists. A very limited number of these are then able to sell works, whether through dealers, auction houses or at art fairs like Art Basel Hong Kong. A tiny proportion of this elite of economically successful artists may be invited to exhibit at events like the Kochi Biennale and perhaps eventually may have their works bought by institutions such as Tate or the Guggenheim Museum. I suggest that the exhibition catalogues for Beijing's Tsinghua University graduates in art and design evidence the development of a widening and "westernizing" process of social and cultural individuation taking place in China, within which contemporary art is an important if relatively minor aspect. I also consider the experience of Chinese students enrolled at Dalian Polytechnic University on a joint program run with a British university. They go through a process of "knowledge internationalization" shaped by their English-language inculcation in Western art and design practices, informed by aspects of its distinctive history and philosophy.

My final chapter is concerned with contemporary art in Palestine, its relations with Israel and the world beyond. To characterize Palestinian lands and people as such is already to court vociferous disagreement over the nameable identity of this place and the character of its legal, political, socioeconomic and cultural existence. But the territory's "dependent state" status was affirmed by the General Assembly of the United Nations in late 2012. Setting these matters aside here, however, the States of both Palestine and Israel must be considered part of West Asia. Yet the use of that term, rather than "Middle East," as I have just noted, threatens to obscure the active political realities of a region where Western (first European) imperial power operated directly for two hundred years (c. 1750–1950) to be followed by economic neocolonialism based on US-led oil extraction businesses, client-state *realpolitik* and West–East Cold War standoff. The civil war in Syria, the murderous incursions of Islamic State fighters and the fate of millions of refugees fleeing violence and reactivation of US–Russian tensions has recently underlined the severe dangers in this region.[35]

The conflict between Israel and Palestinians since 1948, setting aside the longer history of territorial dispute and violence, is inexplicable without knowledge of the wider imperial, then neocolonial and Cold War politics of the region as these were played out in alliances that the United States and the Soviet Union established after the Second World War. The opposing superpowers chose proxies for their military/security and socioeconomic strategies. The United States contracted Israel and the Soviet Union Egypt and Syria—until the 1980s when the United States entered into a now longstanding pact with the Egyptian army and that country's successively corrupt dictators. This agreement enabled the United States to stabilize Israeli–Egyptian relations (these two previously warring states have since signed peace and co-operation agreements). Yet this arrangement has only further delayed and deferred the finding of a real, lasting solution to the situation of Palestinians living under occupation in the West Bank and Jerusalem in parts of the state of Jordan captured by Israel in the 1967 war; in Gaza—now effectively a giant sealed refugee camp controlled by Israeli military forces; and in Israel itself, where Palestinians have lived in conditions of gross inequality since the 1950s.

This chapter examines the basic conditions of existence of the contemporary art world that manages to survive in major Palestinian towns such as Ramallah, as well as in east Jerusalem. Its chief focus is on the impact of the "aid culture" fostered since the 1990s by the work of transnational NGOs, mostly of European and US origin. This influx of resources, experts and organizations increased substantially after the signing of the 1995 Oslo Agreement accords by the Israelis and Yasser Arafat's Palestinian Liberation Organization (PLO), which was transformed into the governing "Palestinian Authority." Given this external aid culture, along with the enormous power that Israel wields over the whole organization of Palestinian society and the impact of *shatat* (Palestinian diaspora) investment in the territory, the State of Palestine has been subject to a very distinctive—perhaps anomalous—experience of globalization. Such a conclusion, however, begs important questions about the cultural impact of globalization anywhere and everywhere, as I have already suggested.

Its local nature and effects, that is, are always specific and differential, dependent on the historical social orders of the places where it takes hold.

Given the complex, traumatic histories of territorial division and sociopolitical crises marking many regions in both west and east Asia, it may be that the contemporary art world managing to subsist in, say, Ramallah is as strange, though in some very different ways, as that which might exist, as far as it is possible to know, in Pyongyang, capital of North Korea. Both peoples have spawned diasporas of artists whose lives and works must, presumably, fit somewhere into an account of the global contemporary art world. We are back to the problems of being "from" somewhere again. Palestinian artist Bashir Makhoul, from Galilee, now in the northern part of the State of Israel, travelled to England in the late 1980s to undertake a degree in art in Liverpool—from the Middle East to the North West, as it were. His artworks since, including the installation *Enter Ghost, Exit Ghost* have been, in direct and indirect ways, about the fate of the Palestinians, meaning both his own family and sense of a people, where ever they have ended up having to live. "Palestinian" is, then, in one sense a global appellation, and perhaps even a test case for examining what identity under globalization actually means for everyone. All of the case studies of border identities and crises presented in this book, however, finally make sense only with an understanding of the interrelations and interdependencies of neocolonialism, Western capitalism, Soviet and Chinese Communism, the Cold War and the recent consequences of global neoliberalization in political and military, but also sociocultural and artistic, terms.[36]

Global Crash, Crises and the Art World

It should be clear from this outline that the global contemporary art world—its producers, forms, organizations, discourses and networks of production, exchange and consumption—is firmly lodged within the historic structures and forces of Western capitalism. The celebration of contemporary art principally as a dynamic and highly profitable "bull market" has been the most striking feature of its rise in public visibility since the 1990s. Irrespective, then, of its aesthetic and many other interests, it began to be constructed in the mass media and by financial consultants as a reliable new "asset class" for investment by wealthy individuals ("High" and "Ultra-High Net Worth" groups, in the jargon) and corporate organizations alike.

Mexico-based collector Cesar Cervantes illustrated this when he explained in 2011, for example, that it was "easier to have ten Damien Hirsts than to have ten yachts... besides, your yacht becomes more interesting with a Damien Hirst on it."[37] The whiff of self-parody in this statement shouldn't obscure recognition of the reality that there are now perhaps thirteen million US dollar millionaires in the world (the art world's primary target "VIPs") looking to buy assets of varying kinds holding financial value that will increase over time and return a profit if sold. The volume and value of the contemporary art market grew exponentially in the early 2000s—particularly in terms of Asian and specifically Chinese art—but then, along with most other sectors of the global economy, collapsed in 2008 following the banks' and mortgage businesses' Crash in the United States and Europe.[38]

"Contemporary" and the older word "co-temporary" share the meaning of something held or experienced together: contemporaries are people who live at the same moment and are co-formed in it. The 2008 Global Financial Crisis—originating in an industry increasingly dependent upon global high speed computer-based trading in finance and other commodities, dominated by exchanges in the United States, Western Europe and Asia—indicated how the global economy was networked in a near-instantaneous, never mind contemporary, worldwide knowledge of prices, values and trends in buying and selling. Once a "contagion" in confidence failure began the system as a whole was threatened with collapse. Although stocks and shares markets had imploded catastrophically in earlier decades, most spectacularly in the 1929 Wall Street Crash preceding the Great Depression, the high technologies of global capitalist trading and interpenetration of bank loans and investments internationally ("exposure") meant that rapid and systemic losses were inevitable, and capacity to control their extent very limited.[39]

The result for most people in the world was a lowering of incomes and standards of living, and the instigation of huge, long-term "austerity" programs carried out by Western governments, such as those in the European Union, ostensibly in order to recover public money paid to bail out the banks, to reduce national debt and to "balance" national state budgets dominated for decades by what rapidly became represented as supposedly unsustainable deficits. The 2008 Crash, however, enabled a wide resurgence and emboldening of neoliberal measures that shifted wealth and resources massively from public (state) control to private individuals and capitalist corporations. This process resumed a long-term shift that the leading Western states had facilitated over about a 35-year period, at varying rates with varying degrees of opposition in particular countries, as governments of marginally differing hue revolved in power in the United States and Western Europe since the early 1980s.[40]

The global contemporary art world simultaneously abuts (that is, borders) this, the brutally hard end to contemporaneity in the global capitalist economy, and is part of it. This is because the entity I am calling the "global contemporary art world" exists both as a specific analytic construct—a kind of model or distillation which I'm proposing here—but is also a set of actual objects, relationships, people and places out there in the real world. The reader should get use to moving between these two senses and seeing their interrelation. The art markets around the world share the same "compressed time and space" as all the other markets (real and virtual) of globalized capitalism. A fetishizing overemphasis of the art market, however, creates a highly partial misrepresentation of the extensive, complex system that comprises the global contemporary art world.[41] Although accumulated buying and selling of artworks certainly has many real and systemic effects, discussion of contemporary art largely in terms of the mediations wrought by market activity threatens to obscure the wider phenomena, processes and significance of art world organizations, producers, products and discourses that may be redescribed in other and more valuably explanatory ways.

For instance, both the border divisions and interrelationships between separated lands, peoples and cultures that preoccupy discussion in the following chapters have created what might be called a kind of "split contemporaneity" in art and societal life. I felt this most strongly in South Korea, while talking to older people, and some artists, who had "lost" relatives and friends in 1953 to the "other side" (to the North) but who went on living, self-consciously and traumatically, in a form of "separated coexistence." A similarly divided contemporaneity has characterized Hong Kong's relationship to the mainland PRC, dating from the time of colonization by the British and, in different ways, since 1997 when the SAR was created. This agreement between the UK and the PRC enabled a form of relatively autonomous though narrowing "separate development" the continuation of which gave Hong Kong people legal–political, economic, social, cultural and even artistic rights significantly different from those of the PRC's own citizens. The status and future of this relative autonomy is now increasingly uncertain, as the mainland government moves to control the political process there more directly.[42]

Border existence and split contemporaneity experientially animates life, too, for the Palestinians and Israelis. The supposed separateness of their "confessional" (religious) and sociocultural histories and allegiances actually masks two enemies held together/held apart in an extended death grip across the wall that now runs the length of Israel's territorial division with State of Palestine areas. Banksy's stenciled graffiti donkey, asked for papers by an IDF soldier, though admirably designed to suggest the human folly of the wall, attracted offense from some Palestinians who thought that it mocked an animal revered by them for its multiple uses. Contemporary artists (and biennial curators) "helicoptered" into such crisis zones, however well-intentioned they may be, can come to constitute another facet of the "West and the rest" mentality. This represents another border and form of split contemporary life at the heart of a global contemporary art world divided between its dominant Western artists, institutions and businesses—multiple, cross-invested proprietors of the idea of Art—and the emergent others from greater Asia and everywhere else. However, like the colonization and Cold War of which they are a trace, such borders mark both a duality, a split, but also an interaction—some form and level of mutually transforming co-determination. There will be evidence (social, cultural, artistic) that the people and their activities on either side of any border, however divided from the other side, have been formed and deformed by the other's existence. Though this may usually be cast negatively, in terms of an antagonism, a hollow inversion or mere mirroring, perhaps here and there a positive attitude or value may also have been created.[43] I've tried to look out for both here.

Other borders exist inside states and territories as well as between them. India's neoliberal triumphalism is particularly egregious given the persisting grotesque structural divisions of extreme wealth and poverty in a country that is lauded and lauds itself for being the world's biggest democracy. Articulation of this attitude found a compelling form in the clear socially excluding rhetoric of the inflight magazine *Jetwings* that I read when travelling to the Kochi Biennale. On one page a story about the exhibition, showcase for the city and Kerala state, on another an advert for new "prestige housing" in Bangalore. "Ultra luxury homes," we are informed, "sculpted to suit only the very upper crust. If you belong here [...]" A later page announced the "privileged sanctuary" of the Taj Coromandel Chennai hotel, owned by Indian global corporate giant Tata Enterprises: "Forever refined. Forever classic. Forever contemporary." The VIP art world of private views and private dinners to meet the artists slides seamlessly into this wider world of luxury, as you move from your private jet to your five-star hotel suite to the limousine that takes you to the exhibition's exclusive *vernissage* event enabling you to see the artworks in privacy and to meet the dealers.[44]

The global contemporary art world is this system of interrelated and interdependent elements which are specific yet continuous with the other worlds and systems of "luxury" global travel, commerce, investment and residential property. *Jetwings* magazine, like the market-focused *Art Newspaper: International Edition* (published in English, Italian, Russian, Greek, French, Spanish and Chinese monthly editions) both announces and mediates one's sense of arriving, and of "having arrived," in the global contemporary art world. And at whatever location within this world the VIP happens to be there will be the limousine, the hotel, the *vernissage* opportunity, "if you belong here [...]" Mediation has this simple sense of something produced but also altered through a particular channel—though one of its earliest meanings was also "to divide," to "split in half."[45] The global contemporary art world's players all, to some degree, mediate and are mediated themselves by the system. The interests of curators, dealers, directors and artists may be different, aligned or antagonistic in particular moments and situations, but they are also dynamic and volatile as moments and situations change.

One certainly experiences the global contemporary art world visibly and physically at events such as fairs and biennials, and in auctions, museum openings and symposia. Press, TV and internet content now routinely mediate the system, in global and apparently instantaneous ways. News of Serota's elevation to the status of No. 1 player in the 2014 system swept around the world via coverage on web sites and mobile internet devices—I found out from a Chinese friend in Chengdu, in southwest China, who got the information from an app on his cell phone. But the contemporary art world also works invisibly and is relatively immaterial. It communicates and coheres across local and globally distanced networks of emotional and social contact, those both public and discreet, well away from the theater of auctions and museum openings. Some of its constitutive glue comprises activities entailing aesthetic, intellectual and sociopolitical commitment.

Perhaps a majority of artists and other agents active in the global system would even profess to hold "anti-capitalist" perspectives, or adhere to some legacy of twentieth-century "avant-garde" political and aesthetic radicalism. Many examples of these are discussed in the chapters that follow. The "public education" ethos of Tate, as well as the work of many private, as well as state-financed, museums and galleries across the world, mitigates, to varying degrees, a fascination with the market and the financial value of contemporary art. My focus in this book, however, is emphatically not on Western artists working in Europe or the United States, where the avant-garde inheritance is still felt and articulated most strongly ("The West and the rest" again).[46] Nor is the focus here on the best-known globally successful artists whose works and reputations may already be familiar to many readers. I am trying not to reproduce the existing system.

These objectives have helped lead me to a focus on some Asian centers and their complex relations with the powerful historical structures of Western art organization. My intention was also partly to radicalize the discussion of how mediation works in the contemporary art world—a wide-ranging topic that has been a staple in many productive and interesting debates over the last two decades. Mediation in my usage here, however, will be repurposed in order to seek answers in the following chapters to two sets of related questions. Firstly, how might the contemporary artworks examined in my case studies be understood as "global" or "globalized" in and through their specific forms, materials, means of production, contexts and meanings?[47] Are certain modes or idioms such as installation or video characteristically global by dint of their claimed intrinsic qualities? Can the analysis of an inevitably very small selection of works sustain the burden of such claims to representativeness? In my Conclusion I offer a lengthier discussion of works by two artists: Bashir Makhoul and Wang Guofeng. This extends aspects of the analyses developed earlier (at the beginning of this Introduction, and in Chapters 2 and 5), but also demonstrates that other perspectives and interests will take interpretative activity decisively away from generalized, if not necessarily reductive, exemplifications of heuristic categories such as "global art."

The second set of questions concern the impact that my own analytic attention, given my specific background as a Western, white, male academic now in the middle of his sixth decade, has in shaping/limiting my understanding and articulation of these works' significance. Is there a kind of culturally determined "explanatory tautology" at work here, as it were, behind my back? How predictable or prejudged will my constructions be—but also yours? Other related and extending questions abound. Can or should these artworks, their makers, related art world institutions and facilitating agents (e.g., curators and critics) resist, and if so in what ways, the corrosive aspects of globalization: endless commodification, fetishism of markets and rhetorical spin presented as serious criticism? By "endless commodification," to make an important clarification, I mean a contemporary art world that seemingly ever-increasingly encourages artists to conceive and make works primarily for sale. This pressure is in sharp contrast with the earlier historical possibility, but not inevitability, even in a capitalist social order, that artworks made for other purposes may then, fortuitously, get sold.[48]

All the Asian countries and centers whose contemporary art worlds I examine here have some degree of access to locally available markets and exhibiting spaces able to operate in order to value artworks and the reputations of their makers. This is part of the "resource infrastructure" I referred to earlier. The global contemporary art market in terms of art fairs, auctions and dealing galleries has either come to town or is operating reasonably nearby. Regular, biennial-type shows of contemporary art occur in or geographically near to all of these centers—including in Palestine, with the Qalandiya and Riwaq regular exhibitions. However, these art world "ecologies" are all at significantly differing stages of material and institutional development. More detailed regional focus indicates even greater variation—as the examples of Vietnam, Myanmar, Indonesia and the Philippines attest.[49]

The term "emergent" can be a useful empirical tool within such analytic differentiation. But it may also act as an ideological barrier erected, consciously or unconsciously, in order to resist considering or valuing other possible or potential qualities in an object or an artist. The even more loaded term "development," as in "Third World development," too often actually meant in practice a process to be controlled by those in the dominant Western states who wished to entrench their power through a selective extension of resources to subordinates encouraged only to emulate their masters. In what ways might contemporary art in a globalized world fit into this pernicious pattern?[50]

Contemporary Art in the Friezer

Since its first "edition" in 2003, the London-based Frieze annual art fair has led the way, at least ideologically, in the celebration of contemporary art as a "global phenomenon." Its own extensions have been emphatically "Atlanticist," however, with the 2011 inaugurations of "Frieze New York" and "Frieze Masters" (also held annually in London, centered on sales of modern art).

These confirm the predominance of the London–New York axis, Western Europe and the United States, as the twin capitals of the global contemporary art world system. Reproducing this, since the mid-2000s the world's two leading auction houses, Sotheby's and Christie's, have coordinated their mid-season sales events to coincide with the London Frieze fair. In addition, the "Frieze Foundation," a not-for-profit arts organization set up to commission projects, became integrated into EU funding mechanisms—recognized, because of its "expertise" and accruing authority—to help allocate public (state) funding to artists and cultural organizations across the EU member countries. This further indicates the structural blurring of public and private sectors characteristic of neoliberal economies and their evolving social orders.[51]

Frieze magazine, established by Amanda Sharp, Mathew Slotover and Tom Gidley in 1991, rapidly became and presented itself as the leading magazine on "contemporary art and culture." This is a strap line that its web site still promotes, across the page from advertisements for other "leading" global galleries Spruth Magers (London and Berlin), White Cube (London, Hong Kong, São Paulo), Hauser & Wirth (London, New York, Zurich), Chisenhale (London) and Victoria Miro (London).[52] *Frieze* magazine's January–February 2014 edition vividly indicates its "global brand" aspirations. Opening glossy advertisements for White Cube, Hauser & Wirth galleries, and luxury fashion by Saint Laurent, the latter in a parody of Andy Warhol's Rolling Stones' 1971 *Sticky Fingers* album cover, give way to apparently serious, though very short, articles on contemporary art and the global art world. For instance, "Roman Ruins," a piece declaring Italy's economic and cultural decline—the country is no player in the contemporary art market despite providing the biennial circuit with its most famous biennial at Venice—gets no more than about 1,000 words.[53]

A longer essay discusses Tate's move into collecting contemporary art from Africa, following a show held at Tate Modern in 2013 and the appointment of its specialist "Curator of International Art." It is reported that the London *Financial Times* has on several occasions celebrated the "hotness" of "African art" as a rising "emergent asset class." London had recently hosted a number of shows on contemporary African art, including a major exhibition at the Saatchi Gallery, though the essay is critical of how this work was presented, with a negative reference back to the Venice Biennale's own attempt in 2007 with its "African Pavilion." Ads follow for biennials and exhibitions in Singapore, Frieze in the Big Apple (*Wall Street Journal*: "Frieze Art Fair electrifies New York"), and Madrid's ARCO art fair. Later reviews include pieces on books about the internet and a round-up of contemporary art exhibitions around the wider world ("38 reviews from 30 cities in 15 countries"). These include Istanbul, "this month's featured global city," the Athens and Thessaloniki biennials, and shows in the US and Australia.[54]

Such quantity/quality issues are irredeemably elided in *Frieze* magazine's own meditations on and mediation of the global contemporary art world.

The words "global" and "art market" perform the same fusing/confusing operation which produces a series of intellectual and experiential conundrums for anyone trying to understand—"get the measure of"—the varied phenomena this world entails. Phrases such as "African art" and "art from Africa," like "emergent" and "peripheral," seem to be simultaneously factual and partisan, truthful and yet troubling in some fundamental ways. Would a magazine or art fair such as *Frieze* ever present contemporary "European art" or "American art" in the same grossly generalizing way? Would not these exoticizing terms be mocked as ridiculously indefensible—intellectually, if not as marketing devices? That seemingly innocent preposition "from" subsumes an alarming set of related interpretative problems, for example when "artists from Africa" who've ostensibly managed to join the main stage in London or New York, may have already spent many years living in the United States or France, and make their work there.[55]

Equally troubling is the statement by Tate's then International Curator, Elvira Dyangani Ose, who professed an interest in telling, through her exhibitions, what she calls "the story of a universal art history." The quantity/quality dilemma surges again. What Tate is doing, she claims, "is increasing the presence and visibility of African art within the Tate collection." This implies both more and different objects, and more and different ways in which these may be presented and understood. At one level this ambition is of course not contentious but laudable. Tate, and other major European and US museums, clearly should radically widen the scope of their concerns and attempt to reach new, different publics—for example, the vast postcolonial diaspora of Africans and their descendants living across the northern hemisphere.

But "universal" here suggests both integration and totalization—an impossible quantitative task that, in all previous attempts in art and cultural history, has always actually been founded on drastic, partial, if often undeclared, qualitative selection. "World histories of art" narratives, for instance, emerged in the nineteenth-century colonial era espoused by the Western national empires, sponsored by leading European and US museum institutions and establishment academic representatives. Their purpose was to make colonized peoples and their artefacts meaningful and valued within the taxonomies of Art and Culture invented by Western intellectual history and its related disciplines.[56]

Tate is aware of these dilemmas. Tate Modern's then director, Chris Dercon, stated: "We are becoming aware that there are different forms of modernities." How this recognition is squared with an ambition to promote "universality" remains, however, unclear. Ose herself indicated recognition of the quantity/quality problem (and its related other dimension, fact/value) in her awkward but nevertheless revealing comment that "Africa is not the only conceptual context in which artists *there* operate." (my italics) "Africa" and "there," it is clear, are both ideas and assumptions as much as terms that refer to an actual place or places. Given the legacies of colonial history and the present order/disorder of globalizing capitalism, how indeed could what Kodwo Eshun called the "complexities" of "African contemporaneity" be made "visible, audible and 'speakable'"?[57]

These are the same problems and questions that confronted me in writing this book. They cannot, however, be "solved" or "resolved" in a study or an exhibition because they actually entail altering—indeed eventually ending—the power relations that operate now, dynamically but asymmetrically, in the world and in the global contemporary art world. The conclusions and answers I've formed here are provisional, "trial-and-error," rough ones, necessarily limited by the interests that I can both declare and others which may operate still without my conscious knowledge or wishes.

Contemporary art has already been subject to an enormous quantity of writing—theoretical, critical, descriptive and anecdotal. I make reference to some of this discourse where necessary and supply further reading suggestions throughout what follows. In *Globalization and Contemporary Art,* as I've explained, I explicitly brought seven theoretical categories into critical alignment with groups of essays based on empirical cases. My idea was that these categories and empirical studies could start to inform, test and critique each other. Phenomena in the world are never simply present to us in some transparent or direct manner. Experientially, and in subsequent attempts at explanation, we need to use and create mediating words and concepts in order to make sense of things—although we can still be rendered speechless and disoriented by experience, and further experience can again transform the ways in which we try to understand the world. *The Global Contemporary Art World* has a similar objective: I have organized its contents partly in order to articulate, but also possibly to destabilize, a set of interrelated and interdependent explanatory concepts.

Several of the most important of these derive from a footnote Karl Marx added to the first volume of his study *Capital,* published in 1863. Human society's transformations, Marx observed, were based on the complex interdevelopmental relations of six elements (both ideas and things in the world). These are: technology, human relation to nature, processes of production, the production and reproduction of daily life, social relations and mental conceptions. These components have always existed in dynamic interaction and are not to be thought of hierarchically. Notice Marx doesn't mention economy or class, two ideas usually held to be at the determining or "causal" center of Marxism's explanation of human history. The relationships between these six elements are open and change historically, but as a dynamic ensemble they have driven the development of the social order of capitalism, its globalization and will drive its future.[58] The global contemporary art world, a component of this wider world order/disorder, yet active within it in specific ways, may be understood to be similarly composed and recomposed. I have used Marx's insight to clarify and articulate my sense of this art world as it exists in its specific forms in Hong Kong, South Korea, India, the PRC and Palestine.

It should become clear, too, that the development of something called "Asian contemporary art" is as necessary and yet problematic a formulation as "African contemporary art." This art is bound into a system of dynamic power relations with the "core" Western art institutions. Some of these I have started to outline here. Along with Marx's six interacting elements, I pursue the related analytic categories put forward in the first book in my trilogy. The global contemporary art world, to reiterate, comprises art *forms*, created by their makers using specific *means and forces of production*, though in a wider context of active and collectively engaged *producers*. A range of historical and new *institutions* exists within which artists and their works are produced, exhibited, disseminated, sold, curated and validated. Validation through institutional collection (thus creating "museum quality," an art fair sales patter cliché) is part of a broader process of critical assessment or *identification*—discourse which includes everything I say in this book. Often produced with other scholars and students in mind, this discourse on art takes a part in the broad social *reproduction* necessary to enable the global contemporary art world to carry on, as part of our planet's now systemic *organization*.

Despite my habitual tendency to put "material" or "economic" before "social" or "aesthetic," I don't intend by it to smuggle in any hierarchy. Words, sentences, paragraphs and chapters have to follow meaningful sequence but this should not be interpreted to mean that the most important always comes first. Sometimes it comes last! The global contemporary art world is a matter, first and last, of systemically interrelated and interdependent elements. Though we may particularly treasure certain artworks, or revile them, they really exist only as an indissoluble part and as evidence of a total human and social order. The Art Basel Hong Kong fair held in 2013, to which I turn now, is my first example.

Notes

1 See Bashir Makhoul, *Enter Ghost, Exit Ghost* (Yang Gallery: Beijing, 2012), catalogue of show curated by Gordon Hon: March 15–April 16, 2012. On military conflict in postcolonial Middle Eastern and Third World urban zones, see Stephen Graham, "War and the City," *New Left Review*, 44, March–April 2007: 121–132, and Mike Davis, "The Urbanization of Empire: Megacities and the Laws of Chaos," *Social Text*, 22 (2), 2004: 9–15.

2 See, e.g., Wouter Davidts, "Art Factories, Museums of Contemporary Art and the Promise of Artistic Production from Centre Pompidou to Tate Modern," *Fabrications: The Journal of the Society of Architectural Historians, Australia and New Zealand*, 16 (1) (2006): 23–42, Davidts, "The Vast and the Void: On Tate Modern's Turbine Hall," *Footprint Trans-disciplinary*, Autumn 2007: 77–92, and Claire Bishop, *Installation Art: A Critical History* (Routledge: New York, 2005).

3 See http://artreview.com/power_100/2014/(accessed March 21, 2017)

4 See Jonathan Harris, "From the Spiral to the Turbine: A Global Warning," in *The Utopian Globalists: Artists of Worldwide Revolution, 1919–2009* (Wiley-Blackwell: Oxford, 2013): 316–332.

5 See Leo Panitch and Sam Gindin, *The Making of Global Capitalism: The Political Economy of American Empire* (Verso: London, 2013): 14–15, and David Harvey, *A Brief History of Neoliberalism* (Oxford University Press: Oxford, 2005).

6 See, e.g., William Blum, *Rogue State: A Guide to the World's Only Superpower* (Zed Books: New York, 2014), and Naomi Klein, *The Shock Doctrine: The Rise of Disaster Capitalism* (Allen Lane: London, 2007).

7 See Patrick Coburn, *The Rise of Islamic State: ISIS and the New Sunni Revolution* (Verso: London, 2014).

8 The literature on contemporary art is vast. See, e.g., Daniel Birnbaum, Connie Butler, Suzanne Cotter, Bice Curiger, Okwui Enwesor, Massimiliano Gioni, Bob Nikas and Hans Ulrich Obrist, *Defining Contemporary Art: Twenty Five Years in Two Hundred Pivotal Artworks* (Phaidon: London, 2011), and Terry Smith *Contemporary Art: World Currents* (Laurence King: London, 2011).

9 See Melissa Chiu and Benjamin Genocchio (eds.), *Contemporary Art in Asia: A Critical Reader* (MIT Press: Cambridge, MA, 2011).

10 See Francis Frascina and Jonathan Harris (eds.), *Art in Modern Culture: An Anthology of Critical Texts* (Phaidon: London, 1992).

11 Lively debate on this issue can be found in James Elkins (ed.), *Is Art History Global?* (Routledge: London, 2007), and James Elkins, Zhivka Valiavicharska and Alice Kim (eds.), *Art and Globalization* (Pennsylvania State University Press: University Park: PA: 2010).

12 See, e.g., What is Contemporary Art?" in Terry Smith, *What is Contemporary Art?* (University of Chicago Press: Chicago, 2009): 241–271.

13 See reference in n4 above.

14 This argument is powerfully affirmed by Peter Osborne, *Anywhere or Not At All: Philosophy of Contemporary Art* (Verso: London, 2013), especially "The Fiction of the Contemporary": 15–35.

15 Jonathan Harris (ed.), *Globalization and Contemporary Art* (Wiley-Blackwell; Oxford: 2011).

16 See, e.g., Ruth Craggs and Claire Wintle (eds.), *Cultures of Decolonization: Transnational Productions and Practices: 1945–1970* (Manchester University Press: Manchester, 2016).

17 See my account of late twentieth-century sociopolitical radicalism in the discipline of art history, *The New Art History: A Critical Introduction* (Routledge: London, 2001).

18 See Osborne, Introduction (especially 5–8), in *Anywhere or Not At All*, and "Nomadic Globalism: *Scenographica* in Christo and Jeanne-Claude's *Wrapped Reichstag*," in Harris, *The Utopian Globalists* (287–315).

19 On "typicality," see "Typification and Homology," in Raymond Williams, *Marxism and Literature* (Oxford University Press: Oxford, 1977): 101–107.

20 See the main Introduction to Harris (ed.), *Globalization and Contemporary Art* (especially 3–7). A select bibliography on globalization is included in the anthology (510–512).

21 This claim or assumption recurs within many of the essays included in, e.g., Hans Belting, Andrea Buddensieg, and Peter Weibel (eds.), *The Global Contemporary and the Rise of New Art Worlds* (ZKM/MIT Press: Cambridge, MA, 2013).

22 See Panitch and Gindin, "A World After Its Own Image," in *The Making of Global Capitalism*: 275–300, and Samir Amin, *Capitalism in the Age of Globalization: The Management of Contemporary Society* (Zed Books: London, 2014).

23 See the essays on Asian contemporary art in Jonathan Harris (ed.), *Third Text* (special edition on "Global Occupations of Art"): no. 123, July 2013.

24 Curatorial aspects of this are diversely examined in, e.g., Mariska ter Horst (ed.), *Changing Perspectives: Dealing with Globalization in the Presentation and Collection of Contemporary Art* (KIT: Amsterdam, 2012).

25 On Courbet's exhibition, see T. J. Clark, *Image of the People: Gustav Courbet and the 1848 Revolution* (Thames and Hudson: London, 1974).

26 See Marsha Meskimmon, *Contemporary Art and the Cosmopolitan Imagination* (Routledge: Abingdon, 2011) and Kobena Mercer (ed.), *Cosmopolitan Modernisms* (INIVA/MIT Press, Cambridge, MA, 2005).

27 See "'Globalization' and 'Globalism' in Theory and Practice," in Harris, *The Utopian Globalists*: 10–16.

28 See, e.g., Saskia Sassen, *Territory, Authority, Rights: From Medieval to Global Assemblages* (Princeton University Press: Princeton, NJ, 2006) and Retort Collective *Afflicted Powers: Capital and Spectacle in a New Age of War* (Verso: London, 2005).

29 The debate over the UK referendum in 2016 on whether to remain in the European Union starkly confirmed this—it became an issue that many nation-states, such as the United States and the PRC, believed they had a stake in. See, e.g., Armagan Goskaman "Perspectives on the United Kingdom's Withdrawal from the European Union," in Engin Sorhun, Umit Hacioglu and Hasan Dincer (eds.), *Regional Economic Integration and the Global Financial System* (IGIU Global: Hershey, PA, 2015): 36–48.

30 On rivalry for control within the Non-Aligned movement, see Neil Padukone *Beyond South Asia: India's Strategic Evolution and the Reintegration of the Subcontinent* (Bloomsbury: London, 2014).

31 See John Clark, "Modern Art in South-East Asia," *Asia Art Pacific* (Sample Issue, 1993), discussed in Patrick D. Flores, "Field Notes from Artworlds: Interest and Impasse," *Third Text* (special issue on "Contemporaneity and Art in Southeast Asia," edited by Patrick D. Flores and Joan Kee), no.111, 25 (4), July 2011: 383–394 (388).

32 See Elena Filipovic, Marieke Van Hal and Solveig Ovstebo (eds.), *The Biennial Reader* (Bergen Kunsthall: Bergen, 2010).

33 See Patrick Williams and Laura Chrisman (eds.), *Colonial Discourse and Post-Colonial Theory: A Reader* (Pearson: London, 1993).

34 On the broader question, see Wu Hung, "Imagining Asia: A Genealogical Analysis," in Chiu and Genocchio (eds.), *Contemporary Art in Asia* (87–106).

35 On the longer history of interventions by Western powers, see William Blum *Killing Hope: US Military and CIA Interventions since World War II* (Zed Books: New York, 2003): chapters 12, 13, 39, 46, 48 and 52.

36 Neoliberalism, as Harvey points out, is the ideology of "free markets" and "deregulation;" neoliberalization is the actual process in which national governments are centrally implicated, taking decisions, e.g., to privatize publically held assets and not to intervene to support industries and jobs threatened by global competition. See Harvey *A Short History of Neoliberalism*: 13 and 19, and David Craven, "'Institutionalized Globalization,' Contemporary Art, and the Corporate Gulag in Chile," in Harris (ed.), *Globalization and Contemporary Art*: 479–495.

37 Quoted in "Collecting Grows among West's Wealthy," *The Art Newspaper*, November 30, 2011: 1. On the history of art as financial investment, see "Art Investment Funds," in Noah Horovich, *Art of the Deal: Contemporary Art in a Global Financial Market* (Princeton University Press: Princeton, NJ, 2011: 143–187.

38 On the number of millionaires, see http://www.telegraph.co.uk/finance/personalfinance/expat-money/10158420/A-record-breaking-number-of-millionaires-in-the-world.html (accessed March 21, 2017). On the 2008 Global Financial Crisis, see Panitch and Gindin, "American Crisis/Global Crisis," and Conclusion, *The Making of Global Capitalism*: 301–340.

39 See Michael Lewis, *Flash Boys: A Wall Street Revolt* (Norton: New York, 2015).

40 See Panitch and Gindin, "The Rule of Global Capitalism," *The Making of Global Capitalism*: 223–271.

41 See Jonathan Harris, *The Myth of the Art Market: Neoliberalism in the Social Order of Contemporary Art* (IB Tauris, forthcoming).

42 Guy Breshears, *Of Papers and Protests: Hong Kong Responds to Occupy Central* (Guy Rubens Breshears: Hong Kong, 2016).

43 The "Real DMZ Project," bringing artists to the demilitarized zone between North and South Korea to make work on the conflict between the two states is an example; see Chapter 2 below.

44 See Chapter 3 n1 for references.

45 See Jonathan Harris, "To divide, to occupy: cancelled mediations in Palestinian video art," in Bashir Makhoul (ed.), *Palestinian Video Art: Constellation of the Moving Image* (Palestinian Art Court—Al Hoash: Jerusalem, 2013): 68–87.

46 See, e.g., Grant Kestor, *The One and the Many: Contemporary Collaborative Art in a Global Context* (Duke University Press: Durham, NC, 2011). My *The Utopian Globalists* traces this lineage back into the twentieth century.

47 On concepts of "mediation" within a radical sociology of culture, see Raymond Williams, *Culture* (Fontana: Glasgow, 1981), especially chapters on "Reproduction" and "Organization."

48 See, e.g., Griselda Pollock and Fred Orton, *Vincent Van Gogh: Artist of his Time* (Phaidon: London, 1978).

49 See Menene Gras, Jonathan Harris and Bashir Makhoul (eds.), *Contemporary Art and Visual Culture in Global Asia* (IB Tauris: London, 2017, forthcoming).

50 See the range of essays in, e.g., Terry Smith, Okwui Enwezor, and Nancy Condee (eds.), *Antinomies of Art and Culture: Modernity, Postmodernity, Contemporaneity* (Duke University Press: Durham, NC, 2008).

51 See Maria Lind and Raimund Minichbauer (eds.), *European Cultural Policies 2015: A Report with Scenarios on the Future of Public Funding for Contemporary Art in Europe* (IAPSIS; London, 2005): 4–13.

52 https://frieze.com/about (accessed March 21, 2017).

53 See Barbara Casavecchia, "Roman Ruins: Reflections on Italy's Continuing Decline," *Frieze*, no.160 January–February 2014: 13.

54 See Basia Lewandowska Cummings, "See Change: The Increased Visibility of Art from Africa in the UK," *Frieze*, no.160, January–February 2014: 17; Reviews, *Frieze*, no.160: 137–167.

55 See Basia Lewandowska Cummings, "See Change."

56 See Basia Lewandowska Cummings, "See Change," and Martin Bernal, *Black Athena. The Afroasiatic Roots of Classical Civilization: The Fabrication of Ancient Greece 1785–1985* (Vintage: London, 1991).

57 See Basia Lewandowska Cummings, "See Change."

58 See Karl Marx *Capital: A Critique of Political Economy* vol.1 (trans. Ben Fowkes; Penguin: London, 1990): 493, and David Harvey, *A Companion to Marx's Capital* (Verso: London, 2010): 191–197.

1

Doing the Business: Producing Consumption in the Hong Kong Art World

My "premium economy" class flight to Hong Kong is delayed due to engine trouble and I spend a mostly sleepless "economy economy" night in a Helsinki airport hotel waiting for the jet's repairs to be completed. I finally arrive at my budget hotel in Soho, near the western tip of Hong Kong island, only about eight hours later than scheduled, though it feels like I've lost a whole day...

Hong Kong Gets the Art Basel Treatment

On that first morning in Hong Kong I encountered a big demonstration in the downtown area protesting against the PRC's plans to vet all candidates wishing to stand for election to the Hong Kong government in 2017. The privately owned, stock market-listed *South China Morning Post* newspaper—once owned by Rupert Murdoch's News International group—noted that this was the "biggest march for a decade," held on the seventeenth anniversary of the British handover of Hong Kong to mainland Chinese rule in 1997. A local version of the global "Occupy" movement had emerged recently and taken a lead in the protests.[1] I skimmed the pages of the *A.M. Post,* a free monthly magazine on Hong Kong contemporary visual arts. Many stories in the June 2014 number were concerned with the second "edition" of Art Basel Hong Kong held earlier and the numerous related art world events that had been arranged to take advantage of the potential buyers who had flown in for the fair. The global contemporary art world is, as many commentators note, predominantly "event driven."[2]

A.M. Post reported, for instance, that a planned show of life-size sculptures by Antony Gormley, intended to be sited at various high vantage points around Hong Kong, was cancelled due to the suicide of a bank employee who had jumped from the JP Morgan building offices... the French and Hong Kong governments had collaborated on the just-opened exhibition "Paris Chinese Painting: Legacy of the Twentieth-Century Chinese Masters" at the Hong Kong

The Global Contemporary Art World, First Edition. Jonathan Harris.
© 2017 John Wiley & Sons, Inc. Published 2017 by John Wiley & Sons, Inc.

Museum of Art... Para/Site, a chic alternative exhibition and meeting space founded by artists in 1996, had paired up with the library, research and education agency Asia Art Archive, founded in 2000, to produce a show about the "colonial legacy" of "sexual conservatism" in the territory ("Sex in Hong Kong: Ten Million Years of Yearning")... Ai Wei Wei's Berlin show 'Evidence' had dealt with the artist's recent imprisonment in the PRC ostensibly for tax evasion and the revelations of official corruption... a show at the newly opened government-funded arts and "cultural engagement" center, enigmatically called "Oi!"—developed on the site of the former Hong Kong Yacht Club—included a nostalgic film installation by Kingsley Ng based on 1950s home movies of the colony's Lunar Park fairground.[3]

This snapshot indicates something of the range of activities within Hong Kong's contemporary art world in the first half of 2014, which was enlivened and considerably enlarged by the takeover of the Hong Kong Art Fair by Art Basel three years earlier. This move helped to encourage several globally active key New York/London dealing galleries to open venues in the city, confirming the centrality of Hong Kong in the Asian contemporary art market. *A.M. Post*'s editorial fairly sang Art Basel's praises. The business in Hong Kong had initiated, it noted, some philanthropic as well as financial partnerships with, for instance, Art Basel's support for the planned "visual culture" mega-museum M+, Asia Art Archive, the Hong Kong Tourist Board, as well as "main sponsor" Deutsche Bank (Germany's largest financial group, holding assets worth more than 1 trillion dollars), whose corporate art collection was foregrounded at Art Basel Hong Kong's first edition in 2013. These organizations constitute something of the usual range of "bedfellows"—some combinations perhaps appearing unlikely—which cohabit or partner-up in the global contemporary art world. Multinational banks come to rub their shoulders here with "anti-colonial" and even explicitly dissident arts organizations. Sounding only mildly sarcastic, *A.M. Post*'s editors reflected in Warholian terms that it was perhaps "time for artists to [...] enjoy the wealth and quality in life that business can bring, so that art can tread its path towards business—towards a better place."[4]

Art Basel Hong Kong's debut fair in 2013 consolidated the premium significance of the territory within Asia's contemporary art world, although the focus of activity there is overwhelmingly on sales rather than on art production or museum and gallery shows. The SAR is geographically contiguous with mainland China—from which much art is brought to be sold to an effective world market—and relatively close to a number of other significant eastern Asian and southeast Asian contemporary art centers, including Taiwan, Japan and Singapore. Hong Kong's key role is in the production and promotion of art consumption: in terms of art buying, selling and branding—these are the defining features of the global art fair business. Setting aside sales of artworks shown at the fair, Art Basel Hong Kong, along with several satellite fairs and auctions in the city, generates and stimulates economic, social and cultural activity at many interrelated levels and points within the system that comprises the Hong Kong art world. The glossy opening pages of the main catalogue published for Art Basel Hong Kong in 2013, a third-tier world art fair now, alongside original Art Basel (first edition 1970) and Art Basel Miami Beach (first edition 2002), emphasize the continuum of "luxury" commodities associated with the art market. These include gold watches, Cuban cigars, vintage French champagne and residential properties in central London and Manhattan. The catalogue also showcased BMW high performance cars painted in the style ("brands") of postmodern and contemporary artists, or their representatives, prepared to be linked to this wider luxury market: from "Andy Warhol BMW M1 1979" to "Jeff Koons BMW M3 GT2 2010."[5]

The Art Basel businesses themselves are marketed as luxury goods, services and experiences—three complementary sets of products central now to the operation and character of the global contemporary art world. If the small city of Basel in Switzerland offered what is described as "limitless culture without going very far," including access to what is claimed to be the "world's oldest public art collection," (the city's municipal collection of art, founded in 1661), then the US city of Miami Beach boasted "premier international art and a high-caliber audience." Part of the unique service offered by Art Basel, then, is the delivery to participating gallery owners of a dense population of serious

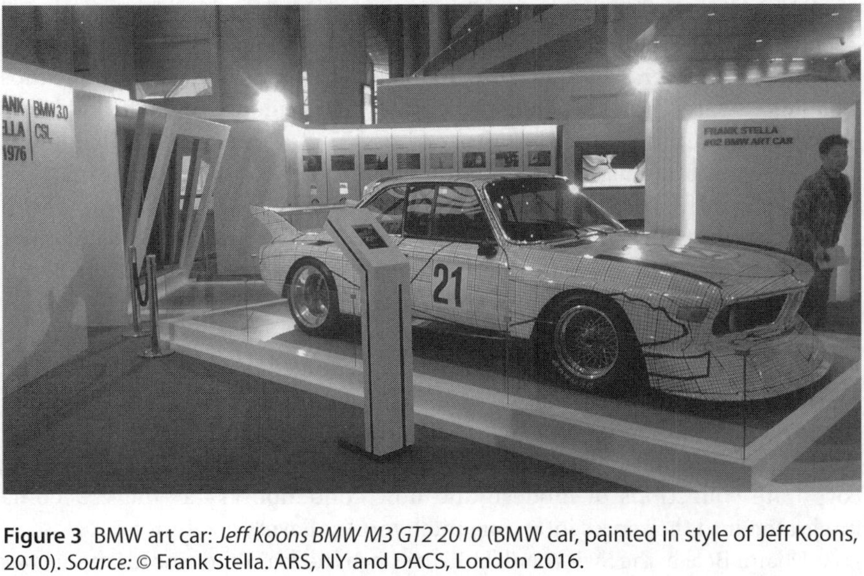

Figure 3 BMW art car: *Jeff Koons BMW M3 GT2 2010* (BMW car, painted in style of Jeff Koons, 2010). *Source:* © Frank Stella. ARS, NY and DACS, London 2016.

potential buyers. Meanwhile, the throng of mere onlookers, though vital to the spectacle of the fair, are kept at a distance from the VIPs.[6]

Time Out Hong Kong's 'Hong Kong Art Guide' to the 2013 Art Basel fair in the SAR also began with multiple pages parading Western luxury brands and fashion models. Then it announced a Jean-Michel Basquiat show at the new Gagosian gallery in town. A few pages later the Chinese performance artist duo Cai Yuan and Jian Jun Xi – based in Britain, famous mostly for jumping on Tracey Emin's *My Bed* installation at Tate Modern in 1999—made an appearance advertising new works at the Shanghai Tang gallery venue in Hong Kong. Yuan and Xi's "interventions," the ad claimed, "reflect upon the phenomenon of globalization and the role of modern China in the 21st century." Celebrity in the contemporary art world is an inevitable adjunct of this kind of marketing activity. *The Art Newspaper* International Edition, commemorating the first Art Basel Hong Kong, presented its own photo-gallery of the most internationally famous Chinese artists: Zhang Peili—reputedly the creator of the first video artwork made in the PRC in 1988—Ding Yi, Cai Guo-Qiang, Zeng Fanzhi, Yu Hong and Ai Weiwei (the latter named as the most influential player in the contemporary art world by *Art Review* magazine in 2011).[7]

Art Basel Hong Kong, following on from the Miami Beach operation, articulates the related worlds of business, city tourism and regeneration, luxury consumption and celebrity media culture. The art fair model has become a global template, encouraging both mutually beneficial and potentially competitive contemporary art world markets. For instance, the main catalogue contains an advert for the 2014 India Art Fair in Delhi, sponsored by "Yes Bank." "Sponsoring," "collaboration" and "partnership" activities have extended deeply into the productive activity of some globally successful artists who've become key players in the world market. These include Jake and Dinos Chapman, represented by White Cube gallery in London, São Paolo and Hong Kong, whose branch opened in the territory in 2012. *Time Out Hong Kong*'s article on the Chapman Brothers' exhibition there, co-timed with Art Basel Hong Kong 2013, partly concerned the "pyjamas project" they had done with fashion house Louis Vuitton's head designer, Clint Jones. This was another mutually beneficial spreading of cash rewards associated with the luxury goods field, with a bit of the Chapman brand's social comment thrown in. "We don't really have a wider interest in fashion [but] it's quite nice to see the work bleed into other areas," averred Jake Chapman, then aged 47 but still billed, and branded, as one of "Les Enfants Terrible."[8] But while diverse luxury commodities, services and experiences proliferate around and in the art shown at Art Basel events, the heavy lifting of "sponsorship" is done by the finance banks, whose corporate collections of modern and now contemporary art have become integrated into the representational pitch for Art Basel's exhibitions.

At Miami Beach, the Swiss bank UBS has been the main sponsor for the art fair since 2002, and at Basel itself since 1994. The bank described its involvement in the 2012 edition in Miami Beach as "an integral part of our long history of supporting the arts through our global sponsorship programs and the UBS Art Collection." UBS presented this involvement tacitly as a form of public penance for the crimes and malpractice within its global business activities. The multinational bank was castigated after the 2008 Crash, investigated and fined several times by the US government for illegal trading and tax evasion practices that were reported widely in the media. In 2011 its former chief executive Oswald Grübel resigned in the wake of the latest scandal worth about US$2.3 billion.[9] At the 2012 fair the catalogue statement from UBS extolled the corporation's extensive charitable and education works in the United States, the diverse public accessibility of its art collection and the copious amounts of work done by its employees—on UBS time—in non-profit public service.

Offshore Art Business in the Global Neoliberal Capitalist Economy

Art Basel decided to contract the main sponsorship of Deutsche Bank for its fledgling Hong Kong fair. The bank's art collections are based at Deutsche Bank Towers in Frankfurt, the Stadel Museum, also in Frankfurt, and in Hong Kong. Other sponsors for the 2013 edition spanned the usual range of luxury goods and "media partner" services—high-end vodka and brandy, five-star hotels, watches, the *Financial Times*—along with, somewhat jarringly perhaps, Para/Site and Asia Art Archive, named as "cultural partners."[10] Deutsche Bank's explanation in the 2013 catalogue of the reasons for its involvement in Art Basel Hong Kong raises the question of some of the "borders" central to this chapter and the book as a whole. The bank's high-minded self-justifications are exemplary of much official art fair rhetoric that constitutes part of what might be called the "global text" of the contemporary art world.

Deutsche Bank's corporate collection, the institution's Art Basel Hong Kong literature explains, consists of over 56,000 artworks; more than 900 branch offices worldwide exhibit examples from it. We are transported once more into the enigmatic world of art quantity/quality issues again. Ninety five percent of the Deutsche Bank collection is "accessible to the public"—but what if this excludes the best 5% of the art? Or does quantity trump quality here in an inversion of usual art critical values? The meat of the matter, however, is in what Deutsche Bank characterizes as its "deep and enduring connection with art globally [which] stems from our belief that creativity transcends borders, challenges the status quo and is a source of innovation and new perspectives."[11] Deutsche Bank's motivation to "invest" in modern and contemporary art has been rooted ostensibly in both economic and public relations concerns. Its collections date from 1978, at the time when fine art was first beginning to be marketed as a viable, or potentially viable, "asset class."

The pioneers of this business development in the mid-1970s claimed that artwork purchases could prove to be a reliable way to "park" capital, in a time of high inflation, with an expectation that their financial value, over time, would at least not decrease—or on the basis that art's volatility or risk as a carrier of durable value was significantly less than that of other kinds of material assets, such as luxury boats or cars.[12] Deutsche Bank's sponsorship of Art Basel Hong Kong enables it (so, one imagines, the bank's chief executives think or hope) to appear cultivated and high-principled in terms of corporate social and community commitments, especially given the 2008 Crash with which it, along with UBS, was directly associated—interestingly, in the Miami area itself.[13] Deutsche Bank's sponsorship role also enables the bank to have its global business activities associated positively, if tenuously, with contemporary art's apparent avant-gardist utopianism and societal radicalism, through the bank's abstracted, ambiguous business-speak of "innovation" and "creativity." This, then, is part of the reason why at Art Basel Hong Kong in 2013 Deutsche Bank came to rub shoulders with local visual arts organizations such as Asia Art Archive and Para/Site—indigenous and initially "grass roots" institutions with considerable connections to post- and anti-colonial traditions in the arts, scholarship and activism.

Deutsche Bank is also interested in the prospect of financial profit through its involvement in the art fairs' cumulative sales in Hong Kong, Miami Beach and Basel which work, directly and indirectly, to enhance the value of the many thousands of artworks in the Bank's own collection. But although the Asian contemporary art market (and "emerging markets" in the Persian Gulf and Brazil) has grown dramatically since 2000, concomitant with a rise in Asia-Pacific based millionaires by 9.7% to 3.3 million in 2010, the total value of art sales in 2011 in European and US markets, despite the 2008 Crash, remained much higher, according to Marc Spiegler, co-director of Art Basel Miami Beach.[14] Another operative border, then, and a veritable economic "iron curtain" operating everywhere in the world, as well as in the global contemporary art world, is that between the rich and the rest. Between, that is, those (the "High Net Worth" and "Ultra-High Net Worth" groups) who can afford to buy art as a form of "investment"—the medieval sense of which, interestingly, meant to besiege or blockade—and the multitudes without that power.

Corporations, galleries and individual collectors made up the bulk of those buying artworks at Art Basel Hong Kong in 2013 (at which 245 selected galleries were represented, attracting more than 65,000 visitors over the four days of the event), though the quality and quantity of information on art market sales remains inadequate in many respects, despite the ever-growing economic significance of world trade in art and antiques.[15] Part of the reason for this is that the contemporary art market is divided between the highly competitive so-called "secondary" public sales done at auctions and at art fairs and the private purchases agreed between dealers, artists and collectors, traditionally termed the "primary" sales forum. "Secondary," however, is a misleading name for an increasing quantity of sales happening at art fairs, where artists in growing numbers have begun directly to send new works—labeled "direct from the studio"—for first time sale. In an overall growing market all competing sectors might benefit from this change; in the time of harsh volatility and slowdown after 2008, however, the auction houses and art fairs sometimes came into conflict over preserving what they considered the legitimate borders of their selling territories.

For instance, in an effort to maintain its profits during this period, Christie's auctioneers took over a dealing gallery of their own, Haunch of Venison, with branches in London and New York, which it operated from 2007 to 2013. After that point the decision was taken that the gallery's resources were to be integrated into Christie's traditional auction-based sales activities. Art Basel decided to exclude Haunch of Venison from taking a booth in any of its fairs during this period as it enabled Christie's to attempt to poach some of the VIP buyers that Art Basel regarded as belonging to its territory – in its fairs at Basel, Miami Beach and Hong Kong. Art Basel also became wary of rival auctioneers and dealers' clandestinely acquiring Art Basel's VIP "passes," allowing continued access to the sales floor, in order to approach potential buyers, within an infrastructure set up and paid for by Art Basel. (My own attempt—finally successful—to gain a VIP pass for Hong Kong in 2013 involved a bizarre telephone interrogation by Art Basel's UK agent who seemed suspicious of my motives and self-declaration as a "critic." Might I be secretly acting for a dealer or auctioneer?) It's difficult to feel too sorry for Art Basel, however, in their attempts to maintain control over what they see as "their" market and having to suffer auctioneers' agents steering potential buyers away from certain gallery booths, organizing, according to one dealer, "dinners around the fair and [taking] the best tables at the best restaurants," where they "exhaust the clients with their dinners and exhibitions."[16]

Art Basel, once it had taken over the Hong Kong Art Fair, was able to bring into play the work and expertise of its global "VIP managers" service, totaling 22 agents based around the world. This number was a massive increase upon the single specialist employed by the Fair's previous owners to tout for potential business. "Globalization" in the contemporary art market partly means this kind of intense and extensive—and continually extending—intelligence-gathering activity. The imperative is to attract and retain the interest of potential buyers, and, especially in hard times, eliminate what is regarded as unfair competition from other sectors in the business.[17] A public debate organized at Art Basel Hong Kong in 2013 drew explicit attention to the business when it considered the motion "The market is the best judge of art's quality." Participants included Amy Cappallezzo, chair of Christie's "post-war & contemporary" art sales and Charles Guarino, US publisher of *Artforum* journal. These influential art world professionals were invited to join the discussion, partly in order to give the fair some intellectual and critical kudos. Such "collateral" seminars lend an element of the "biennial experience"—shows more apparently akin to serious museum exhibitions than to the hype-driven selling fairs—and thus cross the border between the two paradigmatic "main events" dominating the contemporary art world calendar.

Guarino encapsulated a prevalent fetishizing of the art market in his preparatory statement for the debate when he claimed that artists "are ever mindful of their audience, of which the market is a logical extension—some might say synonymous [...] Selling work may not be the primary motivation, but it's surely there before brush touches canvas. The real question is 'do good artists ever ignore the market?'"[18] In the context of Hong Kong, rather than, say, London or New York, the primary homes of the global contemporary art market but also of art production and its museum validation, this debate had particular significance. (Guarino's revealing phrase, "before brush touches canvas," also underlined the predominance of paintings in the objects put up for sale at art fairs: many more pictures get sold than all other kinds of objects put together.) Another border, then, is that between the market's activities on the one hand and the museum and related academic bases of contemporary art on the other. In Hong Kong and Asia generally, the former—though still dominated by Western interests—is much stronger and more influential than the latter, a situation creating serious asymmetries that further skew the power relations in the global contemporary art world.[19] Astute commentators in Hong Kong were aware at the time of the 2013 fair that the SAR, despite enjoying "an enviable degree of artistic freedom [...] compared to the Mainland," had little historical or recently developed institutional infrastructure needed to sustain art production and the related curatorial/critical processes of museum validation.[20]

The two most recent ambitious exhibitions of new work by Hong Kong-based artists, for example, took place well outside the city. These were the "Horizons" show at the Shanghai Museum of Contemporary Art in 2007 and "Hong Kong Eye," held at the Saatchi Gallery in London, that attracted more than 200,000 visitors in 2012. The historic diaspora of Chinese around the world means that there cannot be just one single location or authentic home for either these people or the works made by Chinese artists where ever they happen to live, or where these artworks might be shown or sold. The development, however, of new high-profile art exhibition venues in Hong Kong has certainly been celebrated by their supporters. They cite the arrival of globally powerful galleries such as Gagosian, White Cube, Perrotin and Lehmann Maupin (from New York and London), and Pearl Jam, Platform China and Peking Fine Arts (from the PRC). A growing number of "alternative" spaces and resource centers such as Para/Site, Asia Art Archive, Osage, Cattle Depot Artists' Village—home to Videotage, a moving image archive and research unit active since 1984—and Spring Artists' Residencies all suggest an indigenous, diverse visual arts culture constituting what has been called Hong Kong's "new amazing art hub."[21] Sceptics point out, however, that the economic success of the SAR has led to continuous rent rises, squeezing artists out of the city, that the PRC's gradual encroachment on the relative political and cultural independence of Hong Kong is a worrying matter, and that most of the new international galleries ("at the moneyed end of the spectrum") have no interest in showing or selling works by local artists. Their sense of the market is predominantly determined by the taste of the rich of mainland China and Asia broadly. Related to this focus, Hong Kong is also home to a local art public in the main intolerant of the kinds of conceptualist interests characteristic of much contemporary art since the 1990s with the rise of the "Young British Artists" Damien Hirst, Tracey Emin and Sarah Lucas.[22]

One exception to the predominance of Western corporate interests in the art market in the territory was the return to the city of Ben Brown Fine Arts in 2009 from London, where the firm's eponymous owner maintains another gallery. Born in Hong Kong, Ben Brown is regarded as one of the first "world class" local dealers to have moved his gallery into the historic Pedder Building in the Admiralty district. Brown claimed in 2013 that the city's art world had moved beyond "pure investment [and] speculation" and was now about "genuine interest [...] a time of great cultural effervescence." His Hong Kong gallery shows a mixture of Chinese and international artists.[23] Both *A.M. Post* magazine and *Time Out Hong Kong's* special edition on Art Basel Hong Kong in 2013 recognized the local art world created, though still under consolidation, there. According to an essay in *A.M. Post,* it constitutes a kind of "art world factory" of key players—the artist, the auction house, the curator, the gallery, the critic, the collector. The author's tone accepted that a necessary system or proto-ecology was at work, but that this can also be "played" or rigged by those with particular interests and may be skewed by those who enjoy more power (for instance, he noted that prospects "for employment remain bleak for visual arts graduates in Hong Kong"). There was a recognition that the contemporary art system in the SAR was vulnerable, even "pitifully weak," at many levels. It was vulnerable to global business pressures, to the economic and political regimes dividing but also connecting Hong Kong and the PRC, and poor in terms of the prospects for the development of good local conditions for educating and employing home-grown arts professionals. It was very difficult for Hong Kong's own artists and their artworks—especially given the lack of a "culture of professional art criticism"—to rise above the status of being a "sideshow" to the city's art market burgeoning under Art Basel's control.[24]

The vulnerability of Hong Kong's art world, though also its specific qualities, is underlined by the character and local reputation of the Sigg Collection of contemporary works. This was gifted to the mega-museum M+, planned for completion in 2019 on a vast "regeneration" site in West Kowloon across from Hong Kong Island. The collection includes many important pieces by mainland artists, such as Ai Weiwei, Fang Lijun and Zhang Pelli, whose video, photographic, painting and installation works have been censored for many years by the Chinese Communist Party government because of their sociopolitical and sexual content. *Time Out Hong Kong* magazine wondered what future for "artistic freedom" there might be in the SAR when the PRC had recently prevented Shanghai's Power Art Station from showing Andy Warhol's silkscreen prints of Chairman Mao in the exhibition "Andy Warhol: 15 Minutes Eternal" that then travelled on to Beijing. If that was not bad enough, the complaint was that some influential local art pundits, including renowned traditional artists such as the oil painter Lin Minggang (chairman of the Hong Kong Oil Painting Research Society) had attacked works in the Sigg Collection as "rubbish." Such criticism, though still occasionally seen in the Western contemporary art world's homelands several decades after the notorious Carl Andre "bricks" media frenzy in Britain in the late 1970s, has largely been banished to a marginal "flat earth" position. This achievement was due in some large degree to the efforts of Tate's Nicholas Serota who relentlessly promoted Britain-based contemporary art as a sign of vigorous national creative health through the gallery's annual "Turner Prize," begun in 1984.[25]

Could a "mature," well-rounded and indigenous art world infrastructure or ecology be established in Hong Kong, given these particular vulnerabilities? The same question could be asked of the prospects for contemporary art in Ramallah in the State of Palestine, a multiply-fractured proto-territory frozen into pernicious dependency on Israel, the subject of this book's final chapter. What, then, are the conditions necessary for the authentic flourishing of contemporary art and the range of agents, institutions and networks needed to support it in such "emerging" centers? That modifier suggests something of the difficulties in a global art world dominated by pre-existing Western interests and resources. Perhaps, one way or another, such a question is inevitably what might be called "occidental essentialist." Based, that is, on a stated or tacit partisan perspective: a set of presuppositions generated by Western art institutions for over two hundred years and embodied in the canonical artworks made, bought, sold, exhibited and critically validated within its core territories in Europe and the USA during this epoch.

Isn't the global contemporary art world system created from, and working to reproduce, a set of asymmetrical power relations and nodes highly differentially placed geopolitically? Isn't this system linked decisively, in economic and cultural terms, to the dominant Western powers, for example, through art market businesses such as Art Basel Hong Kong? This global system also manifests the historical legacies of imperialism, colonialism, neocolonialism and Cold War division that still act to determine (forming and limiting) the kinds of regional and local art worlds that have developed, and can, in places such as Hong Kong—now a part of mainland China and yet, for the moment, still relatively autonomous from it. It is to the territory's divisions and borders, products of this history, that I turn now.

Combined and Uneven Development in the Hong Kong Art World

The "handover" of Hong Kong by the British authorities to China in 1997 meant that the people of the former colony became citizens of the PRC, and ruled by a government for which they had not, ever, voted. This outcome actually replicated the historical disposition of the British regime that had always denied Hong Kong residents general elections and which only introduced very limited popular representational democracy through the Legislative Council in 1985—a cynical late-Cold War gambit—with the knowledge that return to mainland Chinese control was imminent. (This measure enabled the British to warn with a smidgeon of truth that the Hong Kong people might now be deprived by the Beijing government of "democratic rights" that they had previously enjoyed, albeit very briefly, under their former rulers.) Hong Kong had grown apart from China in all ways since the beginnings of British rule—though especially during the 1966–1976 "Cultural Revolution"—and many residents thought of the territory's delivery to the PRC as a second colonization. But the PRC was itself, by 1997, in a process of dramatic change as the capitalist reforms of Mao's successor, Deng Xiaoping, the "modernizer," had radically transformed the country over the previous 20 years. The PRC was invited to join the World Trade Organization four years later—conditional on agreeing to a range of international treaty obligations that regulate global capitalism—and began huge growth that has continued, if after 2014 at a slower rate, making China's the world's second biggest economy.[26]

Art Basel's corporate owners wanted control of the Hong Kong Art Fair because it brought the Swiss business very close to what is now also the second biggest market for art of all kinds in the world (up massively from 6% in 2006 to 25% by 2012, due to a huge rise in the size of a Chinese middle class prepared to spend some disposable income on artworks). It remains unclear, though, how many committed, systematic collectors of contemporary art there are in the PRC—one estimate put it as low as 30. What evidence there is quite firmly demonstrates that they mostly buy contemporary "traditional" ink paintings and calligraphic works made by Chinese and other Asian artists. Not all newly made art is, then, equally contemporary, or contemporary in the same ways: choice of media and themes are key to the varied and partisan definitions of contemporaneity that new works attract. (This is a question that I pursue further in Chapter 4, concerned with the passage from modern to contemporary art in the PRC.)

While Hong Kong by the 1990s had become a highly significant marketplace globally—especially for intercontinental financial dealing—development of the trade in material commodities such as contemporary art via enterprises such as Art Basel Hong Kong and recently arrived London/New York-based global galleries such as White Cube and Gagosian remains a speculative, risky venture.

Western art businesses hope that the cosmopolitan mainland Chinese buyers' tastes will gradually become more what might be termed "global contemporary"—that is, derived from the Western European and US modern/postmodern art era of c. 1860–1990. Christies, for instance, decided to move squarely into the PRC market, establishing a permanent auction house base in Shanghai in 2007 and thus began to compete directly with "state backed" local auction businesses (although the government imposed restrictions on Christie's sales of certain kinds of works).

Contemporary Chinese artists renowned in the west, such as Zhang Xiaogang and Fang Lijun, mostly still sell their works outside of the PRC, where they can achieve much higher prices: 211% higher on average, in fact, for works sold abroad in a period studied recently.[27] In contrast, Sotheby's, along with PRC-based auction houses Poly and China Guardian (which both opened branches in Hong Kong in 2012), sold the vast majority of their lots of Chinese calligraphic works at 2013 auctions there, further indicating Chinese buyers' relative aesthetic conservatism. Calligraphic works accounted for a huge 88% of all Chinese fine art sales at all auctions in PRC in 2011. According to one report, over 90% of all contemporary art pieces—though acknowledging the serious ambiguities of that term—sold at auction by PRC businesses in Beijing in the last few years went to Western buyers.[28]

Though Hong Kong's assimilation into the PRC has been partial in all respects, China, the British and Hong Kong's own elite indigenous ruling groups have sought since 1997 to maintain the benefits of the SAR's economic and financial arrangements for attracting global business. Hong Kong had the world's sixth-highest GDP per capita in 2004 and supported 33% of all foreign capital flows into the PRC.[29] The territory's continuing attractiveness in these terms is obvious. Hong Kong's free trade policy includes no taxes on art imports or exports, though PRC cross-border trade in art and antiques is regulated. By contrast, the PRC operated a 12% import tax for artworks until 2011, which was then halved for a trial period if the work's country of origin had a preferential trading agreement with China. Value Added Tax (VAT) remains at 17%, so the overall import tax is 23% compared to zero in Hong Kong, although the SAR does apply a 15–16.5% profit tax range on businesses. It has been very difficult, therefore, for mainland auctioneers to compete with Hong Kong's contemporary art business given China's comparatively high tax regime. Many PRC collectors prefer to keep their artworks in the SAR in order to avoid these payments. Not surprisingly, art insurance, storage, transport and conservation businesses have also thrived in Hong Kong.[30]

Nevertheless, developments indicate that a kind of globalization of contemporary art sales within the PRC has taken place since the mid-2000s, in the sense that the disparities in price between works sold at auction there and externally, including in Hong Kong, have decreased, though the reasons are complex and the quality of the evidence is patchy. Business professional opinion, reported in *The Art Newspaper* in 2013 at the time of Art Basel Hong Kong confirmed, for instance, that New York and London no longer maintained an iron-grip "duopoly" on contemporary art sales. It suggested that the move of Art Basel and major dealing galleries into Hong Kong is a kind of recognition of this, as well as of the rising power of mainland China's own art market.[31]However, too much focus on the art market runs the risk of ignoring and underplaying significant cultural and social developments bound up with the transformation in relations between the PRC and Hong Kong, but also within these two interconnected but still separate entities.

For instance, according to Philip Tinari, director of the Ullens Center for Contemporary Art at "798" in Beijing, much more varied and distinct senses of "Chineseness" are now experienced and expressed by the Chinese people in the PRC. These are clearly distinguishable from those of people in Hong Kong, Taiwan and in the greater Chinese global diaspora. Multivalent and mutating identities have been produced out of China's own profound and rapid globalization since the 1990s.This transformation comprises an emerging contemporary generational identity that has grown, Tinari observes

> out of a shared citizenship, education system, consumer culture and set of historical memories filtered through their parents [...] rather than some immanent notion of a cultural identity [...] this "China" is itself an extremely wide category [...] that today, in an era of atomised subjectivities [...] contains multitudes."

If the Beijing central government rather unintentionally legitimized contemporary art precisely by treating it "as a market," and as a small part of the nation's economic modernization, then it also helped enable it to become an available and potent form of representation and self-representation.[32] (Chapter 4 explores this development further.)

Art Basel is not the only Swiss business operating in Hong Kong. International Social Services Hong Kong (ISS-HK) is a "global aid" company and non-governmental organization (NGO) specializing in providing contract welfare services and payments to refugees, or "asylum-seeking clients," living in the SAR. The Refugee Union—an asylum seekers supporters' organization—was involved in the street protests in Hong Kong in 2014. This group launched a campaign attacking ISS-HK for allegedly taking $280 m in its contract with the Hong Kong government but paying welfare support 25% below the SAR's legal poverty line and then colluding in a series of corrupt deals with food suppliers and landlords.[33] Neoliberalization measures within the global economy have centrally involved nations privatizing such government services and cutting social and welfare provision budgets—especially since the 2008 Crash. In Hong Kong this policy is part and parcel of the same "investment strategy" that attracts contemporary art market business by charging low profit taxes and no import/export taxes. (Only relatively small or zero reductions in national debts and deficits in the European states have actually been achieved by making large programmatic cuts to state spending—"austerity"—rather than by raising progressive taxes, especially on corporations and the super-wealthy, in order to maintain welfare provision for their citizens.)[34]

Magnus Renfrew, then the director of Art Basel Hong Kong, in his "welcome" statement in the main catalogue to the 2013 edition, claimed that the European-US domination of contemporary art, manifesting what he called a "broadly unified aesthetic," had actually given way to a "plurality" of art in Asia. He then observed that Hong Kong, Asia's finance capital, had an "opportunity to become a defining force in the international art world." The regional significance of Hong Kong included its status as the center for the Asia and Asia-Pacific "collector base" for modern and contemporary art. In addition, Renfrew said that the SAR's own emerging visual arts organizations would help to "cement" Hong Kong's position "as a cultural hub of global stature." Of the 245 galleries from "35 territories" present that year at the fair (selected from over 600 applications) over 50%, he noted, had "active gallery spaces in Asia and the Asia Pacific region." This was actually a tacit acknowledgement, however, that a majority of this "over 50%" were, in fact, European and US-owned, despite the "Asian Tiger" rhetoric.[35]

Ben Brown Fine Arts' arrival in the SAR in 2009 represented one of the most practical means through which support could be provided directly to Hong Kong's indigenous artists. Brown's gallery and, later, the Lehmann Maupin Gallery began to show the work of local artists—such as Simon Birch, Tsang Kin-wah and Pak Sheung Chuen—as well as North American and European artists, including Tracey Emin. Lehmann Maupin also began to offer internships for Hong Kong arts graduates in New York City, the global contemporary art world's "mother ship." This development was part of a scheme by the gallery intended to promote what it called "dialogue between East and West." The other Western galleries' move to the city around the time of Art Basel Hong Kong in 2013 has clearly helped to promote the growth of "cultural industries" infrastructural support companies of varying kinds, as previously noted. The long drawn-out plans for the mega-museum M+ have been very ambitious—a US$2.1billion development intended to rival Tate Modern and the Museum of Modern Art in New York.[36]

Art production in Hong Kong, due to the high and perpetually rising rents since 2000, has substantially turned, of necessity, into a "post-studio," "post-medium" practice, favoring digital forms, and often requiring an outsourcing of production as a consequence of the space limitations, frequently with the use of modest quantities of materials, typical of the SAR's general "just-in-time" economy. This mode is sharply contrary (sometimes intentionally so) to the eruption of contemporary art production in Beijing since 2000, based on the use of generously sized converted factory spaces available in the outer suburbs, especially those along the city's eastern corridor to the Capital Airport. The Hong Kong conditions arguably neither guarantee nor foreclose anything in terms of the potential quality of work produced though, as one commentator has suggested, they may lead to assimilations of some "fine art" production to wider commercial design activities in the city. This consequence, in turn, may have provoked, or could provoke, a backlash where artists come to favor working in a traditional studio context, seen precisely as a kind of retreat from Hong Kong's advertising and graphics business culture.[37]

Space and money issues do not trouble Wang Wei Lui's collection of modern and contemporary art. Along with her husband, luxury handbag manufacturer Yiqian, she owns two private exhibition venues—together comprising the Long Museum—located in Shanghai, spaces open since 2011 and 2014 respectively. These institutions exemplify a trend in super-rich Asian wives' cultural philanthropy (enjoying favorable state land purchase and tax benefits) which also includes the private Kiran Nadar Museum in Delhi, India, discussed in Chapter 3. In 2009 Wang Wei Lui spent over US $58 million buying Western and Asian art while the two buildings, the Long Museums in Pudong and West Bund, cost over US $48 million dollars to construct. Lui has bought installations by Elafur Eliasson and Mona Hatoum and, earlier on in her collecting career, so-called Chinese "red classic" paintings with post-1949 socialist-realist revolutionary themes. These works, she claims, are really early "pioneers of Chinese contemporary art," existing in attenuated, traumatic continuity with the art world of Art Basel Hong Kong and the SAR's complex, symbiotic relationship with the PRC.[38]In 1949, according to one source, there were only 21 museums in the whole of mainland China, 348 by 1978, but more than 4,000 in 2013. Of these, 175 are visual arts specialist institutions funded by the government. The PRC, like Western nation-states, now sees its "cultural industries" as a significant sector of the country's economic expansion. In 2010 this sector had an output of US $178.9 billion, up 221% from 2004, and comprising 2.75% of China's GDP. The PRC's five-year plan begun that year had the target for the nation's cultural industries sector increasing to 5% of GDP by 2015.[39]

One of the problems this extraordinarily rapid growth has created, however, is a huge amount of exhibition space with often little to fill it. Many new venues lack permanent collections of artworks, trained staff of all kinds (paid a decent salary) and exhibition program budgets able to turn these museums into permanent functioning institutions. The Power Station of Art, Shanghai, for example, was converted into a museum in 2012 at a cost of US $64 million, paid by the city government. Like Tate Modern, it is a renovated energy-generating plant. The building was converted in order to host the 9th Shanghai Biennale that year, but since this event finished the museum has had long periods without any exhibitions at all. In addition to budget, staffing and planning problems, policy and political controversies recur. The "15 Minutes Eternal" show of Andy Warhol works, as noted earlier, took place at the Power Station of Art in April–July 2013 but the authorities removed the silkscreen prints of Mao which they regarded as "unsuitable."[40]

The privately owned Shanghai Museum of Glass (or SHMOG, an unfortunate acronym given the chronic environmental problems in the PRC) opened in 2011 with a specialist focus on this construction, decoration and expressive material. It is housed in a former factory renovated in spectacular fashion by corporate designers Coordination Asia, a German design and architecture firm based in the city. SHMOG exemplifies a trend in businesses opening museums effectively as "fronts" for public relations efforts. SHMOG is one of the planned 100 museums to be launched in a decade as part of the city authorities' campaign to turn Shanghai into what it calls a "global cultural and creativity center." Despite these ambitions, the museum's "Keep It Glassy" exhibition held in the spring of 2013 appears to have been the last show the institution managed to organise.[41]

While many new permanent exhibition spaces in mainland China have emerged rapidly from within a generally poor visual arts infrastructure, some much more innovative shows have been produced by the organizations running biennales and annual art fairs across the whole of Asia, and beyond, in recent years.[42] Commentators also claim that these events now offer some of the most important and stimulating shows in the global contemporary art world calendar, compared with the exhibitions organized by the historic museums of modern art based in the "core" Western countries—especially when those still funded significantly by governments, such as Tate in Britain, have faced deep "austerity" budget cuts of their own over recent years.[43]

In particular, Manifesta 3 (2000), Documenta 11 (2002) and some biennial exhibitions (e.g., the Havana Biennials of 1984, 1986 and 1991; the Venice Biennials of 1999 and 2001) received high critical acclaim for mounting shows that challenged and helped transform understanding of the meanings of "contemporary," "postcolonial" and "global" in relation to art made around the world since the 1980s.[44] Partly in emulation, the art fairs organized by Art Basel began to more explicitly "thematize" their displays in the early 2000s and organize "collateral" discussion events. The intention was to add intellectual and experiential texture to, and heighten the cultural status of, these essentially sales-driven events. In a wealthy city such as Miami Beach, able to attract many of the richest and most influential players in the global contemporary art world, and boasting many nearby high-quality museums, galleries and publicly accessible private collections, this was not a difficult task to undertake successfully—in the richest country on earth supporting a very well-developed visual arts infrastructure. Accordingly, there was a considerable "curatorial accent" to Art Basel Miami Beach held in 2011, through 30 sponsored "special exhibitions" organized in the fair as a whole dedicated to themes such as "The Two of Us" (artist couples "working together and apart") and "Repetitions—Art Works in Plural," along with focus on conceptual and performance practices.[45]

Art Basel Hong Kong in 2013 organized a section of its show called "Encounters." This consisted of large-scale sculptures, installations and photographs placed at various places in the exhibition arena—a decision which included siting 17 works whose scale worked, it was claimed, to "transcend" the usual art fair size stand for commercial galleries. Art Basel's marketing for the Hong Kong event was based on the idea that the fair was no longer simply a narrow opportunity to buy and sell art, but rather a bigger "event of cultural importance." The "Encounters" show was curated by Yuko Hasegawa from the acclaimed 21st Century Museum of Contemporary Art in Kanazawa, Japan. In addition, Art Basel Hong Kong made the decision to allow some politically sensitive issues to be broached at the fair. One of the "Encounters" works, for example, was provided by the Hong Kong-based gallery Osage (which also possesses exhibition spaces in Beijing and Shanghai). Osage displayed large-scale photographs taken anonymously by Filipino domestic workers, in a 2009 show by artists Sun Yuan and Peng Yu called *Hong Kong Intervention*. The works depicted these Filipinos in their employers" homes in Hong Kong and in other locations in the SAR.

These photographs offered a commentary on employer–servant relations in a globalized world where both legal and illegal migrant workers along with asylum refugees move (and are moved on) from state to state, across real yet sometimes relatively porous borders, seeking employment and personal safety. Given UBS's and Deutsche Bank's longstanding sponsorship of Art Basel, and its Miami Beach and Hong Kong events, it seems that contemporary art in a globalized social order has come to depend upon key players within the financial system—in terms of both the fairs' subvention and their occasional presentation of "cutting edge" social commentary artworks. This is a very fine line to

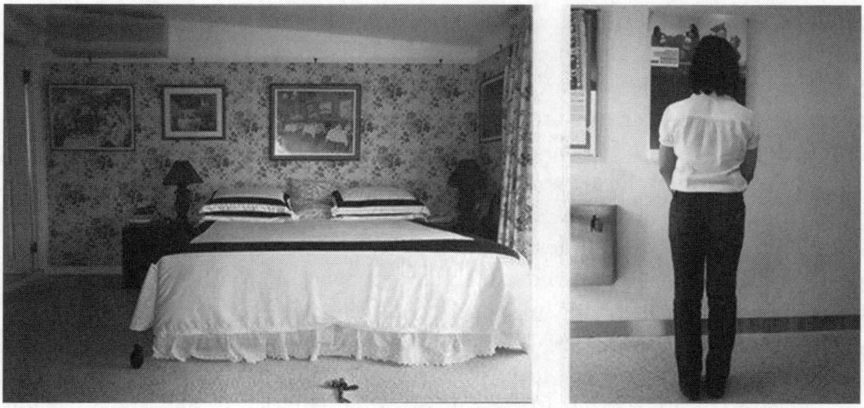

Figure 4 Sun Yuan and Peng Yu *Hong Kong Intervention* (anonymous photograph of Filipino workers in Hong Kong, 2009).

walk, however, given the structural asymmetries, inequalities and iniquities of the system evidenced by both these banks' recent criminal prosecutions and fines for persistent wrong-doing.[46]

Hong Kong's Art World Inside and Outside China

Was the art exhibited for sale at Art Basel Hong Kong in 2013 somehow actually globalized, or made "global," in and through its presentation at this event, where hundreds of galleries based in Europe, North America and Asia presented several thousands of works made in many different places? The visitor's first, though in my case recurring, experience of the sheer overwhelming mass of works on display at art fairs, in the giant sheds of space provided at these industrial scale venues, prompts this and related questions. "Global" can stand simply as a synonym for absolute volume or totality. In what ways does the art fair event create and mediate the presentation and intelligibility of contemporary art? Once again, the quantity/quality issues raised earlier resurface. All the catalogues and related booklets published for Art Basel's fairs offer a literal written text and furnish a presuppositional context for making some provisional sense of the mass of works on sale. The physical size and density of the fairs along with their discursive representations constitute a key component of the global contemporary art world's marketing and branding system.[47]

The main catalogue's introductions, welcomes, information sections and adverts for luxury goods finally give way to short sections on the hundreds of galleries taking part written by gallery staff themselves. Some of the works for sale are illustrated, accompanied by short texts of differing kinds, such as an artist's biography, or a note on the work's content and other works for sale, or background information on the gallery itself. As this advertising space in the catalogue is bought by galleries there is leeway in what their managers decide they want to include. But the galleries are highly selectively chosen, Art Basel constantly emphasizes, on the basis of their "quality" and "representativeness" in terms of what it claims are the highest global standards of creativity and innovation.[48]

This mediation of the artworks on sale through the catalogue format accompanies the "experiential" tours organized for buyers of the galleries' booths by both legitimate art fair guides and, as mentioned earlier, the occasional unofficial ("hostile") strikes carried out by undercover auction house and dealing gallery professionals trying to poach potential buyers. The highest-profile works are often bought ("pre-sold") before the fair even opens. Galleries send "jpeg" illustrations of them to buyers, partly in an attempt to forestall their money going to other artefacts for sale by other galleries at the fair. In a shady practice castigated by some, these might be works reserved for what Marc Spiegler, co-director of Art Basel Miami Beach in 2011, called the "top clients."

But there is also an attempt to keep other works available for what is called "building relationships with new clients"—those, that is, who might become regular buyers.[49]

Some of the "collateral events" held in Hong Kong in 2013 debated the merits of these practices and the wider geopolitics of the art fair form under globalization. The Asia Art Archive had run a three-year project on the nature of "the global." Several of its sessions in Hong Kong with speakers such as the Indian critical theorist Geeta Kapur, artist Vivan Sundaram and Iranian filmmaker Abbas Kiarostami looked at contemporary art and visual cultural production from a broader Asian perspective. Might the inclusion of these powerful voices be seen as a form of "repressive tolerance," enabling the corporate owners of Art Basel Hong Kong to neutralize potential criticism by drawing those who are actually likely to articulate it into the event itself? Or can such an event, given its evident and tacit imbrications within global capitalism, genuinely respond, for instance, to neo-Marxist postcolonial critiques?[50] How would we know if this had been achieved?

This question raises the matter of the diverse and possibly antagonistic interests present at Art Basel Hong Kong in 2013, including the perspectives of academics and the institutions for which they work. A group of Art Basel-funded sociologists from the University of St Gallen in Switzerland have studied the social impact of all the fairs. I encountered them at the "collateral event" I was speaking at in Hong Kong. Professor Franz Schultheis, their leader, was understandably diplomatic, given their benefactors, in the remarks he'd previously made about the Miami Beach fair to *The Art Newspaper*. "There is cultural globalization here," he observed, not giving much away. With a now-obligatory genuflection to the French sociologist Pierre Bourdieu's research in the 1960s and 1970s, Schultheis talked about contemporary art's "cultural capital" (rather than its financial value, though he claimed art and money are "antagonistic"), identifying the art fair, anthropologically, as a form of life and an instance of a "habitus," with the implication that, presumably, it deserved to live just like any other life-form.[51]

What Art Basel's business and organizational expertise brought to the Hong Kong fair was really a "technics," a hyper-rationalized means of operation designed radically to increase its quantity and quality in terms of branding, marketing, sales and profitability. This expertise included three innovations. Firstly, the "24 hours art night," held the day before the fair opened in order to generate interest and excitement in and about Hong Kong (sometimes portrayed as "the New York of the East"), when visiting potential buyers were bussed to as many openings and shows as they could physically stand. Secondly, the attraction to Hong Kong of numerous serious collectors from Europe and the USA along with a much higher number of core Western galleries to sell them artworks. Thirdly, super-efficient "VIP dining arrangements" that meant much better networking amongst potential buyers, artists and dealers.

In short, Art Basel brought accumulated professionalism from the west (all those VIP agents allocated countries to "work") and offered a commitment to professionalize Hong Kong's part of the global contemporary art world via the growing, if admittedly still very weak, infrastructure stimulated by the Swiss corporation's arrival.[52]

Leap, the self-billed "international art magazine of contemporary China" produced an intelligent, partly satirical commentary on this transformation process, or at least the promise of it. It recognized, as did *The Art Newspaper*, that Art Basel Hong Kong, despite its own rhetoric, was "less an Eastern fair, more an international brand in an international, free-trading city" able to attract some of the wealthy, the powerful and sundry celebrities from Europe and other parts of Asia, as well as mainland China. "People loosen up when speaking Chinese in Hong Kong," *Leap* noted:

> This first Art Basel Hong Kong has all the feeling of an Asian celebration. Once they get a few Laphroaig 18 [whiskies] inside their belly, the Mainland [Chinese] gallerists slip raucously into their native dialects. With a good day's trade behind him, you can hear the pride of the rich man in his language. There haven't been so many Chinese and international big name galleries in one place for a long time [...] the tycoons like to buy from power galleries, not even knowing the artists [...] Artprice rankings are what drive most people. Basquiat is first, Fangzhi Ceng second. Liu Wei is showing at White Cube.[53]

Within the globalization of visual arts "creative industries" businesses in the contemporary art world, Art Basel Hong Kong is an instance of the kind of cross-continental socioeconomic event that neoliberal public/private liaison organizations such as the Asia–Europe Foundation (ASEF), underpinned by EU and the Association of South East Asian Nations (ASEAN) intergovernment services, exist to sponsor. ASEF's "Creative Encounters" program, for instance, is designed to bring together cultural organizations in Asia and Europe by supporting artistic exchange between the 49 countries of the "Asia–Europe Meeting" group (ASEM). Its declared aim is to reinforce "dialogue between cultural professionals from the two regions," initiate "capacity building workshops" and develop long-term cooperative projects.[54] But might these forms of "NGO-type" developments effectively constitute another form of insidious Western neocolonization, given the structural asymmetries in the power relations between the Euro-American "core" and "peripheral" Asian nations? Can there be a mutually, equally beneficial result?

The Hong Kong-born and -based curator Johnson Chang, founder of the territory's Hanart TZ Gallery in 1983, and co-founder of Asia Art Archive, saw the task of those primarily interested in indigenous visual arts development as that of understanding the degree of "self-colonizations" that Asian countries have generated and to which they have succumbed. Early twentieth-century Chinese nationalists, he has noted, were dazzled by an image of Western modernization powering the "May Fourth" movement that sought to bring in Western culture and values, as a reaction against Japanese imperialism after the First World War. A similar bedazzlement by Western capitalism and its promise characterized the "modernizing" ambitions of leading factions inside the Chinese Communist Party after the death of Mao with the leadership of Deng Xiaoping.

Art Basel Hong Kong may be seen, then, as a by-product of this longer history and of the ties and divisions that characterize the complex historical relationship between the SAR and the PRC. For Chang, a way for Asians to be liberated from this obsession with the West is to work to build closer ties with other countries in the broader region, as part of a continuing construction of practical opposition "to Western cultural colonialism." India's contemporary postcolonial social theory, Chang suggested, was China's "most relevant object for reference and cultural exchange." This was because its scholars, such as Geeta Kapur, Homi Bhabha and Dipesh Chakrabarty had made the most complex study of "modern Western thought," which was a necessary precondition to understanding "contemporary Western thought."[55] (India's contemporary art world and its relation to both Western modernity and the country's own recent socioeconomic neoliberalization since the 1990s is the subject of Chapter 3.)

Chang curated the influential exhibition "China's New Art Post-1989," first shown at the Hong Kong Arts Festival in 1993, which then toured in the USA. It seems that Hong Kong's global success has always been and remains intimately tied to both the West and the PRC. Divisions of many kinds—economic, social, cultural and political—are as constitutive of its identity as its links to these places, states and peoples. The work of Chinese artists in the SAR and on the mainland is shaped now by global market forces (within and beyond art) that have dominated the PRC's development since the 1990s. Ai Weiwei went so far as to claim in a review of London's Hayward Gallery's 2012 retrospective show of performance and installation works, "Art of Change: New Directions from China," that "the Chinese art world does not exist [...] Chinese art is merely a product."[56] Though this is polemic overstatement, a lot of art produced has been for and about the market. For instance, Henry Chu's 2007 interactive installation work, *The Sound of Market*, converted Hong Kong stock market data into music tunes programmable by the user. In what other revealing or enjoyable senses can the art world be reduced to or represented as a market? The artist Li Liao, for his 2012 piece, *Consumption*, famously went underground at an Apple computers assembly line in China in order to document in photographs and text how long it would take him to buy an I Pad on the wages he earned there.

But the longer-standing "alternative" visual arts organizations in Hong Kong—long pre-dating Art Basel Hong Kong, with a sometimes explicitly dissident attitude to the establishment culture of British colonial power and postcolonial influence there—have, for many years now, been attempting to build a sophisticated critical art culture and material infrastructure to support indigenous art and artists. Along with Asia Art Archive, the gallery Osage (founded in 2004) and its associated design businesses operating worldwide has a mission to promote contemporary Asian art and culture. Its galleries in Hong Kong, Beijing and Shanghai have shown some of the most challenging and thought-provoking Asian conceptual/installation-based contemporary art. Osage was the first Hong Kong gallery to be selected to take part in Art Basel in 2011 and Frieze Masters, London, in 2012. Osage also runs a range of visual arts service businesses, as well as producing fashion and accessories marketed and sold across the globe. At the same time it operates some "not-for-profit" cultural programs—"Creative Communities," "Cultural Cooperation" and "Creative Capacities"—intended to improve regional co-operation within Asian countries and the world beyond, some co-run with the City University of Hong Kong.[57]

Osage's 2014 two-site exhibition "Market Forces—Erasure: From Conceptualism to Abstraction," curated by Charles Merewether, was held at its East Kowloon base and at the Hong Kong City University's temporary gallery in the north of the SAR territory. This show also dealt with the powers of the contemporary art market, the kinds of use of materials commercial factors tend to impose on the way artists produce "for" a market, and questions to do with the continued domination of Asian contemporary art by Western values. The exhibition included works by artists from Hong Kong, the PRC, Japan, South Korea, Thailand, the Philippines, Singapore and Indonesia. Merewether—born in Scotland but a long-term Asian resident—has long had a particular interest in forms of materiality present in contemporary "Eastern conceptualism" that are not reducible to market commodification. This was demonstrated by another of his recent exhibitions held at Osage, "Poetics of Materiality," featuring new works by four Asian artists: Ringo Bunoan (the Philippines), Young Rim Lee (South Korea), Ng Joon Kiat (Singapore) and Yu Ji (PRC).[58] While Osage gallery maintains a strong interest in the active legacies of materiality and materialism in contemporary Asian painting and sculpture forms—exploring their evolution into recent "globalized" mixed media and installation art configurations—Hong Kong's Videotage moving image collective, in contrast, has sustained a commitment to supporting new technologies for critical representation and documentation practices in contemporary art.

Videotage is a not-for-profit video collective that has documented the territory's transformations through processes of globalization, the end of British rule and Hong Kong's return to mainland Chinese control since 1997. It's both an archive resource center and a cultural agency that supports individual artists and groups based in the SAR. Its original home, at what became known as the Oil Street Artists' Village (an abandoned government supplies depot at

North Point, on the eastern side of Hong Kong island) was closed down to make way for high-value residential development in 1999, after an occupation to resist this move enforced by the initial SAR government. This was the same year that Hong Kong resident artist Tammy Cheung made her first documentary film about the lives of three Indian women working in the city, *Invisible Women*, which explored gender inequalities and the lot there of ethnic minority groups. Many other video works have since dealt with what has been described as Hong Kong's "constant identity crisis" brought on by its location, attraction as a destination for both legal and illegal Asian migrants and its complex relationship to the PRC.

These works include Linda Lai's *Voice Seen, Images Heard* (2009), a collage of film clips about Hong Kong's past and Eric Siu's witty three-part video film critique of global consumerism *Made in China* (2011).[59] The territory's shifting identity has been characterized by one of the founders of Videotage, artist Ellen Pau, maker of the 1999 film *Recycling Cinema* which micro-focused on the activities she documented along an expressway close to the Hong Kong seashore, as moving from an "insecure postcolonial status to the humbling embrace of the great motherland [but] society seems ever confused at how to react to cross-border connections."[60]

Videotage curators, in statements written for its "One World Exposition" video screening event in Hong Kong in 2012, declared a particular interest in engaging, via media art practices, with the PRC from what they called the "strategic location" of the SAR—which they characterized as always both "inside" and "outside" China.

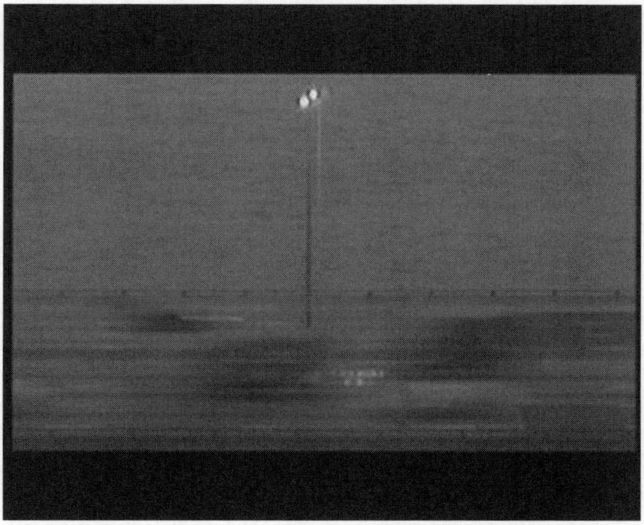

Figure 5 Ellen Pau *Recycling Cinema* (still from video, 1999). *Source:* © Ellen Pau/Videotage.

Videotage offered what they claimed was an important "attempt to rethink our identities through different concepts of Chinese culture." With the looming presence of the first edition of Art Basel Hong Kong in mind, Hong Kong-born curator Isaac Leung wondered if his city could be imagined "not only as an offshore location of the "national Chinese art market," but also as a complex "mediator" proposing, via media art, "a mode of thinking that is different from other forms [enabling us potentially to] rethink our history, memory, subjectivity and citizenship." The PRC-born co-curator Li Zhenhua developed this theme of the "Parallel Worlds" that Hong Kong and the PRC constitute in his review of the development, in both territories, of film, video and "integrated media art." He noted that the years immediately before the 1997 handover had been a critical moment in the development of video art in mainland China. In this period a sizeable group of artists using video for experimental short films and animation projects had emerged and the PRC's "independent film circle" began to receive increased international attention. What understanding of Hong Kong before the 1997 "return" to China could PRC citizens have had of the territory, only seeing images of it in archive film, asked Zhenhua.[61]

One answer to this question would be that the people in the PRC and Hong Kong share a common experience of very rapid and continuing urbanization since the 1980s. Ou Ning's and Cao Fei's 2003 film *San Yuan Li*, commissioned for the 50th Venice Biennale, presents a multicamera portrait of a mainland Chinese village on the edge of the urban sprawl from the mega-city of Guangzhou, home to 12 million people. Another shifting border, then, is that between such urbanization processes and the transformations in what was once a rural life where subsistence farming and craft culture had been able to survive. Within these ongoing global developments lie the contradictions, tensions and traumas that have accompanied PRC and Hong Kong Chinese working population concentrations and related sociopolitical marginalization. Ellen Pau's explicitly political film, *For Some Reasons*, made in 2002 as a response to the PRC's attempt to impose new "anti-subversion" laws in Hong Kong—against the Sino-British agreement at handover—helped to mobilize opposition to the bill which eventually was abandoned because the elected Legislative Council would not support it.[62]

Twelve years later, the demonstrations that I encountered when I visited Hong Kong in July 2014 also concerned the governing powers that the PRC wished to extend to the ex-colony. The British, remember, had only introduced elected representation in 1985, when it was clear that handover to mainland China was imminent. This late-Cold War act—though highly cynical in one respect, but now vital to the actual popular freedoms of Hong Kong's citizens in another—provides a telling link to the next chapter. This is concerned with the state of the global contemporary art world in South Korea, a country divided in 1953 from its northern region and people by the civil war and then Cold War superpower conflict fought between the Soviet Union and China on one side and the United States and its allies on the other.

Notes

1 *South China Morning Post*, July 2, 2014: 1, 4, 5, 6, 12 and 14. On the protest movements in Hong Kong, see Joshua Wong, "Scholars on the March," *New Left Review* 92; March–April 2015: 43–52, and Sebastian Veg, "Legalistic and Utopian: Hong Kong's Umbrella Movement," *New Left Review* 92; March–April 2015: 55–73. On the Occupy movement, see W. J. T. Mitchell, Bernard E. Harcourt and Michael Taussig, *Occupy: Three Inquiries in Disobedience* (University of Chicago Press: Chicago, 2013).

2 Art Basel's parent company, the MCH Group, bought a 60% stake in Asian Art Fairs—the owners of the Hong Kong Art Fair—in 2011. See "Collecting Grows among West's Wealthy," *The Art Newspaper*, 30 November, 2011: 1. On the global role of art fairs, see, e.g., Noah Horowitz, *Art of the Deal: Contemporary Art in a Global Financial Market* (Princeton University Press: Princeton, NJ): 16-17, and Don Thompson, *The Supermodel and the Brillo Box: Back Stories and Peculiar Economics from the World of Contemporary Art* (Palgrave Macmillan: Basingstoke, 2014): 233–242.

3 See *A.M. Post*, 107, June 2014: Gormley statues 5; French–HK show 30–37; Para/Site exhibition 54–57; Weiwei exhibition 68–70; Oi! Art Center 71–75.

4 *A.M. Post*, 107, June 2014, Editorial: 89.

5 See catalogue *Art Basel Hong Kong May 23–26, 2013*: 14–20. On Art Basel Hong Kong's draining of Taiwan's contemporary art market, see *A.M. Post*, 95, May 2013: 20–21.

6 See catalogue *Art Basel Hong Kong May 23–26, 2013*: 32 and 24; catalogue *Art Basel Miami Beach 1–4 December 2011 The 10th Edition*: 38.

7 *Hong Kong Art Guide 2013 Edition*: Basquiat advertisement: 9–10; Cai Yuan and Jian Jun Xi advertisement: 12. *The Art Newspaper International Edition*, May 22–24, 2013: "Up close and personal: the stars of Chinese art": 10–11.

8 India Art Fair: *Art Basel Hong Kong May 23–26, 2013*: 452; Chapman Brothers: *Time Out Hong Kong*, no. 131; May 22–June 4, 2013: 18–19.

9 UBS statements in *Art Basel Miami Beach 1–4 December 2011 The 10th Edition*: 11 and 13. On UBS corruption, see *International Business Times*, September 24, 2011, http://www.ibtimes.com/ubs-chief-resigns-ramifications-likely-spread-211651 (accessed March 22, 2017), and for a contextualized account of UBS involvement in banking malpractices associated with the Crash, Alex Brummer, *Bad Banks: Greed, Incompetence and the Next Global Crisis* (Random House: New York, 2015): 179 and 267.

10 Deutsche Bank statements in *Art Basel Hong Kong May 23–26, 2013*: 11. Luxury goods advertisements: e.g., 14–16.

11 On the bank's collections see, for instance, Deutsche Bank USA, The Americas Collection: https://www.db.com/us/content/en/1097.html (accessed March 22, 2016).

12 On the early days and subsequent development of corporate art investment, see Horowitz, *Art of the Deal*: 9–12 and Chapter Three: 143–187.

13 See, e.g., "Deutsche Bank's Illegal Foreclosure Practices," in *Dialog International: German-American Opinion: Politics and Culture*, http://www.dialoginternational.com/dialog_international/2009/03/deutsche-banks-illegal-us-foreclosure-practices.html (accessed March 22, 2017), and "Deutsche Bank will pay $554 Million for Illegal Tax Shelter Activity", *Forbes* https://www.forbes.com/sites/nathanvardi/2010/12/21/deutsche-bank-will-pay-554-million-for-illegal-tax-shelter-activity/#7ae296a465f7 (accessed March 22, 2017). On Deutsche Bank's involvement in legal suits over, and federal indictments for, reckless subprime lending practices, mortgage-backed securities and predatory short-selling, see, e.g., Charles H. Ferguson, *Predator Nation: Corporate Criminals, Political Corruption, and the Hijacking of America* (Crown Business: New York, 2012): 55, 71, 85, 105, 138–139 and 302.

14 *The Art Newspaper International Edition*, "Collecting Grows Among West's Wealthy": 1.

15 On the reliability of art sales data, see Horowitz *Art of the Deal*: xxi–xxii, and for a wider range of methodological issues in art sales research, see Iain Robertson, "Price Before Value," in Iain Robertson and Derrick Chong (eds.), *The Art Business* (Routledge: London and New York, 2008): 29–54. On the recent growth and character of the Chinese art market, see, e.g., "China's Billion-dollar Domestic Art Market," *The Art Newspaper International Edition*, May 22–24, 2013: 2.

16 "Is This Fair Big Enough For The Both Of Us?" *The Art Newspaper International Edition*, November 30, 2012: 4.

17 *Art Basel Hong Kong May 23–26, 2013*: 13.

18 "In the Name of Art," *Time Out Hong Kong*, no. 131; May 22–June 4, 2013: 64.

19 See Hammad Nasar, Head of Research and Programs at Asia Art Archive, *Hong Kong Art Guide*, 2013 Edition: 48.

20 "Is Hong Kong Ready for Contemporary Art?" *Time Out Hong Kong*, no. 131; May 22–June 4, 2013: 20–24 (22).

21 See Lars Nittve, then director of Hong Kong's long planned M+ museum of visual culture, *Hong Kong Art Guide* 2013 Edition: 13.

22 "Is Hong Kong Ready for Contemporary Art?" 20–24, and *Hong Kong Art Guide* 2013 Edition: 18.

23 *Hong Kong Art Guide* 2013 Edition: 39.

24 See *A.M. Post* 95; May 2013, "Art Ecological Chain": 24–25, and David Elliot, quoted in "Where Next for Hong Kong, Asia's Art Hub?" *The Art Newspaper International Edition*, May 22–24, 2013, 1–2.

25 See "Is Hong Kong Ready for Contemporary Art?" and, on the Andre "bricks" (*Equivalent VIII*) controversy, see David Hopkins, "The Death of the Object: The Move to Conceptualism," in Hopkins, *After Modern Art: 1945–2000* (Oxford University Press: Oxford, 2000): 144–145.

26 On the impact of the PRC's Cultural Revolution in Hong Kong, see artist and writer, Kurt Chan, in *Hong Kong Art Guide* 2013 Edition: 18, and Jiehong Jiang, *Burden or Legacy: From the Chinese Cultural Revolution to Contemporary Art* (Hong Kong University Press: Hong Kong, 2007).

27 "China's Billion-dollar Domestic Art Market": 2 and "China's New Art Sold for 200% More Outside China," *The Art Newspaper International Edition*, May 22–24, 2013: 4. On Christie's in Shanghai, see "First in China: Christie's to Hold Sales Independently in Shanghai," *A.M. Post* 95, May 2013: 7.

28 "China's Billion-dollar Domestic Art Market": 2, and "Arts Globalized," *A.M. Post* 95, May 2013: 19.

29 CIA gov. *HK GDP 2004.* Retrieved March 6, 2007; see History of Hong Kong, wikipedia.org/wiki/History_of_Hong_Kong.

30 "How to Look After Your Latest Acquisition," *The Art Newspaper International Edition*, May 22–24, 2013: 7.

31 "China's New Art Sold For 200% More Outside China": 4.

32 "The Art of the Matter," *Hong Kong Art Guide* 2013 Edition: 26.

33 See *South China Morning Post*, February 12, 2014, http://www.scmp.com/news/hong-kong/article/1426463/protest-asylum-seekers-food-provisions-not-worth-ISS-HK?page=all (accessed March 22, 2017). See also "ISS-HK, the aid group which is the focus of the protests, went to the High Court on Monday 17 February [2014], to obtain an injunction against the occupation [of the NGO's offices]. In yet another example of the class-bias of the judicial system, the judgement also prevents those who took part in the protest from entering ISS-HK welfare offices without written permission. ISS-HK is a subsidiary of International Social Services, a Swiss-based NGO, which combines the roles of 'aid group' and limited company. In 2006 it won the lucrative HK$203 million per year government contract to administer aid to around 5,000 refugees in Hong Kong." http://chinaworker.info/en/2014/02/17/5977/(accessed March 22, 2017). For response from ISS-HK see http://www.isshk.org/e/default_home.asp Press Releases 2014 (accessed March 22, 2017), and the Refugee Union at www.facebook.com/refugeeunionhk (accessed March 22, 2017).

34 On the post-2008 recession-led "short-termism" of government arts funding in Hong Kong, see, e.g., Robert Ho Yau-Chung, "Nurturing Through the Arts," in *Leap: The International Arts Magazine of Contemporary China* May 23, 2013–May 26, 2013 (Art Basel Hong Kong special edition): 32–35 (35). On the failure of austerity policies to deliver significant reduction in budget deficits and national debts, or to provide conditions for sustainable economic growth, see, e.g., Yanis Varoufakis, *The Global Minotaur: America, Europe and the Future of the Global Economy* (Zed Books: London, 2015): Chapter 9.

35 See "Welcome," main catalogue *Art Basel Hong Kong May 23–26, 2013*: 6.

36 On the Lehmann Maupin gallery, see *Hong Kong Art Guide* 2013 Edition: 55; on Ben Brown Fine Arts "The Art Fair Is Crowded and Galleries Are Buzzing,"

The Art Newspaper: International Edition, May 25–26, 2013: 9; and on M+, see *Hong Kong Art Guide* 2013 Edition: 61and http://www.westkowloon.hk/en/mplus (accessed March 22, 2016).

37 Robin Peckham, "Vast as Factories—Or Mostly In the Mind," *The Art Newspaper International Edition*, May 22–24, 2013: 14.

38 See Aimee Lin, "Great Collectors and Their Ideas No 6: Wang Wei," *Art Asia* vol.2 no.1, May 2014: 42–44 and "Build first and find the art to fill them later," *The Art Newspaper International Edition*, May 22–24, 2013: 9. See The Long Museum web site at http://thelongmuseum.org/html/index_en.html (accessed March 22, 2016).

39 "Build First and Find the Art to Fill Them Later": 9.

40 "Build First and Find the Art to Fill Them Later": 9, and timeoutshanghai.com/photo/11669/Andy-Warhol-15-Minutes-Eternal-highlights.html#prettyPhoto.

41 "Keep it Glassy," *A.M. Post*, 95: May 2013: 003. The exhibition offered "a glimpse of the museum boom in China—of how corporate interests commission international design firms to devise museum concepts and strategy, despite somewhat meagre content."

42 See, e.g., Maria Hlavajova, "How to Biennial? The Biennial in Relation to the Art Institution," in Filipovic, van Hal and Ovstebo (eds.), *The Biennial Reader: An Anthology on Large Scale Perennial Exhibitions of Contemporary Art* (Bergen Kunsthall: Bergen, 2010): 292–305 and other essays in the same volume.

43 See, e.g., Hans Belting, "The Plurality of Art Worlds and the New Museum," in Belting, H., A. Buddensieg and P. Weibel (eds.), *The Global Contemporary and the Rise of New Art Worlds* (Center for Art and Media Karlsruhe/MIT Press: Cambridge MA, 2013): 246–254.

44 See a range of essays on the historical legacy of these, and other, exhibitions in Filipovic, van Hal and Ovstebo (eds.), *The Biennial Reader*, and Barbara Vanderlinden and Elena Filipovic (eds.), *The Manifesta Decade: Debates on Contemporary Art Exhibitions and Biennials in Postwar Europe* (MIT Press: Cambridge, MA, 2005).

45 On the collateral program and special exhibitions at Art Basel Miami Beach 2011, see main catalogue *Art Basel Miami Beach 1–4 December 2011 The 10th Edition*: 36–37, the section on local museums 585–609, and, on the curatorial focus of the fair, *Art Basel Miami Beach 1–4 December 2011: Art/Kabinett*: 3. On "Encounters," see main catalogue *Art Basel Hong Kong May 23–26, 2013*: 26 and "Bigger and Better," *Art Map Express Art Basel 2013* May 2013: 1.

46 On UBS's central involvement in the 2008 Crash, see, e.g., Varoufakis, *The Global Minotaur:* 148–149.

47 See Theodor Adorno's classic *Culture Industry* (Routledge: London, 2001 [1972/76/81]). On "global = total," see Harris, *The Utopian Globalists*: 21–23, 51–56.

48 See, e.g., Magnus Renfrew, Director Asia for Art Basel, "Welcome," main catalogue *Art Basel Hong Kong May 23–26, 2013*: 6.

49 Spiegler quoted in "Sold on a Jpeg?" *The Art Newspaper International Edition: Art Basel Miami Beach Daily Edition,* December 1, 2011: 1.

50 See Asia Art Archive publicity materials *Unpacking Global 23–24 May 2013.*

51 See "Deconstructing Art Basel Miami Beach," *The Art Newspaper International Edition: Art Basel Miami Beach Daily Edition,* November 30, 2011: 2.

52 See interview with Hong Kong-based collector Rudy Tseng, in *Leap: International Art Museum of Contemporary China (Art Basel Hong Kong special edition),* May 23, 2013–May 26, 2013: 40–41, and Elizabeth Currid, *The Warhol Economy: How Fashion, Art and Music Drive New York* (Princeton University Press: Princeton, NJ, 2007).

53 "Brand New: The Name is the Game in Hong Kong," *The Art Newspaper: International Edition,* May 25–26, 2013: 1–2, and "Wild Nights at Art Basel Hong Kong," *Leap: International Art Museum of Contemporary China (Art Basel Hong Kong special edition),* May 23, 2013–May 26, 2013: 18–19.

54 ASEF, *Call for Proposals* leaflet. See www.asef.org.

55 "From 'Post-1989' to Asian Thought: An Interview with Johnson Chang," *Leap: International Art Museum of Contemporary China (Art Basel Hong Kong special edition),* May 23, 2013–May 26, 2013: 36–37. See, e.g., Geeta Kapur *When Was Modernism: Essays on Contemporary Cultural Practice in India* (Tulika Press: Delhi, 2002), Homi Bhabha *The Location of Culture* (Routledge, London: 1994) and Dipesh Chakrabarty *Provincializing Europe: Postcolonial Thought and Historical Difference* (Princeton University Press: Princeton, NJ., 2000).

56 Weiwei quoted in "Pity the Poor Privileged 'After 80s' artists," *The Art Newspaper: International Edition,* 25–26 May 2013: 14–15.

57 See, e.g., *About Osage* (Osage Art Foundation: Hong Kong, 2014) and *Works by Au Hoi Lam* (Osage Art Foundation: 2014). See also www.osagegallery.com.

58 See. e.g., the event/publication *Symposium: Art and Values* (Osage Art Foundation and City University of Hong Kong: Hong Kong, 2014), part of the exhibition project including 22 Asian artists featured in *Market Forces—Erasure: From Conceptualism to Abstraction* curated by Charles Merewether (Osage Art Foundation and City University of Hong Kong, May 16–June 30, 2014). *Poetics of Materiality,* curated by Charles Merewether January 4–February 16, 2014 (catalogue published by Osage Art Foundation: Hong Kong, 2014); *Ng Joon Kiat: Towards a Horizon* (Osage Art Foundation: Hong Kong, 2013), with essays by Charles Merewether, Isabel Ching and David Ho Yeung Chan.

59 See the exhibitions, film showings and discussions that comprised *One World Exposition,* presented by Videotage at Hong Kong oneworldexpo December 8, 2011–January 8, 2012, in collaboration with Asia Art Archive, Hansart T Z Gallery, Osage Art Foundation, City University of Hong Kong and Spring

Workshop, supported by the Hong Kong Development Agency (catalogue: 14–15; 19–20). On Tammy Cheung's *Invisible Women*, see Ellen Pau "The Discourse of Moving Images in Hong Kong in the 21st Century," in Jinsuk Suh (ed.), *Moving On Asia 2004–2013* (Alt. Space Loop: Seoul, 2012): 420–426 and, for a broader account of the history of moving image works in the PRC, Hong Kong and Taiwan, see Guo Xiaoyan, "How to Self-Construct: The Primary Facts and Narration about Moving Image in China," in Jinsuk Suh (ed.), *Moving On Asia 2004–2013*: 394–407.

60 Ellen Pau "The Discourse of Moving Images in Hong Kong in the 21st Century": 425.

61 Isaac Leung, "Curatorial Statement: In-between Hong Kong and China—Mediation as a World-making Process," *One World Exposition*: 1–3 (3); Li Zhenhua, "Curatorial Statement: One World Exposition: Film, Video and Integrated Media Art in Mainland China and Hong Kong," *One World Exposition*: 6–7.

62 *One World Exposition* (catalogue: 17).

2

New Media Art and Cultural Globalism in South Korea

Consulting the inflight map on the screen on the back of the seat in front of me as the plane finally dips down into Incheon airport I am alarmed to see quite how close Seoul is to the border—the "Demilitarized Zone" or "DMZ"—with North Korea. In the dark, however, it is all one Korea to me. Respite on the ground is short. Seoul is only an hour's flying from Dalian, a city in northeast China where my university maintains a campus at which we teach 800 Chinese students in partnership with a local university. Four hours later I fly on to Dalian for two days of meetings with our staff and students then back to Seoul to give a lecture at the "Video Art Archive Network Forum" conference. After Dalian—an international city, by the PRC's standards—Seoul feels very "Pacific-American," very corporate.

The Chic of Global "New Media Art"

The 2013 Video Art Archive Network Forum in Seoul brought together leading organizations from around the world with specialist interests in "new media" and "new media art." Taking part in the conference were representatives from the institutions FACT (Foundation for Art and Creative Technology, Liverpool, UK), ZKM (Zentrum Fur Kunst und Medientechnologie, Kahlsruhe, Germany), Video Data Bank (Chicago, USA),Videotage (Hong Kong, PRC), Inter-Communication (Tokyo, Japan), Minsheng Art Museum (Shanghai, PRC) and the Loop Alternative Space in Seoul, which hosted the conference. I attended the conference with a colleague, Menene Gras, from the visual arts organization Casa Asia—a department of the Spanish government based in Barcelona and Madrid. The Forum in Seoul included, as part of its collateral displays program, an exhibition of recent video works by Spanish artists curated by Gras. The global contemporary art world, to reiterate, is a networked "event driven" entity.[1]

The Global Contemporary Art World, First Edition. Jonathan Harris.
© 2017 John Wiley & Sons, Inc. Published 2017 by John Wiley & Sons, Inc.

The categories "new media" and "new media art" are simultaneously intellectually vague and rhetorically significant within the global arena of the contemporary art world. In one sense, the term "new media" may appear simply to nominate a technological specialization: photographic, film, video, digital and internet-circulated images and image-production processes. But photography, traced to its origins, emerged nearly two hundred years ago and film much more than one hundred years ago. The modifying prefixes and suffixes "new" and "art" provide important clues to the complexities and confusions surrounding these terms. In another sense, then, "new" isn't—indeed is never—a neutral, adjectival term: "new" virtually always suggests an evaluative judgement, although it may be tacit. This surreptitious, and often ideological, usage is indicated, for example, by the way that "new" is routinely used as a synonym for "modern" meaning "advanced" or "up to date"—as in the phrase "economic modernization" (i.e., changes to industry that end what are held to be old "restrictive labor practices" such as closed-shop trade unions).

The "new" in "new media" is partly a matter, then, of emphasis on the claimed innovative technological and labor processes within and through which images or a representational idiom—e.g., a photograph or film—has been produced. But the modifier "new" also affects our understanding of the product of these processes, which is claimed, by virtue of its ostensive novel character, to be somehow better, or more truthful, or more interesting, or a significant breakthrough (and a decisive break from the "old" or the past) in some other way. In another direction, the suffix "art" works as a specializing proper noun, wherein certain "new media" works are selected and assimilated into this specific aesthetic and institutional order, which is also held to afford a distinct form of experience and knowledge. Philosophers have called this the "art episteme."[2]

The absorption of some "new media" processes and products to the category of "art" erects another border, through which specific photographic, film and digital–internet representations have been divided from other institutionalized orders of representation and forms of knowledge, such as the "mass media" and, over about the last ten years, "social media."[3] "New media art" organizations, however, though they are necessarily tied to traditional museum practices through their affiliation to the "art episteme," have increasingly wished to manifest a break away from the kinds of establishment institutions that have hitherto collected, exhibited and validated historical art. In this sense, "historical" can be used as a synonym for "traditional" meaning old, reactionary and out-of-date; the emphatically not new.[4]

While new media art organizations since their inception in the 1980s have usually offered public displays of their artefacts, conventional notions and practices of exhibition—connoting a unidirectional process of interpretation dictated by expert curators—always appeared anachronistic and inappropriate for their objectives. Correspondingly, new media art institutions rarely inhabit (or wish to inhabit) buildings or create display spaces that look like traditional art museums and particularly not like the neoclassical structures of the Louvre in Paris or the national galleries of London, Washington and many other Western capitals.[5] The rhetoric of new media art organizations tends to be what is termed "post-museum" (sometimes even "anti-museum"), despite the important continuities with some kinds of modern—but now also contrastingly "old"—art that these organizations usually claim. Despite the fact also that, increasingly, some of the "traditional" art museums have themselves increasingly adopted a "post-museum" stance in how they have begun to revise and extend their self-definitions, "mission statements" and core activities, often as part of an explicit discourse on the meanings and consequences of globalization.

Seoul Museum of Art (SeMA) is an exemplary case in this regard, to which I shall turn shortly.[6] Since the 1980s South Korea has become one of the leading high-tech "emerging" economies and societies in eastern Asia—associated particularly with automobile and digital communications media innovation and production. Much of the country's contemporary art world, and one-fifth of its population, is based in or near to the capital, Seoul, close to the border with North Korea. One of the world's most explicitly "globalist" biennials takes place in the South Korean city of Gwangju, 200 kilometers to the south of the capital. Both Seoul and the Gwangju Biennial (first held in 1995 and 39th to be founded in a total of 149 surveyed in 2013) have long manifested strengths in "new media art."[7]

These have drawn on the global success of Nam June Paik (1932–2006), by far South Korea's most influential and well-known twentieth-century artist, internationally acknowledged as one of the leading precursors in the development of contemporary and "new media" art. Paik's major retrospective exhibition held at the Guggenheim Museum in New York in 2000 sealed the artist's validation by one of the most powerful of all the Western gatekeeper visual arts organizations. In 2008 the Nam June Paik Art Center was established within the Gyeonggi Cultural Foundation, a complex of museums and exhibition spaces in the city of Suwon close to Seoul. Later, a dedicated building—emphatically "post-museum" in its design, in this case resembling a standard office block—was constructed to house the institution's collection of Paik's artworks.[8]

South Korea (officially The Republic of Korea) was divided from North Korea (The Democratic People's Republic of Korea) in 1953 along the 38th Parallel or Demilitarized Zone—the "DMZ." South Korea endured autocratic and effective military rule from then until 1993 when the first civilian president was elected. The Gwangju Biennial, founded two years later, was partly inaugurated in order to memorialize a civilian protest against the regime in this city in 1980—South Korea's own Tianenmen Square massacre—that was put down by the army, killing about 150 demonstrators.[9] Nam June Paik's family, like many others, had fled what was to become "South Korea" during the civil war.

The artist settled in Japan, then Germany, before moving to New York in 1964 where he began to experiment with the use of portable video equipment. Widespread interest in film and video art developed in South Korea during the 1970s. It emerged partly as a form of resistance amongst artists and activists to both the mass import of US Hollywood commercial film and the authoritarian surveillance carried out by the military regime at home.[10]

Loop Alternative Space in Seoul, founded in 1999, inherited and propagates this belief in video as a practice—whether linked to the "art episteme" or not—that carries inherent "democratic potential," a claimed capacity to encourage what one of its director's has called "participatory [...] autonomous direct democracy." Other early new media centers (all eschewing the title "museum" altogether) also operated, alongside Loop, to support this effort. Art Center Nabi, IlJoo Art House, Ssamzie Space, Art Space Pool, Project Space SARUBIA and Space Beam all appealed to what one commentator has called a "digital aesthetic" opposed to the established, conventional gallery culture in South Korea.[11]

During the 1990s a sophisticated film culture developed in the country linked to forms of leftist and socially liberal political movements. These included the Seoul Women's International Film Festival (founded in 1997) and the Korea Queer Culture Festival (founded in 2000). The Incheon Women's Biennale of Art first took place in 2004, following social and cultural liberalization policies gradually enacted by the civilian governments that replaced military rule in the country. Since then, video and multimedia works have constructed a revisionist account of the country's historical development. These include Hwayeon Nam's 2007–2010 extended multimedia work *Operational Play*—a kind of anti-war filmic history of military activity in Korea over the centuries. Other moving-image works have critically investigated the extensive use of documentary film and photography by military regimes themselves in South Korea during the twentieth century. Hyunsuk Seo's *The Hanging Garden* (2009), for instance, satirizes official state propaganda histories of Korea. Yeondoo Jung's feature-length video work *Documentary Nostalgia* (2007) offers a witty deconstruction of hackneyed representations of the Korean national landscape created by official state media over the decades.[12]

Analogous critiques of military-rule documentary film and TV propaganda can be found in video works produced by artists in other eastern Asian countries following the tentative and often reversed beginnings there of less repressive civilian democratic social orders. Works made in Thailand, for instance, have examined the role of military moving-image representations in creating dominant notions and images of Thai (formerly Siamese) national identity. Others include Chieh-Jeh Chen's 2003 film *Factory*, dealing with capitalism, Cold War and neoliberalism in Taiwan, and Michelle Dizon's 2009 film *Empire* that examines recent globalization processes, urban development and corrupt corporate power machinations in the Philippines.[13]

It may be that a coherent "pan-Asian" development is discernible here, despite hugely significant differences between the states, cultures and peoples across the continent's southeast and eastern regions. Artists and arts organizations—new-media-focused and others—have worked together for several decades in an effort to build supportive networks. Do these activities exemplify Johnson Chang's call, discussed in the previous chapter, for Asian states to learn from themselves and each other about the extent of their "self-colonization," as part of a necessary preliminary stage before being able to create sustainable real societal and regional independence from the West? Or should the contemporary art world's presence within a country such as South Korea rather be understood as a form of cultural neocolonization characteristic of the global neoliberal capitalist social order? I turn to this issue now and begin by looking at the international activities of a visual arts organization funded by a Western European government.

Contemporary Art as Global Cultural Diplomacy

As Casa Asia's name indicates, this Spanish government funded agency operates a "cultural liaison" network linking visual arts organizations in Spain to those in Asian countries such as South Korea through public exhibitions and film screenings, related publications, conferences and other events. Casa Asia's activities contribute to the broader work of implementing what has been called "the cultural cooperation policy of the Spanish Agency for International Development Cooperation." In Seoul, Casa Asia organized the exhibition "Language and Aesthetics of Spanish Video Art: Ten Years of Critical Practices," held at the Songwon Art Center, near the Seoul Museum of Modern and Contemporary Art, which opened in 2013. Casa Asia's exhibition was presented in collaboration with Loop Alternative Space, the Spanish Embassy in Seoul, Cooperacion Espanola, and the Spain-based media and video art distribution agency, HAMACA.[14]

Why does the Spanish government believe Casa Asia's activities to be worth funding? Before exploring this question it is worth pointing out that for historical reasons—given Spain's central role in colonizing Latin American countries over several centuries—the Spanish government still regards its strategic economic and cultural relationship with the Americas to be primary. In a globalizing world, however, no continent or region can be ignored by nation-states defending their economic power and pursuit of this goal through external sociocultural (and sometimes political and military) activities. Art Basel's penetration into North America at Miami Beach and into eastern Asia through its take-over of the Hong Kong Art Fair embodied a global extension of the "premium" art fair experience that greatly benefits Switzerland economically, directly and indirectly. The ARCO art fair, held annually in Madrid, is another contemporary art world event entailing transcontinental ambitions, this one highly beneficial to Spain. Though ARCO has traditionally sustained its strongest intercontinental links with galleries based in Spain's ex-colonies in Latin America, its actual and potential reach now also includes several Asian centers.

ARCO is the brand name for the Feria Internacional de Arte Contemporáneo (International Contemporary Art Fair). ARCO is backed by the Spanish national government and is also the recipient of Madrid and surrounding region state funding. It operates simultaneously as a commercial art fair and, effectively (along with most art fairs and biennials), as a hybrid quasi-state apparatus designed to promote global economic, social and cultural developments beneficial to the host nation. Through such forms of intervention into the "cultural industries" sphere of the global economy the borders between "public" and "private" interests and activities have been both redefined and radically blurred within the state-capital nexus.[15] Routine involvement in the activities and objectives of this intervention now characterizes the work of many strata of professionals, including museum directors, government "cultural regeneration" advisors, academics and specialist "enterprise" staff in universities, business people as well as art fair managers.

No less a figure than the king, Don Juan Carlos I of Spain, for example, in his welcome address to ARCO visitors, printed in the main catalogue for its February–March 2013 edition, spoke, in his role as honorary president of the art fair, of the significance of what he called the event's "usual vitality and innovative spirit, consolidating our region as a tourist destination and a major focus of creation and cultural diffusion." The president of the regional government of Madrid, throwing his hat into this ever-faster spinning rhetorical ring, raised the stakes beyond the significance of the nation's capital and its environs. "Spain," he noted, "is a leading cultural power, and the prestige that comes with this is also measured by our capacity to renew and strengthen our presence in international contemporary art circuits."

Finally, sounding rather like a director of Art Basel (or perhaps more like one of its global bank sponsors), the mayor of Madrid appeared to equate contemporary art entirely with global business development. "This commitment to art" represented what she called

> one of the best targets for investment, as it offers a safe bet of increasing value for individuals and businesses. That is why ARCO Madrid is presented as the best way to boost a sector that complements its pronounced economic nature with other values, such as the promotion of culture and knowledge, by giving priority to the marketing of works of art as well as raising the international profile of art galleries and artists.[16]

As noted in the previous chapter, some of the bedfellows in the world of global contemporary art would appear sometimes, ostensibly at least, to be at crossed purposes. Politically dissident or simply "edgy" artists—remember Jake and Dinos Chapman's luxury pyjama designs publicized at the time of Art Basel Hong Kong in 2013—still articulate the language of avant-gardism and political opposition to capitalism, yet find themselves now habitually sharing the art world duvet with billionaire collectors and business-hungry government advisors. A mostly tacit acknowledgement of sufficient (or extensive) shared interests suggests that they all manage—most of the time anyway—to rub along.[17]

Though the majority of the video artists included in the Casa Asia show at the Songwon Art Center in Seoul may have been Spanish citizens, their films were partly chosen because they focused on Asian countries. These included Sergi Aguilar's short video on Cambodia, Dionisio Gonzalez's on Vietnam and Marisa Gonzales's film on the Philippines. Aguilar's 2005 *From Phnom Penh to Srepok W. Area* explores from a helicopter viewpoint the still devastated Cambodian landscape—a country subjected to secret US aerial "carpet" bombardment in the early 1970s. Dionisio Gonzalez's 2008 film short *Thinking Hanoi* narrates the urban environmental damage in this Vietnamese city caused by a miasma of internal combustion engine fumes and polluted humid air. Marisa Gonzales's 53 minute-long video portrays the life of an estimated 150,000 Filipino women working in exploitative domestic service jobs in Hong Kong and their one day off a week lived out on the streets at weekends before they return to their employers' homes (see the related discussion of this topic in Chapter 1).

Others films in the show examined global terrorism. For instance, Joan Leandre's and Toni Serra's 40 minute *Babylon Archives 2005* (2005) probed, in a fictional mode drawing on video game conventions, terrorist attacks on Western interests including embassies, corporate headquarters and retail businesses in US, European and Asian territories. The critical claims made for films shown in the exhibition echoed those made by South Korean film-makers and commentators that video is a privileged idiom particularly suited for such politico-aesthetic representation. Moving image works were asserted, for example, to be uniquely both global and local ("glocal") in terms of their aesthetic–critical potential. Part of this power lies in their capacity, Gras claimed, for instance, to offer a challenge to "the art system and art market and the economy of society in general." This is restatement of the familiar idea that, distinct from traditional painting and sculpture forms, film and video (often also used as elements within installations) are in some ways quintessentially global contemporary art forms.[18]

Some leading South Korean visual cultural organizations have internalized this language, equating contemporary art (though not just film and video) with a new phase in a globalizing—though also democratizing—modernity to which the nation must be committed. This commitment is evident, for example, in mission statements made by Seoul Museum of Art (SeMA). These include its Nanji Residency project that has been housed in a converted sewage treatment plant and its grounds on the city's outskirts since 2006. Selected artists invited to live and work at the residency, from South Korea and the world beyond, are funded by SeMA to make and regularly exhibit new work in a dedicated collective living/ studio complex and adjacent gallery. An exhibition of Nanji Residency artists' works took place during the Video Art Archive Network Forum conference.

The 2013 7th Residency Program, as the catalogue for the exhibit declared, showed how SeMA had adopted what it called a "globalized management system" as part of its vision as a "post-museum" institution.Within this, these younger artists—including 16 chosen from outside South Korea—were said to be "incubating" their artistic interests. Use of this term, with its strong biological sense, suggests the organization of a kind of controlled aesthetic experiment with varied, and globally inclusive, cultures of production. Every month in the residency's exhibitions and discussion sessions the artists would reveal and discuss how their work was developing. They also took part in pan-Asian events hosted in South Korea, such as the 2nd "Asian Arts Space Network (Hub City of Asian Culture, affiliated to Korean Ministry of Culture and Tourism)" and collaborated with Alternative Gallery Loop and the Video Art Archive Network Forum conference itself.[19]

SeMA's Nanji Residency initiative is intrinsically globalist in outlook. It announced (sounding a bit crypto-imperialist in the process) what it called an "overseas expansion" in its activities. While partly competing with other such schemes around the world, Nanji, through elaborating a "network with international residency programs," was trying to offer the best facilities to lure the most promising young artists to South Korea. Rather like the global landscape of fairs and biennials, museums and artists' residency centers form part of the "ecology" of the contemporary art world system, wherein benignly cooperative relations appear overall to hold sway. But these symbiotic relationships may enter phases of antagonism, if the interests of these interacting components—or those of their funding patrons—begin to clash. This potentiality was exposed in the volatile relationships that sometimes come to exist between art fairs and auction houses (discussed in the previous chapter) when their respective sales territories are perceived to have become threatened or are actually impinged upon for one reason or another.[20]

Seoul has a wealth of museums and galleries, along with the Nanji Residency program and several university-level institutions offering visual arts provision. This relative plenitude is evident especially in comparison with Hong Kong's acknowledged imbalance, where market institutions strongly overshadow other parts of the SAR's generally weak visual arts infrastructure. Nevertheless, more than three-quarters of the artists in the 2013 Nanji Residency program had actually studied for their MFA or Masters degrees in universities or art schools outside South Korea. This suggests an underlying systemic weakness that could explain SeMA's attitude of defensive competitiveness about the country's future visual arts development and profile in the global arena.[21]

SeMA's rebranding exercise in 2012 also entailed a revealing introspection (reminiscent of twentieth-century Communist Party political self-critiques, those both voluntary and forced) expressed in its new mission statement. As a self-designated "post-museum," for example, the institution, its leaders asserted, "strives to become a humanistic space [a] living space [...it will] do its best to communicate with citizens of Seoul, endeavoring to become a world-class art museum." The institution was now working to build a "global network;" it was "strengthening curating power" and "increasing community activities." The post-museum will be reorganized in order to respond to its users "various preferences" and will need to shift from a focus on "past art and classic works" to "developing timely projects, anchored in the contemporary and modern."

Central to this endeavor was the task of "promoting the globalization of regional and local art." Diagrams accompanying this key statement indicated the relations between the different parts, functions and building styles of the SeMA "post-museum" institutional ensemble as a whole (SeMA has five centers in Seoul). "Communication" with its user-groups is central to the success of all its ventures, the statement asserted, along with the "drive to build an international network." Like Tate in the United Kingdom (which pioneered strategies for collecting and displaying international contemporary art), SeMA wished to lower the hitherto disabling borders existing between curation and the permanent collection on the one hand and the role of education and societal engagement on the other. "There is an endeavor," the statement proceeded, "to explore global symbiosis as a study place for international exchange, advocating non-mainstream art as an alternative space displaying a variety of experimental works." Central to this project would be Seoul's hosting of the 8th Media Art Biennale—Mediacity Seoul 2014, focused on "cutting edge media art." These forms, idioms and artefacts were identified to be essentially "cross-genre" and declared to embody a necessary "hybrid culture."[22]

"Glocal Video": Conventions and Critiques

Complementing and contextualizing this focus on contemporary media art in Seoul was the exhibition of "historic" video works that accompanied the 2013 Video Art Archive Network Forum hosted by Alternative Gallery Loop. This consisted of works selected by the eight participating international organizations from their respective archives. The conference was held, in part, in order to discuss the problems these leading organizations have faced in attempting to create coherent, standardized global archiving conventions which would enable video works to be conserved and made accessible through a unified, singular system for international—indeed, truly global—use.

Intellectual Property Right laws vary considerably from country to country, as do technical and other practical systems that make such potentially universal, or "arbitrary," use impossible. Getting basic international cooperation has proved difficult, making it hard to introduce what have been termed "sustainable archive sharing projects." The "post-museum" conundrum preoccupying Seoul Museum of Art also raises key questions concerning the public exhibition role of new media art organizations. Digitally preserved "paleo" video artworks (those made in the 1960s, 1970s and even early 1980s) must still be shown through analogue systems in the main, requiring a whole period technology of antique reception devices to be maintained against succeeding decades of digital innovation.[23]

Such practical and related policy issues and problems challenge the characteristic globalist perspective of new media art organizations committed to the universalism of these representational practices and their concomitant sociopolitical radicalism: video art's claimed "democratic," "participatory" and "autonomous" capacities.[24] It was this belief that helped power the emergence of a formation of "alternative visual culture" in South Korea, able, it has been claimed, aesthetically and ideologically to deconstruct the dominant "modes and basic framework of fiction film, documentaries, commercial media art, and mainstream art." New media organizations could thus project themselves as representing what one commentator calls a "microscopic sociopolitical alternative to the sociopolitically macroscopic ideologies of capitalism, patriarchy, heterosexism, and nationalism."[25] In terms of mainstream South Korean media output, for example, the term "foreigner" is usually reserved to refer to white Westerners, and TV commercials endlessly present whiteness (and whitening) as the key to success and accumulating wealth. In contrast, the term "immigrant laborer" is used to refer to a manual worker from a poor third world country.[26]

The simple "alienation effects" used in some of the early video works may be thought to create a clear contrast with—and offer a kind of blocking of—such mainstream narrative film and commercial TV conventions (not just in South Korea). Included in the Alternative Gallery Loop exhibition, for example, was Zhang Peili's 1988 piece *30 × 30*, reputed to be the first video artwork made in the PRC. It shows a mirror being smashed, repeatedly mended and smashed again over a three-hour period. Such works, at one level, thus starkly, if also enigmatically, draw viewers' attention to the passage of real, as opposed to fictive, time through such emphatically repetitive, "non-narrativized" actions. Peili's 9½-minute video *Water-Standard Version from the Dictionary Cihai*, made three years later, displays a different tactic. Peili wholly recreated the CCTV studio newsreading environment but employed the announcer—Xing Zhibin, "the voice of China's media broadcasts"—in the task of simply reading words out from a dictionary. This ambiguous action highlighted the announcer's usual role in providing the government's selection and account of the news as well as provoking questions about the authority and meaning of public communication.[27]

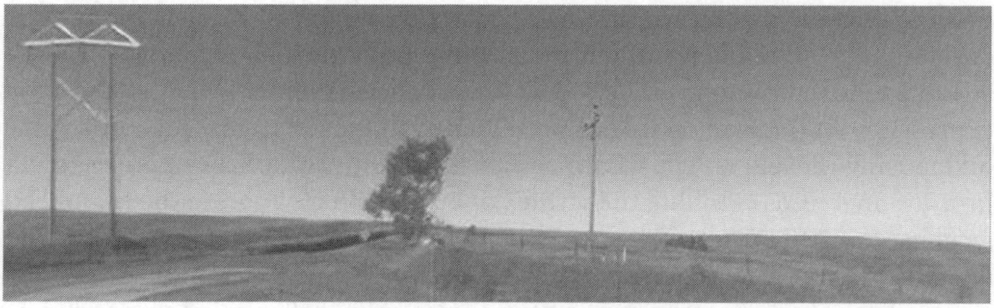

Figure 6 Tamura Yuichiro *Nightless (ver.5)* (still from video, 2010).

Some video works shown in this exhibition appropriated, sampled or "remediated" conventional narrative moving-image techniques, "bending" or drawing out from them nonstandard or anomalous effects. These alienation devices also act to produce elements of ideological and social critique. For example, Japanese artist Tamura Yuichiro's *Nightless (ver. 5)*, made in 2010, is a kind of "road movie," but it is made entirely from still images taken from the "Google Street View" facility. The audio track is taken from Youtube sources, so the artist himself has actually neither filmed nor recorded any pictures or sounds. The transcontinental journey of scenes in *Nightless (ver. 5)* takes the viewer from Nebraska to Chiba, from Alaska to Portugal, Marseilles and beyond. All the scenes occur in daytime, creating an unsettling continuity which defies usual moving-image depictions of "fictional" and "historical" narrative, installing instead a kind of frozen global contemporaneity/simultaneity of action and location.[28]

This effect offers parallels with the experience of using actual web sites which live-stream data, creating virtual images of the whole world for various purposes. These include "live tracker" visualization systems representing aircraft movements around the world, with "3D," "cockpit view" and other display options that also show an endless virtual day of real-time landings, take-offs and flights through cloudless blue skies.

Other works premised on the globalist, democratic role of "video-as-critique" have scrutinized predatory global neoliberal capitalism across Asia, where migrant labor, corporate outsourcing, downsizing and asset-stripping practices are characteristic of the social–economic order. Chieh-Jen Chen's 2003 film *Factory*, for example, deals with the impact on Taiwan of US corporate power, the Cold War and "glocal capitalism" since the 1990s. Chien-Jen Chen asked the workers he had met in 2002 to return to the abandoned Lien Fu Garment factory at which they had worked for years until sacked, and to perform a re-enactment of their labor there. Corporate investors in the factory had closed it down in 1996, withholding severance pay and pension contributions while maintaining ownership of the company's assets. In Taiwan's low-wage economy based on offering corporations "attractive" conditions to set up their businesses—including few laws protecting workers—these laborers were regularly left unemployed when industries simply moved away to find more advantageous conditions. The video work concentrates on the gestures and expressions of the women workers re-situated in the long-empty factory, while juxtaposing these with clips from earlier black and white Taiwan government promotional films extolling the virtues of business relocation to the island.[29]

Singapore-American artist Ana Prvacki's 2007 film *Money Laundering* is an effective satire on financial and political corruption. Her 1 minute 38 second single-channel video work literally shows wads of US dollar bills being scrubbed clean in real time—demonstrating another critical "anti-narrative" technique. Filipino-American Michelle Dizon's short video *Empire (ABS-CBN)*, made in 2009, deals with corporate power and socioeconomic globalization in Manilla, referencing Andy Warhol's iconic eight hour 1964 film of the Empire State Building in New York. Dizon's *Empire*, however, substitutes Manilla's communications tower, described by a critic as "surrounded by haphazard development and a makeshift democracy stunted by the rule of the rent-seeking elite. It is a tower of a media conglomerate that controls water, light, broadcast and cinema" in the city. South Korean film-maker Soyoung Kim's *Two Doors* is a "transmedia" documentary made in 2010. Through combination of a range of media sources (including video film, public TV footage and newspaper articles) *Two Doors* portrays a sit-in protest over rent rises on a factory roof in Yongsan, South Korea, the previous year that ended in violence when a government paramilitary squad entered the building and shot dead several of the protesters. The title refers to a fatal flaw in the planning of the raid (which door to break down?) that led to the deaths of both protesters and police officers sent into the building with erroneous information about the actual location of the demonstrators.[30]

Culture, Contemporaneity and the Postcolonial Artwork

The claim that such video art practices are quintessentially globalist rests on a particular characterization of their material-technological features and lack of traditional origin in or from any one particular location or culture in the world. That is, they emerged and grew up with, as part of, recent globalization processes themselves. They authentically "belong" both everywhere and nowhere at the same time and attain—through what might be called this radical geographically dispersed ontology—a kind of heterogeneous purity of potential meaning and reference. Wherever in Asia video work as a formal–aesthetic means and practice of representation has been developed it has seemingly become implicated within a radical sociopolitical critique of these postcolonial societies and the globalized neoliberal capitalist social orders that have developed, but which remain contested, within them, since the 1990s.[31]

A similar case has been made for installation art. The two idioms have also been combined, with video being incorporated into installation works, as in the example of Mark Boulos's "video sculpture" practice. Boulos's works have focused on postcolonial situations in Asian and African countries, examining socioeconomic structures of exploitation linking Western corporate capitalism to the extraction of raw materials such as oil, for export from poor southern hemisphere rentier states such as Nigeria. For example, his 2008 video installation *All That is Solid Melts into Air* dramatically set two large video screens off each other—one depicting the lives of brokers on the floor of the commodities exchange in Chicago and the other local people fighting the Shell corporate multinational in the Niger Delta. Boulos has also made work, with an anthropological dimension long present in Western documentary film history, on the social life of the revolutionary Marxists groups living, with *No Permanent Address* (the title of his 2010 video installation work) in the jungles of the Philippines.[32]

A different sensibility characterizes the work of South Korean artist Jewyo Rhii, who was born in Seoul in 1971. Her installation works are concerned with the quotidian materials and domestic spaces of contemporary Seoul and South Korean society, explored through what might be called Rhii's "systemic itinerancy" which is core to all her activities. She disavows the idea of a permanent home and moves from location to location—sometimes in receipt of arts grant income to fund these living projects. Rhii collects, fabricates and assembles objects which are then presented in more or less obviously orchestrated ways for public viewing and consideration, both in declared conventional exhibition locations, but also in her abodes and other less conventional venues and receptacles for display. For her piece *Ten Years Please* (2006, ongoing), for example, she carried round a group of disparate objects (her "works") in a shopping trolley, unwilling to destroy them after an earlier exhibition. After finally deciding to display them all at once, she then invited friends to "look after" them for ten years. Themes of anomie, city life and alienation arguably dominate her installations, in, for example, *Night Studio*, exhibited at the Artsonje Center, Seoul in November 2013. This installation was a partial recreation of the contents and layout of her apartment in the Itaewon district of the city which is home to thousands of immigrants, "at the end of a cramped market street of shops dealing in bags, socks, Korean souvenirs, old US army paraphernalia, and imitation designer goods." Her 2009-13 installation *Moving Floor*, built for an exhibition in Germany, was another recreation of part of her apartment in Itaewon.[33]

In a way these installations of things Rhii has made or collected stand for (represent) her living space and her actual living or life. Their "readability" or significance, however, is inherently unstable, volatile—viewers can make of them what they will and there is certainly no clearly or even loosely intended authorial meaning. These objects, their selection and arrangement for display are signs of specific and generalized condensations and displacements of

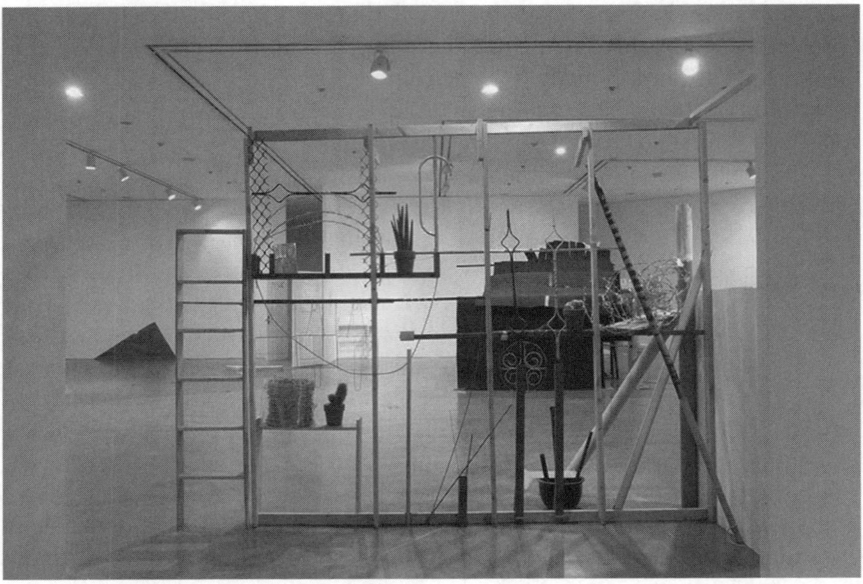

Figure 7 Jewyo Rhii *Night Studio* (mixed media installation, 2013). *Source:* Courtesy Wilkinson Gallery, London.

possible meanings and affects (feelings)—in Rhii's own life, the life of the district where she happens to be living, Seoul, South Korea, the world beyond. "The works," she notes, "are each displaced in divergent times and spaces."[34] Copious notes are presented alongside the myriad objects in the installations in order to aid, but also to make more complex their understanding. There is a kind of quiet, unannounced historical and archival investigation going on in Rhii's works. She has discussed the development of Seoul after the Korean War and its impact on the older city and its inhabitants (for instance, in her 2008 mixed media work *Lie on the Han River*, a compendium of drawings and photographs exhibited at the Bildmuseet, Umea, Sweden). But her installations are caught somewhere between being analytic and fantastic constructions, containing elements of both which, in their interaction, further confute simple or singular readings. This is a defining feature, one is tempted to say, of cultural displacement as contemporary experiential reality—that of people, and of objects, places and relationships within our globalizing social order.

This, of course, is not only an eastern Asian reality. Displacing and disrupting borders like the one dividing the two Koreas continue to exist all over the postcolonial, post-Cold War Asian world following the last century's imperialist and civil wars, along with the neo-imperialist and internecine conflicts of this one. These include, as I showed in the last chapter, the border that still both divides but now increasingly connects Hong Kong's SAR and the PRC.

The borders separating but also joining India, Pakistan and Bangladesh (the three former components of "British India") are discussed in the next chapter. A third is what the Israeli authorities prefer to call the "security fence" or "security barrier"—actually a monstrously ugly concrete wall—dividing what they have mostly arbitrarily designated as the Palestinian areas from legally or illegally held State of Israel territory (see Chapter 5).[35] Highly dangerous, virtually closed borders and "no-go" buffer zones also characterize Israel's contiguous relations to its northern neighbors, Lebanon and Syria. These countries, like the Koreas, have been traumatized and torn apart by civil wars and Cold War politics, regional fighting over several decades and now by the broader religious and ethnic violence engulfing Iraq, the Kurdish region, Iran and Afghanistan. The old Cold War regional and global superpowers—Russia, Turkey, the United States and the European Union—once more intervene from the skies.

Artists in Lebanon, including Walid Raad, Akram Zaatar and Walid Sadek, have produced works in photographic, moving-image and installation modes that underline what Charles Esche, in his discussion of Rhii's art, called the "unreliability of the past to shape the present and the possibility to open up both to artistic invention." Sadek's writings, in addition, have dealt with major filmic accounts of the 1975–1991 Civil War in Lebanon—for instance, Ghassan Salhab's 1998 *Beyruth Fantome* and Ziad Doueiri's *West Beirut* (1998). These feature-length films establish the immanent personal and societal chaos of the conflict and yet also work to create some stabilizing narratives of the war's meaningfulness to its survivors. However, displacement and disjunction are mass as well as minority artistic experiences and materials under the conditions of globalization—in the violent and relatively peaceful, or just pacified, parts of the world—when rapid social, political, economic and geo-spatial change/movement potentially disorients everyone and everything.

Rhii, for one, doesn't appear to think of herself as ever "having" a home or being "at home" and never stays in one place for very long. Cosmopolitanism used to be the positive name for this incessant mobility. Her 2008 *Airport Romance* installation is a witty commentary on an aspect of this globalized nomadism. This installation work was a simulation inside a Dusseldorf gallery of some of the material props of moving and living between countries drawn from the liminal spaces of airports. Rhii impressionistically recreated check-in, immigration and security areas in the gallery, suggested through provisional arrangements of roped-off areas, desks, piles of luggage and seating. *Airport Romance* succinctly evoked the quotidian alienations but also perhaps the fleeting pleasures of people-moving and people-processing systems and spaces.[36]

At the Gallery Hyundai in Seoul the Iranian artist Farhad Moshari exhibited some extraordinary beaded knives. These were formed into patterns to create words made up of menacing blades and multi-colored handles attached to the gallery walls. As such, Moshari's assemblages equally inhabit an at least metaphorically violently disjunctive world. These artefacts lie somewhere between an approximation (or even kitsch recreation) of a traditional "Persian aesthetic" on the one hand, and a version of Iranian-inflected contemporary pop culture, on the other. The knives comprising, for example, Moshari's *My Flower* (2012) are at once apparently practical and decorative objects that simultaneously belong to both and neither of these realms. Questions and doubts about what an artwork is "of" and where an artist might be said to be "from" (and what "traditional" itself signifies) are raised and radically problematized by the objects, assemblages and installations created by Moshari and Rhii. An analogous fundamental questioning has gone on, I've argued, within many of the "new media" works made by eastern Asian artists discussed earlier in this chapter, setting aside the question of whether these practices have any special claim to "global" or globalized" status. Issues and senses of identity, history, meaning and violence are bound up together in this wide range of contemporary artistic products and practices.[37]

The "Real DMZ Project": Conflict Art in the Korean Peninsula

Within the context of the formation of South Korea the identity of the country's people, and the divided history of the peninsula they cohabit, requires scrutiny. The Artsonje Center in Seoul supported the "Real DMZ Project" that brought artists from South Korea and other parts of the world (though not from North Korea) in 2011—2013 to the border zone to make artworks about the circumstances, experiences and meanings of the division. This project, also known as the Gangwon-do Art Project (after the nearby town), is located in the border area of Cheorwon province, in central Korea. This province is close to the 38th Parallel where the states later to become known as North Korea and South Korea were truncated in the 1953 Armistice that established a ceasefire—a temporary suspension of fighting, but no formal end to the civil war.

Several other de-militarized zones have existed, and some continue to exist, within Asia (as well as in other continents). DMZs are a material and societal residue, though with still powerful continuing effects, of twentieth-century colonialism and Cold War superpower conflicts. The DMZ dividing West and East Berlin, for example, ended with formal German reunification in 1990—part of the process that saw the termination of the USSR and the "Soviet Bloc" states, including what had been the German Democratic Republic ("East Germany"), the following year. Persisting, highly volatile militarized and demilitarized border divisions characterize much of western Asia (or the "Middle East," in received imperial parlance). These include, for example, Lebanon's border with Israel, and the longstanding conflict between the

Palestinians and Israel, operating inside the State of Israel and between Israel and State of Palestine areas, the illegally occupied West Bank and besieged Gaza territories.[38]

War, consequential societal chaos and general penury now characterize life across several Middle East states. This has followed US and European interventions in the Gulf Wars in the early 1990s and during the last decade, the occupation of Iraq in 2003, the eruption of Islamic State's attempt to carve out a regional caliphate (Islamic religious state) since 2012, along with civil conflict and ethno-religious fighting within the so-called "failed" or "failing states" of Syria, Lebanon, Egypt, Libya, Afghanistan and Yemen. Terrorist attacks linked to Islamic fundamentalism have taken place at an increasing level in Europe, Africa and the United States over the past twenty years.[39] Closer to South Korea, the fading British Empire's hasty, arrogant and ignorant division of India from Pakistan (West and East) in 1947 and the later declaration of Bangladeshi independence from Pakistan in 1971, produced one of the bloodiest social traumas of twentieth -century decolonization.[40]

The Delhi-based Raqs Media Collective was invited to take part in the Gangwon-do art project, given the parallels between the divisions within the subcontinent in the late 1940s and the Koreas a few years later. The collective exhibited a short video work made in 2005 called *Door to the Sky*. This depicted an aircraft door, torn from a crashed/bombed plane and starkly shot against clouds—an image, they declared, of a "frontier between worlds," resilient yet fragile. Despite the abstract symbolism, the door is something through which humans routinely have to move. The India–Pakistan and Korean divisions, by implication, may be national, international, and "super-power political" in significance, but the physical fact and direct personal experience of a closed border (and door) starts, and, in human terms, ends, with the planned blocking of an actual road, an intended sealing and preconceived prohibition of people on the ground from being able to meet, pass by each other, and live together.[41] For the same reasons, the Irish government and British Northern Irish arts organizations also supported the South Korean DMZ Project, recognizing some familiarity with the situation people on the western edge of Europe faced until the eventual fruition of the "peace process" and putatively permanent cease-fire called by the terrorist organization, the Provisional IRA, in 2005.[42]

The anti-imperial war in Vietnam waged by the indigenous population against the colonizing French, like the Korean conflict, became another Cold War civil conflict, this time in which the United States and the Soviet Union provided military resources for their proxy allies and fought directly on Vietnamese territory. When this war ended in 1975 the consequences of the victory for the nationalist Vietnamese (led by "the Vietcong," or communist guerrilla soldiers) would be global isolation and impoverishment until "independent" Vietnam eventual re-entered the global capitalist system in 2007, when it was permitted to join the World Trade Organization. The journalist John Pilger noted that in this year:

> Vietnam was allowed to join the WTO and qualify for World Bank loans provided it embraced the "free market," destroyed its free public services and paid off the bad debts of the defunct Saigon regime: money which had helped bankroll the American war. The Vietnamese were financially being granted membership of the "international community" as long as they created a society based on inequity and exploited labor, and abandoned the health service that was the envy of the developed world [...] along with a free education system that produced one of the world's highest literacy rates. Today, ordinary people pay for health care and schools, and the elite send their children to expensive schools in Hanoi's"international city" and poach scholarships at American universities.[43]

South Korea became a major beneficiary of US and other Western "development aid" in the form of gifts, direct loans, preferential government contracts and corporate capitalist investment during the Cold War and in the period since 1991. It attained membership of the international Monetary Fund in 1955 (shortly after the end of the Korean War), the General Agreement on Tariffs and Trade (GATT) in 1967, and the WTO in 1995.

The contrast with North Korea—heavily supported by the USSR in the past but now, practically, only in large measure by the PRC—is extreme. North Korea remains a closed and self-enclosed social order, divided from most forms of relationship with most other nation-states, and from most world trade, travel and tourism, which have become the dominant forms of globalizing socioeconomic interaction that now shape, in both profound and small ways, every country's culture, peoples and societal development. North Korea's dictatorial political system, self-identified as autarkic "state-socialism," and its profoundly entrenched cult of personality centered on a dynastic, ruthless authoritarian power base, marks it out as probably now the most systemically draconian social order in the world. Its officially self-declared "socialist-realist" painting, print, sculptural, photographic and filmic modes form a public propagandistic visual arts realm developed at the inception of the state in the mid-1950s. These practices and products remain interesting in what now appears as their archaic historical quirkiness but they represent the morally blank obverse of a highly puritanical and literally murderous state-censoriousness towards apparently all other kinds of art and its producers—as far as this can be known, given the secrecy of its social order.[44]

The artworks commissioned or exhibited by the DMZ Project in 2013, along with related discussion sessions, were selected in relation to a set of themes based on five key words set by the organizers. These were "Heart, " "Earth," "Iron," "Rice" and "Water." These were chosen in order to enable a socio-aesthetic excavation of the origins of the divided Koreas—without, however, the involvement of any artists or critics from the North—and a concomitant critical examination of the social order built in the South since 1953. The basic material survival of the two Korean states established in 1953 depended on food production and its distribution, along with very basic infrastructure development.

This rival state building phase followed a civil war, killing up to 5 million people, which came soon after the Jeju Uprising in 1948–9 that led to the deaths of about one million people who'd fought against both US occupation and pro-Japanese Korean collaborators (Jeju is an island to the south of the peninsula). The two Koreas of the post-1953 era were—and remain—societies built from these violent depopulation events, setting aside the further traumas of personal and societal displacement that the creation and maintenance of the DMZ itself has caused. It has been argued, however, that these founding traumatic events have been displaced—officially, if partially—within the dominant positive narratives of the South's national development since the war. These accounts continually celebrated industrialization, material infrastructure and, later, high-tech development, marginalizing the highly destructive societal legacies of state repression of popular dissent, civil war and territorial division.[45]

For example, tongil rice, a special variety of carbohydrate-rich grain, was created in South Korea, with US expertise, as a staple crop to feed the growing population and ward off, it was believed, growth or resurgence of popular support there for Communism. A similar project was initiated in North Korea at the same time, for the same reasons, sponsored by the Soviet Union. This development required a rapid intensification of industrial-agricultural production and the extended use of chemical fertilizers. Artworks made for the Real DMZ Project 2013 alluded to this process: Sunkyong Kim's 2008–2011 photographic project *Rice Fields in Cheorwon* explored the meanings of the idea of people "living in harmony with nature"—in the DMZ itself, where the artist's home town is located—given the historical imperatives of technology-driven food production. Water provision and dam-building are closely related issues that both unite and divide the interests of the two Korean states. (Water security is an issue that also profoundly affects the day-to-day life of Palestinians, whose supplies are controlled entirely by the State of Israel.)[46]

At earlier moments in the post-separation history, ties between the two Koreas had been closer and some mutually beneficial co-developments occurred. For instance, the Kaesong Industrial Park development, in the northern part of the DMZ, set up in 2002, involved economic and social cooperation by both governments. This stalled, however, and led to an entrenchment of separate and further separating destinies, influenced increasingly by the competing regional interests of the US and the PRC. Other artworks created in the 2011–2013 period for the project in mixed media, architectural and installation forms have addressed a variety of related themes. These included works on the material structures of the DMZ buildings as well as the homes and shops in the town of Cheorwon. South Korean architect and designer Taehyung Kim, for instance, produced a series of detailed drawings exploring residential buildings in Cheorwon, looking to identify what he called a potential "new type of alternative social and cultural space [beyond] occupation and domination, beyond exclusion and conflict, beyond commercialization and development."[47]

Artists made works for the Project on the social psychology of border conflicts and divisions, about "security tourism" in the DMZ, and reconstructed and filmed Korean War battle scenes. Other pieces were concerned with the day to day existence of soldiers on both sides who police the DMZ, examined life in the surviving, stranded civilian areas, and considered the torture of anti-communists by North Korean state forces.[48] Some of these artworks are witty and seemingly trivial, such as Sean Snyder's photographs and installation pieces concerned with showing North Korean leader Kim Jong Un lower legs and platform heels, revealing a shortness scrupulously hidden in official state media representations. Snyder's 2007 work *Korean Central News Agency, Pyongyang, DPRK* elides six photographs of the trouser legs of the leader with the name of the organization responsible for propagating his image—thus tellingly illustrating the interdependency of one with the other. Snyder's broader and underlying serious interest, however, is in such globally circulating propaganda imagery and the forms of its stage-management.[49]

South Korean Suyeon Yun's 2004–2006 photo-documentary project *Incomplete Journey* dealt with the lives of North Koreans who had managed to escape to the South. *Way to Eden* is the title of one work in the series ironically showing North Koreans who have settled in the South standing in front of a giant advertisement showing cartoon Adam and Eve figures. But Suyeon Yun critically compares and possibly even equates the different kinds of societal shabbiness and shallowness that exist, according to the artist, in both states. Noh Suntag's *Red House # 1-13* photographs from 2005 illustrate the massive set-piece collective gymnastics displays held in North Korea, designed to indicate the cohesiveness and resilience of the nation. But Suntag reminds viewers in his statement for the exhibition that South Korea has also organized large-scale sporting events such as the 1988 Olympic Games for similar propagandistic ends. The two states, he claims, are finally "not unlike mirrors reflecting one another." Chien Chi Chang's 2007–2008 film work *Escape from North Korea* examines the very dangerous journey North Koreans have to make if they wish to get to the South, travelling north and then west, illegally, through the PRC, down to Laos and then back up to South Korea.[50]

Other works have dealt interestingly with aspects of earlier détente—and apparent or failed détente—between the two countries. For instance, Chankyong Park's 2005 hour-long single-track video film *Flying* depicts the journey made by South Korean leaders in 2000 for the first peace talks ever held between the two countries. Part of the film shows the jet flying from Seoul to Pyongyang, but Chankyong Park turned the flight scenes upside down, so that the plane appeared to fly under North Korea—a gesture underlying the "creative ambiguity" of the détente mission, according to the artist.[51] Yang Ah Ham's 6-minute 30-second video film *Tourism in Communism* (2005) is about a moment in the late 1990s when South Koreans were given permission to visit a border area in the North regarded as sacred to all Koreans—though this ended in the shooting of a tourist by Northern soldiers, which put paid to the cooperation.

Magnus Bartas's 2009 video film *Madame and Little Boy* (2009), based on bizarre factual events, concerns a South Korean actress kidnapped and abducted to the North where she went on to make films with her husband, who was also kidnapped, before both managed eventually to claim asylum in the USA.[52] Video works not included in the DMZ Project have highlighted the continuous "interrelationality" of the two Koreas and other contiguous territories, such as Japan and the PRC. Yangachi's 2009 film *Middle Corea Trilogy* explores the adventures of a mythic family that comes to symbolize a kind of self-sustaining "pre-national" state collectivity. Its members over three generations were able to move between all these countries, crossing closed borders and creating, in a sense, an effective border between the family itself and these external states. The title name "Middle Korea" suggests neither North nor South Korea, but rather a territory—also neither entirely real nor imagined—hovering somewhere between both.[53]

Contemporary Art Across Global Asia

The "Real DMZ Project 2013" and the exhibitions I've discussed accompanying the Video Art Archive Network Forum in Seoul all indicate how South Korea's visual arts organizations—those "new media"- and "post-museum"-focused, as well as the conventional galleries—had shared an ambitious pan-Asian emphasis. These shows presented works by artists living and working in a wide range of Asian territories all of which have experienced actual, postcolonial and now neocolonial histories, protracted sociopolitical crises and violent conflicts bound up with the Cold War and subsequent global neoliberal capitalist exploitation. The borders created—those relatively open or closed, peacefully policed, "demilitarized" or mired in state and popular violence—have been literal and physical. The disputes they symbolize, entrench and embody are also deeply rooted in factors of class, gender, nation, ethnic, political and religion affiliation. These, in turn, are bound up with vast regional and global labor migration processes, issues of personal and group safety, and access to resources for people of all kinds, including artists.

The "Asia Curator Network"—a project closely linked to the *Moving On Asia* publishing initiative—has brought together dozens of curators and artists over a ten-year period through involvement in a series of annual exhibitions and related events. *Moving On Asia*'s plan was explicitly to work on projects "transcending any regional limitations" within the continent, operating a decentralized "horizontal structure" bringing together its members "based on independence and autonomy." Its intention, its spokesman–curator Jinsuk Suh has claimed, was to "spearhead a new type of moving image confined by no boundaries and signifying the integration and expansion of different media art genres"—building "a new cultural identity in the 'glocal era' of the 21st century and [breaking] down stereotypes of Asian culture."[54] Territories such as Singapore and the Philippines, in addition to Hong Kong and South Korea, as we have seen in this chapter, have all produced moving-image works dealing with the complex legacies of their respective colonial pasts, diversely postcolonial histories and presents. These cannot be reduced to a single or simple point of origin, such as the myth of a "Raffles" colonial figure in Singapore, displaced from this founding role as the British colonialist is in Tzu Nyen Ho's 23-minute single-channel video film *Utama: Every Name in History in 1* (2000) which explores another figure—Utama—reputed to be the first indigenous "king" of the Malays. Other recent films by Tzu Nyen Ho have excavated broader mythmaking aspects to Singaporean history and identities.[55]

Singapore, as much as South Korea, has been the site of a kind of hypermodernity of industrial high-tech development in the global neoliberal era emergent since the 1980s. Its video artists, responding to this history, have focused on themes of social alienation, migration and multiculturalism. The city-state has highly complex relationships with contiguous Malaysia, the PRC and the vast greater-Asian diaspora of "sino-culture" prevalent in the region. At the same time, Singapore hosts surviving oral performance traditions amid the territory's swiftly modernizing mass media. Once again, digital video/cable/satellite and internet practices have been used by artists as tools of political critique—in a "remediation" process, as one commentator calls it—in order to assess how the still authoritarian Singapore state used such technologies itself as major propaganda weapons in the period of 1960s–1990s.

Ka Fai Choy's 2010 research-based installation *Lan Fang Chronicles*, for example, used video to survey an area of Indonesia (once West Borneo) involved in a republican experiment for over 100 years by Hakka Chinese living in the area. This work critically illuminated, through implicit contrast, Singapore's own authoritarian political order, as well as its diasporic foundations.[56] To the north, in Vietnam, the DOCLAB center for new media in Hanoi—like Loop Alternative Space in Seoul—has begun to try to encourage local audiences and an alternative political and cultural scene, exhibiting a commitment to "cultural democracy" through use of new media technologies and innovative forms of social engagement. However, government censorship of artists and visual arts organizations there continues to inhibit this process.[57]

If such moving image and installation works (and those works combining these practices) are the primary "global art forms" then this is perhaps because in some fundamental ways they must embody/signify nowhere and everywhere at once—and by so doing radically problematize inherited, preglobalization notions and myths of "origin," "in-ness," "of-ness" and "from-ness." These arguments have been highlighted recently in a study of Palestinian contemporary art, subject of this book's final chapter.[58] Critic and curator Johan Pijnappel identified the same complex of problems in an essay on contemporary art "in" India, noting that "the whole question 'Who or what comes from where, and what does it mean?' has become much more complicated."

Nationality is not a reliable guide, Pijnappel observed, as many artists—based in Asia and elsewhere—have what he called a "cross-cultural biography" inflected by experiences of immigration, colonization, dislocation, ethnic identity and language negotiation.[59] The artists Nalini Malani and Shilpa Gupta, for instance, often referred to as "contemporary Indian artists," in fact have much more complex social identities. Malini was born in Karachi in 1946 (when it was still part of India, not Pakistan) and Gupta comes from the Agrawal community of cosmopolitan traders in northern India. Both artists have highly differentiated senses of personal and group identity, origins and interests. What do the seemingly once assured prepositions "in" and "from" come to mean, then, given this inter- and intranational complexity, setting aside the many other forms of possible identification and affiliation? I turn to artworks by Malani and Gupta in the following chapter.

What meaningful distinctions between "Western" and "non-Western" art and artists are tenable now, given the deracinating processes and consequences of globalization? Could the differences and oppositions this dyad once clearly represented have been eradicated, even though the world's leading galleries and museums are still generally held to be those in the United States and Europe? But how is this assumed "lead" or "superiority" to be defined, measured and assessed? In what does it consist? Is the claim of Western superiority in the visual arts actually just a prejudicial supposition made by certain critics and commentators (including this one)?

It is factually true that up to 2008 the highest prices for contemporary artworks made and sold by Western artists—those, that is, "from" the United States and Europe—certainly still towered above those made by artists "from" South Korea, India and the PRC. But what is the final or long-term historical value of this quantitative measure in making critical, evaluative judgements? Might it not just enable some influential players in the art world system to reconfirm and have reproduced their own values, backgrounds and interests (the view expressed in the debate about the art market held at Art Basel Hong

Kong, discussed in the previous chapter)?[60] The organizers of the first Kochi Biennale in India, held in 2012–2013, certainly wanted their event—involving 50% of works, they declared proudly, made by artists "from" India—to be seen to rank alongside the best of such exhibitions held in the West. They drew explicit, ambitious parallels with Venice, no less—the home of the first biennial exhibition in 1895, a city with which Kochi, the organizers claimed, shared an historic trading and cultural tradition. Was such a comparison just rhetoric and sales pitch?

But Pijnappel's concerns, however, were not just about cultural and artistic relations between nation-states, regions and continents. They were about all the borders involved in "West-versus-East" thinking—including neo-orientalism and a "reverse-orientalism" (Occidentalism) produced when, for instance, Indian artists have made what Pijnappel called superficial work while on grant-aided visits to Western countries. But what then, under globalized conditions, do really "deep" and meaningful artworks look like? How can they be recognized? Publics inside India for contemporary art can be as divided (and venues as divisive) as publics and venues anywhere else. The background to the establishment of the Kochi Biennale in traditionally "communist" Kerala province demonstrates this.

Pijnappel himself chose not to show Malani's 2008 work *Remembering Toba Tek Singh* in the elite space of the then new extension to the National Gallery of Modern Art in Delhi, an institution which mostly attracted Western tourists and the Indian capital city's cultural elite. Malani's video/play installation project was concerned with India's and Pakistan's aggressively competitive nuclear testing programmes in the 1960s. The work's title refers to a town in the Punjab province of Pakistan renowned for its religious and social tolerance (the name of which wasn't changed, as most were after Partition in 1947, to reflect the dominant Muslim population). Instead, in an attempt to reach a much wider public, Malani's installation was displayed in the Coomaraswarmy Hall in Mumbai—key location of India's historic proto-national debates in the 1930s and 1940s—in order to attract a larger number and diverse mix of visitors from all classes, religions, ethnic groups and castes.[61] It is to these wider historical and societal conditions of the global contemporary art world in India, within and out of which the Kochi Biennale has emerged, that I turn now.

Notes

1 See Don Thompson, *The Supermodel and the Brillo Box: Back Stories and Peculiar Economics from the World of Contemporary Art* (Palgrave: Basingstoke, 2014): 1. On the transformations in museum organization and displays under globalization, see Peter Weibel and Andrea Buddensieg (eds.), *Contemporary Art and the Museum: A Global Perspective* (Hatje Cantz/ZKM: Ostfildern, 2007).

2 See Michel Foucault, *The Order of Things: An Archaeology of the Human Sciences* (Tavistock Publications: London, 1970), and particularly his opening discussion of the painting *Las Meninas* (1656) by Diego Velazquez. Foucault's account summarizes and exemplifies the understanding of visual art as a special kind of cognition. Note, however, that painting in oils was itself an earlier technological mode of representation which at its inception and development between c 1450 and 1750 in Western countries was credited, like photography—"new" a hundred years later—with dramatically modernizing human vision and understanding.

3 On the interrelation of these domains, see, e.g., Geeta Kapur "A Cultural Conjuncture in India: Art into Documentary," in Terry Smith, Okwui Enwezor and Nancy Condee (eds.), *Antinomies of Art and Culture: Modernity, Postmodernity, Contemporaneity* (Duke University Press: Durham, NC, 2008): 30–59. On the role of social media in the uprisings in Tunisia and Egypt in 2011, see Franco "Bifo" Berardi, "The Paradox of Media Activism: The Net is not a Tool, it's an Environment," in Anthony Downey (ed.), *Uncommon Grounds: New Media and Critical Practices in North Africa and the Middle East* (IB Tauris: London, 2014): 39–46.

4 For a fairly programmatic statement of this position, see Mark Tribe and Reena Jana, "Art in the age of digital distribution," in Uta Grosenick (ed.), *New Media Art* (Taschen: Hong Kong, 2009): 6–25. Tribe and Jana date "new media art" precisely from 1994, the year when the first web browser was introduced which turned the internet into "a popular medium" with global reach (6). For a critique of such perspectives, see Astra Taylor *The People's Platform: Taking Back Power and Culture in the Digital Age* (Fourth Estate: London, 2014) and Evgeny Morozov "Socialize the Data Centres!" *New Left Review* 91: Jan/Feb 2015, 45–66.

5 See Carol Duncan *Civilizing Rituals: Inside Public Museums* (Routledge: London, 1995), and Carol Duncan and Alan Wallach "The Universal Survey Museum," *Art History* December 1980: 3, 447–469.

6 See Hans Belting, "Exhibiting Cultures," in Weibel and Buddensieg (eds.), *Contemporary Art and the Museum*: 164–172. Consider, for instance, emphasis on the idea of "emancipation" through art and learning developed recently at Tate Liverpool: http://www.tate.org.uk/about/our-work/tate-research/research-centres/curatorial-practice-and-museology.

7 See "Mapping: The Biennials and New Art Regions," in Hans Belting, Andrea Buddensieg and Peter Weibel (eds.), *The Global Contemporary and the Rise of New Art Worlds* (ZKM/MIT Press: Cambridge, MA: 2013): 101–107 (104).

8 See http://eng.ggcf.or.kr/about/history.asp (accessed March 23, 2017). For a critical review of developments in contemporary art museum design, see Hal Foster, "After the White Cube" *London Review of Books*: 37 (6); March 19, 2015: 25–26.

9 See Andrew Salmon *Modern Korea* (John Murray: London, 2014): 51–53. Mass arrests followed the killings and 60,000 people were sent to "re-education camps."

10 See Yeunho Kim Jang, "Towards a Social Role for Korean Moving Image: A Proposal towards a Political and Aesthetic Korean Alternative Visual Culture" (350–357) and Hyunsuk Seo, "Digital Heterotopias: Historical 'Elsewhere' in Korean Video Art of the 2000s" (358–367), in Jinsuk Suh (ed.), *Moving on Asia*, vol. 6 (Alt. Space Loop: Seoul, 2013).

11 See Jinsuk Suh, former director of Loop, "A New Sphere for Public Discourse and Media Art," in Jinsuk Suh (ed.), *Moving on Asia*, vol. 6: 476–479 (479), and Yeunho Kim Jang, "Towards a Social Role for Korean Moving Image: A Proposal towards a Political and Aesthetic Korean Alternative Visual Culture," *Moving on Asia*, vol. 6: 354.

12 See Hyunsuk Seo, "Digital Heterotopias: Historical 'Elsewhere' in Korean Video Art of the 2000s": 359–360 and 364–366.

13 See Gridthiya Gaweewong, "State Ideology vs. the Rise of Small Narratives: Discourse of Moving Images on the 21st Century Thailand," in *Moving On Asia*, vol 6: (388–393) and accounts of *Factory* and *Empire* in *Moving On Asia*, vol. 6: 28–29 and 50–51.

14 On the role of AECID, see the booklet *ARCO/Madrid* produced by ARCO Art Fair Madrid, February 13/17, 2013: 91. Songwon Art Center exhibition held November 15–30, 2013, catalogue leaflet, np.

15 See David Harvey, *The Enigma of Capital and the Crisis in Capitalism* (Profile: London, 2010). On the blurring of definitions of "public" and "private" in state and supra-state cultural funding arrangements, see the groundbreaking critique edited by Maria Lind and Raimund Minichbauer, *European Cultural Policies: 2015: A Report with Scenarios on the Future of Public Funding for Contemporary Art in Europe* (Iaspis, Stockholm, 2005).

16 See *ARCO Madrid International Contemporary Art Fair 2014*, 33rd edition: 12, 14, 16. There is, however, little secure consensus on the soundness of using contemporary art as a financial investment. See, e.g., Noah Horovitz, "Art Investment Funds," in his *Art of the Deal Contemporary Art in a Global Financial Market* (Princeton University Press, Princeton, NJ, 2011) : 143–187.

17 For another Yba example, see Don Thompson "Damien Hirst, Artist and Marketer," in *The Supermodel and the Brillo Box*: 95–104.

18 Gras, exhibition leaflet, np. See also, e.g., Caroline Jones, "Globalism/Globalization," in James Elkins, Zhivka Valiavicharska and Alice Kim (eds.), *Art and Globalization* (Pennsylvania State University Press: University Park: PA: 2010): 129–137.

19 *SeMA Nanji Residency 2013* (Seoul Museum of Art: Seoul, 2013): 8–9.

20 See, e.g., "Christie's, Sotheby's, and Their Competitors" and "When Auction Houses and Dealers Collide," in Thompson, *The Supermodel and the Brillo Box*: 137–146 and 195–206. For SeMA's global plans, see Kim Hong-hee, Director of Seoul Museum of Art, in *SeMA Nanji Residency 2013*: 5.

21 See the CVs of the 7th Nanji Residency artists in *SeMA Nanji Residency 2013*: 234–252.

22 Seoul Museum of Art information leaflet, 2013 exhibitions: np. Tate's international collecting activities could also be perceived to be crypto-imperialist. For an historical account of the development of Tate inside England (where it operates four sites) and beyond, see Harris, "Curatorial Imperialism? From 'Tate in the North' to 'Capital of Culture,'" in Jonathan Harris (ed.), *Identity Theft: The Cultural Colonization of Contemporary Art* (Liverpool University Press/Tate Liverpool): 9–27.

23 See Chiara Marchini Camia (ed.), *Digital Art Works: The Challenges of Conservation* (ZKM/Espace Multimedia Gantner/CEAAC: 2012).

24 Jinsuk Suh, "A New Sphere for Public Discourse and Media Art," *Moving On Asia*, vol. 6: 476–479.

25 Yeunho Kim Jang: "Towards a Social Role for Korean Moving Image: A Proposal towards a Political and Aesthetic Korean Alternative Visual Culture," *Moving On Asia*, vol. 6 (350–357): 354.

26 Ibid.: 355.

27 See exhibition catalogue *Analog Welcome, Digital Archive* (Seoul Museum of Art: Nanji, 2013): 20–21 and 24–25.

28 *Analog Welcome, Digital Archive*: 36–37.

29 See *Moving on Asia* vol. 6: 28–29.

30 *Moving on Asia*, vol.6: 236–237, 50–51, and Soyoung Kim, "How Films in the 21st Century Respond and Adopt to the Digital Era: *Two Doors*—a Transmedia Documentary" (346–349).

31 See, for instance, the many examples—including still photographs—set out and examined in Anthony Downey (ed.), *Dissonant Archives: Contemporary Visual Culture and Contested Narratives in the Middle East* (I.B. Tauris: London, 2015).

32 See Jonathan Harris, "Love Stories" (interview with Mark Boulos), *Art Monthly* November 2013; no. 371: 1–4.

33 See exhibition pamphlet *Jewyo Rhii: Night Studio* (Artsonje Center: 2013), n.p. On *Night Studio*, *Moving Floor* and *Ten Years Please*, see *Jewyo Rhii: Walls to Talk to* (Koenig Books: London, 2013): 125–126, 265–274 and 198 respectively. Also see, in the same volume, Rhii's interview with Peter Gorschluter (42–55) and the essay by Charles Esche, "What remains… ambivalent relationships (with people and things)": 87–124.

34 Exhibition pamphlet *Jewyo Rhii: Night Studio* (Artsonje Center: 2013), n.p.

35 For a useful synopsis of the socioeconomic and political consequences of territorial divisions between Israeli and Palestinian areas following the Oslo Peace Accords of 1993–1995, see Perry Anderson "The House of Zion," *New Left Review*, 96; Nov–Dec 2015 (5–37): 10–11.

36 See Walid Sadek, "Peddling Time When Standing Still: Art Remains in Lebanon and the Globalization that Was," in Harris (ed.), *Globalization and Contemporary Art*: 43–55, and Tarek Khoury, "The Art of the Written Word and New Media Dissemination: Across the Borders between Syria and

Lebanon," in Downey (ed.), *Uncommon Grounds:* 302–317. On Rhii's work and Lebanese parallels, see Charles Esche, "What remains…:" 96, and on cosmopolitanism, Marsha Meskimmon, *Contemporary Art and the Cosmopolitan Imagination* (Routledge: Abingdon, 2010).

37 Farhad Moshari, *My Flower*, Gallery Hyundai, Seoul, November 1–December 1, 2013.

38 On the relationship between Asia's experience of Western colonialism and its regional intracolonial wars (especially amongst China, Japan and Korea), see Jung-Sun Ni Han, *An Imperial Path to Modernity: Yoshino Sakuzo and a New Liberal Order in East Asia 1905–37* (Harvard University Press: Cambridge, MA, 2015).

39 On the links between mass poverty, unemployment and "failing states" across Asia, Africa and South America, see Mike Davis, *Planet of Slums* (Verso: London, 2006), which also offers a succinct social history of the "Third World." See also, e.g., Sarah Tobin, *The Syrian Refugee Crisis and Lessons from the Iraqi Refugee Experience* (Institute for Iraqi Studies: Boston, 2013).

40 On the division between India and Pakistan, see the exhibition and catalogue by Iftikhar Dadi and Hammad Nasar (eds.), *Lines of Control: Partition as a Productive Space* (Green Cardamon/Herbert F. Johnson Museum of Art, Cornell University: Ithica, NY, 2012).

41 See *Real DMZ Project 2013* exhibition at Artsonje Center, Seoul July 27–September 22, 2013 and catalogue (Samuso: Seoul, 2013): 32–33.

42 Funding for the DMZ project was made available by The Arts Council Ireland, the Centre for Contemporary Art Derry–Londonderry and Culture Ireland, see *Real DMZ Project 2013*: 91.

43 John Pilger, quoted in Khalil Nakhleh *Globalized Palestine: The National Sell-Out of a Homeland* (Red Sea Press: Trenton, NJ, 2012): 1. Nakhleh is drawing an explicit parallel with the State of Palestine's assimilation into global capitalism following the Oslo Accords of the mid-1990s. This development is discussed in Chapter 5 below. For a brief account of US intervention in Vietnam, see William Blum *Killing Hope: US Military and CIA Interventions since World War II* (Zed Books: London, 2003): 122–132.

44 Seoul Museum of Art in 2015 held a groundbreaking exhibition about North Korean visual arts as part of its display program marking the liberation of (the then unitary) Korean state in 1945 from Japanese occupation. See *The 70th Anniversary of Liberation Day: NK Project* (SeMA: Seoul, 2015).
The exhibition took place July 21–September 29, 2015. The show included substantial numbers of paintings, posters and postage stamps held in private collections never seen before in South Korea. See also the varied discussions of posters in the Ou Yang collection, in Menene Gras (ed.), *Corea del Norte: el peso de la historia* (*North Korea: The Weight of History*) (Casa Asia/Alhondiga Bilbao: Madrid, 2011), and Andrei Lankov *The Real North Korea* (Oxford University Press: Oxford, 2013).

45 See Gwi-Ok Kim, untitled talk at the DMZ 2013 "Monthly Forum: DMZ Humanities—Cheorwon" event, in *Real DMZ Project 2013*: 64–65.

46 On the development of Tongil rice, see Tae-Ho Kim, "Burning Rice: the economics of the division and rice," *Real DMZ Project 2013*: 89–91, and on Sunkyong Kim's project, 52–53. On Palestinian water security and sewage needs, see Eyal Weizman *Hollow Land: Israel's Architecture of Occupation* (Verso: London, 2007): 18–22.

47 See *Real DMZ Project 2013*: 44–45.

48 See the full account of all artworks and artists in *Real DMZ Project 2013*: 16–72.

49 *Real DMZ Project 2013*: 18–19.

50 *Real DMZ Project 2013*: 22–23, 28–29 and 24–25.

51 See *Moving On Asia* vol. 6: 222–223.

52 *Real DMZ Project 2013*: 36–37 and 38–39.

53 See Dooeun Choi "Mulling over the social role of the Korean moving image: Moving images, expecting the images that move society," in *Moving on Asia*, vol 6: 340–344.

54 *Moving on Asia*, vol. 6: 6–7.

55 See *Moving on Asia*, vol. 6: 86–95.

56 See David Teh, "The 'Sea State': Notes on Video Art in Singapore," *Moving On Asia*, vol. 6: 440–445.

57 See Nguyen Trinh Thi, "Discourse on the Moving Image in Vietnam in the 21st Century," *Moving on Asia*, vol. 6: 414–419.

58 See Gordon Hon and Bashir Makhoul, *The Origins of Palestinian Art* (Liverpool University Press: Liverpool, 2013).

59 See John Pijnappel, "Moving Images in the 21st Century in Indian Video Art and beyond," in *Moving on Asia*, vol. 6 (428–434): 428

60 On the important relationship between the highest and average market prices in 2008, see Malcolm Bull, "The Two Economies of World Art," in Harris (ed.), *Globalization and Contemporary Art*: 179–190. Note especially the pyramid diagram of individual sales prices: 184.

61 John Pijnappel, "Moving Images in the 21st Century in Indian Video Art and beyond," in *Moving on Asia* vol. 6: 433.

3

Globalizing Indian Contemporary Art: The Biennial as Rhetorical Form

"Every morning before facing the world, I face myself. Every morning as I get ready to meet my every day challenges, I look at myself in the mirror. The crystal clear image fills me with confidence. Inspires me to go ahead and take the challenges, head on. In a moment I know that nothing is beyond my reach. And no goal too far. Much like Modiguard mirrors. The face of a confident and vibrant India. Bringing the world's finest technologies to give you unmistakably clear and distortion free mirrors." Peering through my own not so clear glasses and rubbing my sore eyes as the cramped seven hour flight from Heathrow to Mumbai nears its end I notice that the young Indian businesswoman pictured in the ad I am reading for Modiguard ("Honest mirrors") has the pallor of someone who's stayed indoors admiring her own image for too long. The Jetwings inflight magazine I've been reading, in fact, seems to feature a surfeit of less than healthy looking individuals, once I begin to examine the range. These nouveau riche entrepreneurs and their families have certainly made it—evidenced by their private gated-community new-build homes, butler service, private schools offering Cambridge University entrance exams and "state-of-the-art security." But many either have the same pallid look as this Echo of Narcissus or—and this is the obverse problem caused by the affluence now besetting the subcontinent's elite—appear increasingly to suffer from obesity. Thankfully, however, as other adverts attest, professionals are on hand to deal with this eventuality. Jetwings also features India's "First Biennale of Contemporary Art," the opening of which I am travelling to attend in Kochi, in the southern state of Kerala. Interspersed between spreads on gated enclaves in Mumbai, six-star hotels such as the Taj Coromandel in Chennai ("Forever classic. Forever Contemporary") and "ultra luxury homes" in Bangalore "sculpted to suit only the very upper crust," is an ad exhorting me to "Take a holiday in Kerala, God's own country"... I sit back, in so far as this is possible in my economy seat. The plane dips down toward Mumbai and I see that

The Global Contemporary Art World, First Edition. Jonathan Harris.
© 2017 John Wiley & Sons, Inc. Published 2017 by John Wiley & Sons, Inc.

the slum-dog houses run right alongside the runway, offering a very different kind of "incomparable lifestyle"...

The Kochi Biennale Big Sell

On the same day that Shri Oomen Chandy, the Honourable Chief Minister of Kerala opened the first Kochi Biennale in December 2012, he also launched what was called the "Grand Kerala Non-Stop Shopping Surprises" event. This was a 48-day "festival of consumption" in which 10 000 local businesses participated, according to *The Hindu* newspaper. Neoliberal capitalism in India was riding high, *The Times of India* confirmed ebulliently, in an article with the breezily rhetorical title "Can You Bet on Consumption?"[1] From one perspective encapsulated in the global neoliberal world order mediated by magazines such as *Jetwings* there is now a pan-Asian continuum of elite consumerism. This comprises the goods, services and experiences of luxury hotels and upper-class travel, private housing, private education, high-performance cars, fashion, accessories and contemporary art.

The magazine *Alef*, for instance, self-styled as the "Cultural Journal to the Gulf," available free at airports across the region stretching from the oil-rich sultanates in the north to Kochi itself near the southern tip of India, recently celebrated what it called Qatar's "first women's luxury brand" range. The creation of this collection of "bespoke" leather goods, shoes, jewelry and couture had been superintended by an imported, and also luxurious, French "master craftsman." A single pair of shoes destined for the state's fashion elite consumers would, the company responsible reassuringly boasted, take their artisans at least three months to make.[2] *Alef* also carried a story about Damien Hirst's first one-man show that had just opened at the Alriwaq Doha gallery in Qatar's capital city. The equally high-end Italian and French curators imported to run the exhibition program of the Qatar Museums Authority reminded readers that Hirst, with his art's vaunted "complex" philosophical themes of life, death and love, was also "one of today's most commercially successful, as well as enduringly popular artists."[3]

Luxury, however, can be made available it seems to the (relative) masses. Organizers of the first Kochi Biennale announced that it had attracted 10 000 visitors in its first three days, and claimed that by the end of its three-month run in March 2013 it should have hit the target of 800 000. The exhibition would "give a new face to Kerala's cultural tourism," an unnamed member of the "Kochi Biennale foundation" board noted. The "Doubting Thomases" who had opposed government funding for the event on the grounds that international contemporary art was elitist would be proved wrong. (Note the religious reference—there is an association of St Thomas the Apostle with the ancient nearby city of Muziris.) Kochi, however, had no reputation as a center for the visual arts in India. Moreover, the communist Kerala state government that had originally pledged financial support for the event fell from power in 2011 and this funding had not materialized. Nevertheless, the new biennial, its organizers and supporters declared, would constitute both a local and a national triumph.[4]

Those responsible for articulating the purpose and character of the first edition apparently saw no conflict of interests within this extension of "cultural tourism." Kochi, after all, was close to ancient but now lost Muziris, the "prosperous seaport" of the first century CE. Muziris, primordial nexus of Indo-Roman Empire-Greek trade routes, was redescribed if not reinvented in Biennale literature publicity as a 2000-year-old "business and cultural center," however much now dilapidated and unvisited.[5] Represented as an intrinsic part of "Kerala's cosmopolitanism in antiquity," Muziris features in the biennial's promotional materials as no less than a powerhouse of globalization millennia *avant le lettre*.

Warming to this theme, the significance of Muziris now, in terms of its inspiration for modern Kochi, was sketched in. Publicity material reported that the lost city's:

> goods, ideas, technology and other creative expressions [accompanied] the movement of people across geographical zones, often crossing socio-cultural boundaries [creating] a unique social platform for heterogeneous cultural practices [...] no single strand [was] responsible for the creation of cultures. Each [was] dependent upon another and the other [...] spread great distances.[6]

The inauguration of the Kochi Biennale would enable Kerala to transcend its hitherto limited tourism trade, largely based on "beaches, back waters and forests"—in other words, the standard Goa India beach holiday offer. Instead, the existing "Muziris Heritage" project, involving conservation, restoration, history, environmental projects and "development of crafts and art forms, occupational and other community activities" was depicted as a kind of omnicultural endeavor of which the biennial would become a natural extension. If the world had once gone to and from Muziris—sent its traders and products through its roads and waterways, to be followed by Jewish, Syrian-Christian, Islamic, Buddhist and Roman settlers—then this "long lost cosmopolitanism," re-presented now as a confluence of "multiple cultural streams," was to be reborn, via "a new social platform" in Kochi, as the biennial opened its doors for the first time to the world, and to the global contemporary art world, on December 12, 2012.[7]

The exhibition took place, however, in a series of buildings and spaces that signify the more recent, less palatable history of southern India—that dominated by the serial conquest and occupation of what is now Kerala state by Portuguese, Dutch and British explorers, soldiers, traders and their "settler" populations in the era from the 16th to the mid-twentieth century.[8] The biennial's opening ceremony took place at Parade Ground, Fort Kochi, an open area along with bordering public spaces where the Portuguese had stored arms and the Dutch and British drilled their troops (Vasco de Gama, who "discovered" this territory and claimed it for Western Europeans, was buried nearby in 1524). Many of the artworks displayed in the first Kochi Biennale were shown in the complex of buildings and open spaces at Aspinwall House—originally the business premises of the English trader Aspinwall and Co., established in 1867. David Hall, a site for more artworks, was a bungalow built by the Dutch East India Company around 1695, named after a Jewish merchant, David Koder, who lived in the house (refurbished recently as an "eco-hotel"). Other artworks were installed in the grounds of the Cochin Club, an early nineteenth-century "exclusive British Gentlemen's Club" which now, though still a private social institution, deigns to admit women.[9]

Durbar Hall was built as a royal court in the 1850s by the Maharaja of Cochin (Kochi's name rendered in English under British rule). It was transformed, exhibition publicity claimed, into a "gallery of international museum quality" for use by the Biennale curators. This institution is run by Lalitha Kala Akademi—India's National Academy of Arts—the organizers of the now defunct "Indian Triennial" exhibition established in the 1960s, whose relation to the Kochi Biennale I consider later. Kerala's chief minister claimed Durbar Hall was "Asia's best gallery." Two further sites for the biennial's artworks and related activities indicated the basis of Kerala's historic economic and trading significance. These were Pepper House, on the waterfront near Kochi, and Mattancherry Bazar Road. The former is a large warehouse facility or "go-down," built by the Dutch. The latter thoroughfare was the hub of the trade in tea, spices, cashews and dried fruits, along with other commodities such as rubber, some buildings along which remain used for freight storage.[10]

Ninety artists were featured in the first edition of the Biennale, representing over 20 countries, though more than half of the total, the organizers explained, were of Indian origin. This selection was intended to signal that the organizers, and their backers, would not be in the business of simply importing generic "global" artists drawn from some generic "global biennial" template. However, some very well-known Indian, and "globally successful" artists, including Sudarshan Shetty, Subodh Gupta and Vivan Sundaram, did participate. The Kochi Biennale, here matching the global template, also included "collateral" programs of performances by musicians and drama groups, film showings, seminars, guest lectures, conversations and panel discussions—intensively so, at least at the outset of the exhibition.[11]

The first edition of the biennial attracted financial support from organizations within the usual spectrum—state/public, private/non-profit and some ambiguously in-between—based in India, the broader Asian region and globally. The Australian government, for instance, was involved, through both its cultural-diplomatic International Council (supporting its own artists taking part in the show) and its department for foreign affairs and trade. The Goethe Institute Max Mueller Bhavan, a German state cultural-diplomatic agency, and the Staatliche Kunstsammlungen Dresden (a provincial state art museum), also provided subvention to Kochi. BMW cars and Tata Enterprises—the giant Indian global multinational corporation—were prominent commercial "partners," a term key to the language and activities of the global contemporary art world. Hong Kong's Asia Art Archive, along with the international Biennial Foundation, based in Switzerland, helped co-develop the Kochi Biennale's symposia program. Several Gulf states-based arts and culture organizations were also involved. The leading practical organizer and funder of the Biennale in 2012–13 was the global advertising agency Wieden + Kennedy, operating from a base in Delhi.[12]

The Biennale attracted support in kind from the Kerala state government and the Cochin Corporation (a Kochi city foundation), along with money from civil society arts and cultural organizations—including the Kerala Lalit Kala Academy, the Kendra Sangeet Natak Academy, the Gurjal Foundation India and Sangita Jindal. No financial contribution, however, was made by the Indian national government. The Kochi Biennale came to be represented as a Kerala state event, set within what the organizers subtly chose to call "the global cultural map"—meaning India as a whole, and the whole world beyond. The previous involvement of Indian central governments in high-profile national arts events, such as the Indian Triennial, defunct since 2008—widely perceived by the turn of the millennium to have become simultaneously lackluster aesthetically and politically propagandistic—inhibited players on both sides in the run up to the first edition of the Biennale.[13] Besides, the proponents and forces of neoliberal India had, since the 1990s, fostered a very different ethos that I turn to later. Nevertheless, the Kochi Biennale organizers certainly understood that sustaining local support for their event required that, as well as emphasizing the important participation of local visual artists, traditional regional cultural practices (here effectively meaning tribal music and ritual performance) had to be foregrounded strongly in the exhibition's "collateral events" program.[14]

Kochi as a Global Venue

Kochi's mayor in 2012, Tony Chammani, in his supporting address at the inauguration of the Biennale, observed that it had become nothing less than "mandatory for a thriving city like Kochi" to have this event. The exhibition, further, would, he claimed, "elevate Kochi to the elite list of cities holding biennales" and enable it to reap "its economic, cultural and trade benefits."[15] Perhaps it was inevitable that its organizers and supporters would attempt to draw parallels with Venice—home of the first biennial and renowned for its intercontinental cosmopolitan trading, arts and cultural significance since the Renaissance. Hormis Tharakan, former director-general of police in Kerala and retired secretary to the Indian national government cabinet, wrote effusively, comparing Venice and Kochi, in the biennial's in-house magazine, *Biennale Leaf*, in December 2012. This essay is exemplary of ubiquitous contemporary art world publicity, combining analytic and rhetorical elements—an instance of well-intentioned "boosterism" that suggests its author had become carried away with an attractive though fanciful conceit.

In the fourteenth century, Tharakan claimed, for example, Cochin (as the city was then called) actually did rival Venice, given its monopoly on "black gold" (pepper) and other spices. Merchants from Venice and Constantinople, Alexandria and Arabia, Java and China visited the city to trade, "pay their respects to the powerful local Kings or just to gawk at the grand palaces, avenues and bazaars."[16] Venice was to lose its independence as a republic in 1797, when the city-state was captured by Napoleon Bonaparte's forces. Two years earlier Fort Kochi had been wrested by the British from the Dutch, on the pretext that the latter had sided with the French dictator. Weaving together the history and fate of the two centers through such sleight-of-hand narrative devices, Tharakan finally asks rhetorically if Kochi, like Venice, can revive itself as an international art capital in the manner achieved by its putative historic competitor since the late nineteenth century. "Will Kochi," he muses, "reclaim its rightful place among the metropolises of the world through the medium of art as Venice did over the last century?"[17]

The fact that now more than 150 biennials operate across four continents indicates, rather, that the international contemporary art exhibition-as-cultural-tourism format has become a staple vehicle for the socioeconomic "regenerative" ambitions of many cities, regions and nation-states. Each biennial, however, entails specific, irreducible originating features, environmental and historical resources, infrastructural aspects and support organizations. An international body, the "not-for-profit" Biennial Foundation, was created in 2009 to liaise between and provide specialist help for members of this growing constituency—which one commentator has called the "global biennial community." At the same time, the mix of state, NGO and commercial agencies involved in funding particular biennials (and to some degree art fairs too) around the world indicates the existence of a complex web of active and interactive political, diplomatic and "aid"/"development" agencies. These operate both in concert, and sometimes less co-operatively, to attempt to secure a range of different though interlinked economic, social and cultural objectives.[18]

Kochi Biennale's originators were two Mumbai-based artists raised in Kerala: Bose Krishnamacahari and Riyas Komu. This enabled the organization they set up to claim with some credibility that its philosophy and ethos was authentically rooted in the place where the exhibition would be held and steered by producers of art, rather than by what might be presented by hostile commentators as an elitist transnational "professional curatorship" parachuted in on expense accounts. This argument was to prove especially significant in the biennial's developmental dialogue with suspicious Keralan groups and individuals. Local writers such as Paul Zacharia, and film-maker Adoor Gopalakrishnan (who selected films for the collateral program), defended the Biennale initiative and Kerala state's financial support for it. Importantly, their testimonies were given credence because the event's organizers had assiduously attended to sectoral interests in the local political landscape. Inclusion of Keralan artists and "traditional" cultural activities really mattered, because the region's dominant Malayalis tribe, which provides Kerala with its local language, regularly holds highly popular festivals of theater, music and cinema. This is another example of how the global art world nests together some apparently odd bedfellows—strange, if not openly antagonistic—for symbiotic benefits that can be social, political and aesthetic.[19]

In the run-up to the Biennale's opening, promised funding from Kerala state sources was interdicted whilst these sometimes testy debates about the purpose, character and value of the biennial were played out. Who or what was it really for? What would be the actual as opposed to the claimed benefits for local people? Wasn't contemporary visual art intrinsically an alien, elite form—irrespective of whether certain Indian artists were themselves now prominent amongst its recognized globally successful practitioners? Arguments about the rights and wrongs of globalization *per se*, projected as an abstract and imposed process, became implicated in these exchanges. They were also related to historical debates about India's colonization, decolonization, its socialist and non-aligned phases in the 1950s and 1960s, and the rise of neoliberal capitalism after the end of the Cold War in the early 1990s.[20]

In the end, the initiative happened because local government, businesses and landowners, acting through the Greater Cochin Development Authority—an example of the classic late modern socioeconomic composite "regeneration agency"—granted the Biennale free use of all its venues. The "munificence of the corporate world of Kochi" also identified, the organizers claimed, a higher good beyond this effort to enhance the region's "cultural tourism." This was that the Biennale would bring what was called "great glory to Kochi, Kerala and India." The real achievement here was that the first edition, according to Ranjit Hoskote (billed by the Biennale's script writers as the "towering" critic and curator who'd organized India's national pavilion at Venice in 2011) exemplified genuine artistic "pluralism."[21] This achievement was also a diplomatic victory of sorts.

Not in Delhi or Mumbai, then—where together the great mass of professional artists based in India live and work—but in Kochi, more than a thousand kilometers away in the rural south, was it predicted by such experts as Hoskote that a new center of artistic activity would develop. The Biennale would offer what he called "a vibrant space and enduring platform which will become one of India's primary artistic and cultural contributions to society"—nothing less than a "sustainable platform for contemporary art in India." The "pluralism" that Hoskote referred to meant the Biennale's astute but precarious balancing of competing interests. This was its declared aim, on the one hand, to "pay homage to India's traditions and heritage by embracing its history of poetry and performance," whilst, on the other, "inviting audiences to experience new cultural and artistic expressions." We enter, here, once again, the world of the rhetorically vague if not ineffable. Claims, that is, that can really be neither proved nor disproved, whose effect, though benign and well intentioned, is really in the end to blur boundaries between facts and hopes—reasonable or otherwise. Such claims have become the contemporary art world's default promotional discourse, the lingua franca of the "global biennial community" which Kochi joined on that iconic date, 12.12.12.[22]

Art at Kochi: Liberal Pluralism Versus Social Engagement with Globalization?

More than forty artists who participated in the Biennale made preliminary visits to the area—ostensibly an indication that they took seriously their stated intention to produce authentic "site-specific" works for the exhibition. These included Subodh Gupta, Nalini Malani, Joseph Semah, Jonas Staal and Amar Kanwar. Some others, such as Vivan Sundaram, chose to use local materials in the fabrication of their commissions. Sundaram took glass, copper and terracotta fragments along with earth from the nearby coastal area at Pattanam and re-assembled them within a large "earthwork" installation entitled *Black Gold* in a warehouse at Aspinwall House on the waterside, accompanied by a video.

The resulting container resembled an archaeological dig that was both a deposit and a manifest: what was the truth, or assumption about truths about the material and historical past of lands and peoples, that this work was trying to tease out?[23] It is worth recalling critic Johan Pijnappel's doubts about the global contemporary art world's language of geographical–cultural "authenticity" and "origination." Malani, as I pointed out, was born in Karachi (now in Pakistan, but once part of an undivided India under British rule), though she is often identified unambiguously as an "Indian artist." Regional and national identities, perhaps particularly in Asian states wracked by postcolonial borders such as those drawn up to divide India, Pakistan and later Bangladesh, are thus often jarringly at odds.[24]

In what senses, if any, can the art form supposedly global above all others, the video installation (a fair number of which populated the first Kochi Biennale, indicating its intent to showcase what its publicity hand out called "new cultural and artistic expressions") be said to originate "from" or authentically "be of" an actual place? Pijnappel's essay was concerned with the development

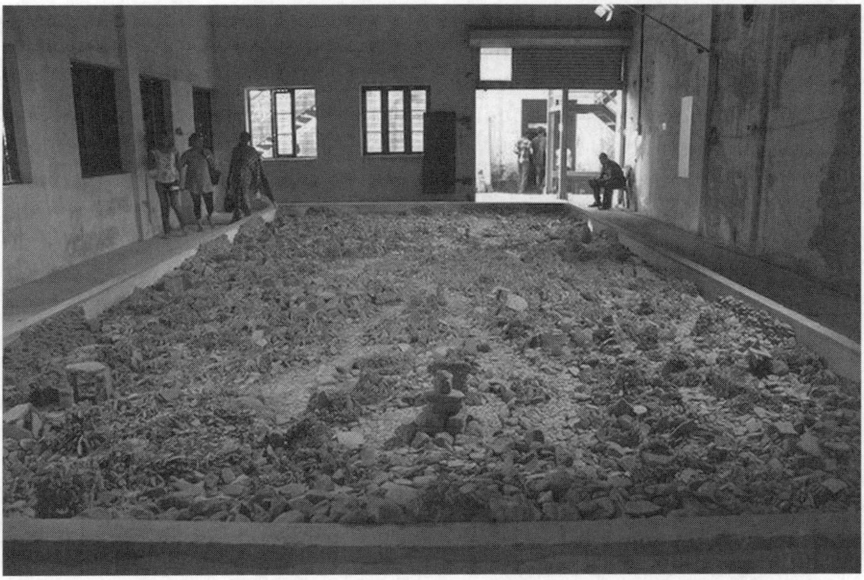

Figure 8 Vivan Sundaram *Black Gold* (mixed media, installation, 2012).

of what he called twenty-first century "Indian video art"—a term which might itself, given his broad reservations, already seem to presume far too much. Two of the artists he discussed had recently made work specifically on this theme of the apparently essential "in-essential" quality to such globalized contemporary art forms that, in technological-aesthetic terms, are necessarily "from" everywhere and nowhere simultaneously. Sharmila Samant's 1998 short animation video *Global Clones* (not featured in the Kochi Biennale) pictured a Dutch clog morphed from the earlier form of a leather *chappal* (slipper) as it travelled, metaphorically, along the Silk Road that runs through Kochi.

Shilpa Gupta's 2002 video *Kidney Supermarket* envisioned another form of apparently magical transformation—that based on the cash nexus—with which the Asian mass poor have had to engage in ever-increasingly extreme ways in an attempt to make ends meet.[25] In this work Gupta placed a model of a seventeenth-century Dutch East India Company ship symbolizing global capitalism on top of a video monitor showing an advert for how Westerners can go about buying Asian human kidneys. Her subsequent work *Blame* (2003)—labelled "bottles of blame" to be bought and sold by Hindus and Muslims—represented the artist's disgusted reaction to the sectarian ethno-religious riots and mass killings of 2002–2003 in Gujurat, stoked by BJP nationalists and Islamic fundamentalists. Texts on the bottles read: "Blaming you makes me feel so good ... So I blame you for what I can't control: Your religion. Your nationality." This work points to another "border zone" of community/caste/class tensions and violence inside the Indian nation-state to be set alongside the existing and sometimes intense georegional disputes with the country's neighbors.[26]

Subodh Gupta's 2008 sculpture *Line of Control* is a spectacular atom bomb mushroom cloud form made out of hundreds of steel kitchen utensils invisibly fixed together. It refers to the Hiroshima and Nagasaki airborne detonations over Japan by the United States in 1945 and to the continuing military standoff between India and Pakistan. These domestic implements of daily life and its reproduction are set together in a drastic contrast with the threat of apocalyptic devastation through nuclear war. The form itself seems to be just on the point of an explosion into formlessness. India's and Pakistan's longstanding dispute has been felt most sharply in the border areas of both countries, and principally in the state of Kashmir (the border dividing the two countries was originally named "the Line of Control" by the British).[27] Gupta's *Line of Control* is housed in the Kiran Nadar Museum of Art (KNMA) in Delhi, the first private contemporary art museum in India, named after the wife of the media and telecommunications billionaire Shri Nadar.

For the first edition of the Kochi Biennale, however, Gupta presented a large traditional boat, suspended at a dramatic angle by wires and filled with fishing utensils and tools of varying kinds which he'd found in the area during his preliminary visits. This choice was clearly an attempt to make his work literally "from" local materials, which was then sited in a storage building just off the central Aspinwall House warehouses on the Kochi dockside (next to Vivan Sundaram's *Black Gold*). Gupta's work, *Untitled*, was low-key in political and aesthetic terms, in contrast with *Line of Control*—the former planned and likely, that is, to appeal to a range of publics, tastes and expectations and not aiming to offend or antagonize anyone.

Untitled presented a sharp contrast with the work by Nalini Malani shown in Kochi. Exhibition of the two pieces indicated the pluralist intent of the Biennale's organizers and backers. Malani's originally six-channel video piece *In Search of Vanished Blood* (2012) dealt with the issue of gang rape of women in contemporary India.

For the Biennale it was shown in a simplified form, with one large screen displaying a map of the world centered on the United States, "the eye of the storm" that is, Malani stated in her commentary, late modernity. With an agitated montaged sound track suggesting violence and malevolence, *In Search of Vanished Blood* attempted an anatomy of global modernization's incitement to sexual abuse and murder of women. It proposed an interrogation of new capitalist commodification of the female body within the geospatial frame of a "traditional" Indian society still rooted in repression and intolerance of sexual, ethnic, religious, class, caste and regional differences. The work's title, indicating Malani's political positioning, was taken from Agha Shadid Ali's translation of the classic Urdu poem *Lahu Ka Surag* by the left-wing Pakistani intellectual and revolutionary poet Faiz Ahmed Faiz. Malani's feminist position has remained

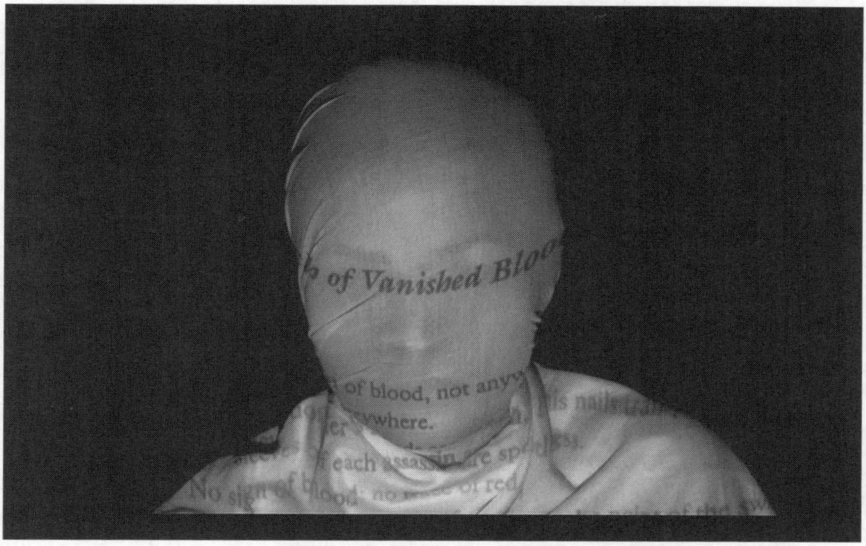

Figure 9 Nalini Malani *In Search of Vanished Blood* (mixed media installation, 2012). *Source:* © Nalini Malani.

consistent over the several decades of her career and her works—paintings, photographs, films, drawings, prints, videos, sculptures and performances—have always dealt directly with the sexual politics of the subcontinent.[28]

Kochi Biennale's first edition also attempted to broaden its representation of Asian modernities beyond India and its bordering states through the commission of what it called the "*BRICS* Project." This brought together eight video films made by artists working in the acronymic countries Brazil, Russia, India, China and South Africa. However, two of these producers were German and the curator of the project as a whole was Alfons Hug, a German critic and director of the Goethe Institute in Rio de Janiero.[29] Shown in a number of small, separate rooms in an area off the central spaces of Aspinwall House, these films demonstrated only a loose thematic or symbolic coherence which, it might be concluded, actually reflect the real natures of the BRICS countries themselves.

The alliance between the first four states had started out in 2006 as an intended challenge to the economic dominance of the US and Western European countries within globalization processes (South Africa joined the BRIC countries in 2010). Though all, apart from Russia, newly industrialized, fast-growing economies with growing affluence—though the disparities of wealth within these states are also egregiously wide, especially in India—these states, with 40%of the world's population by 2014, have also been subject to rapid and often powerfully destabilizing forces of societal change, both before and after the Crash in 2008.[30]

One of the two Chinese videos featured in the BRICS project at Kochi was made by Gao Shiqiang. Called *Revolution* (2007, 42 minutes), it features a group of people discussing the clash of interests always present within the workings of the worldwide capitalist system. Such "antagonistic co-operation" understood as the basis of the global economy was symbolized by the juxtaposition of two different videos shown in the same room on different walls. Here, in his work *Castell* (2012, 18 minutes), the Brazilian artist Pablo Labato staged a large crowd of men and women attempting, with limited success, to form a human pyramid, while Chen Chieh-Jen's *Pushing People* (2008, 22 minutes) also dealt with human collective strenuous physical activity. But in this adjoining work we only see fragmented hands, arms and shoulders enlisted in order to attempt to push an unidentified large and heavy object across a dark room. Is the alienated labor of the global masses in the BRICS countries likely to be rewarded with general prosperity and a sense of collective ownership of society, these films seem to ask and to answer immediately in the negative (note the double meaning of the word "pushing" in the title of Chen Chieh-Jen's video). The conditions of economic globalization within neoliberal capitalism in Asia include both maximum exploitation of the weakest and reproduction of the division of the interests of the masses—or "the multitude," as two recent influential commentators have termed them. These objectives help to maximize profits for corporations and the accumulation of substantial private wealth for the comparatively tiny professional elites that have emerged in these societies since the turn of the millennium.[31]

The regenerative "cultural tourism" ethos that the organizers claimed underpinned the Kochi Biennale was a familiar one, based on the hope that the rising tide of corporate and professional elite affluence in India would eventually "raise all boats" in the state of Kerala, with additional "trickle down" benefits for the country as a whole. The event's promotional literature asserted that, for instance, "cultural and heritage visitors spend, on average, 35% more than the non-cultural tourists" and it was expected that 5 million visitors would come to Kochi during the three month period of the exhibition. What the organizers called the new model of "art-tourism and cultural diplomacy" had worked, they observed, as a form of regional regeneration in what they took to be comparable biennial cities such as Singapore, Gwangju in South Korea, Denver, USA and Liverpool in England. Their claim was that locating the biennial event in Kochi would draw "a significant number of national and international" arts projects to the region, creating significant employment and tax revenue for investment in Kerala. The director of the Singapore 2011 Biennial was quoted approvingly, and it was claimed that what was called, without definition or justification, "civic wellbeing" would improve once citizens were exposed to such a "major cutting-edge international exhibition of contemporary art." Kochi would receive what was alleged would be "a huge facelift in terms of glam and glitter cutting across social and cultural spectrums."[32]

Corporate sponsorship levels for the Biennale were set in order to encourage many different kinds of involvement and resulting benefits. No doubt the organizers were assisted in this calibration by expert advisors at the Biennial Foundation. "Founding Patron," "Friend," and "Official Partner" categories, for example, solicited support in a range of development areas included in the sociocultural remit of the Biennale. These included schools and colleges, learning and resource, arts award, ecological and regeneration, music, film/documentary, and virtual/digital.[33] As I've noted, partners were identified internationally, across an ambiguous public-private spectrum, including some in the United Arab Emirates in the Gulf. India's market for contemporary art remains comparatively very weak—based almost entirely in the two major cities of Mumbai and Delhi—when set alongside, for example, Dubai. Here, for instance, *Alef* journal recorded sales by Christie's in January 2014 of modern and contemporary Arab, Iranian and Turkish art worth over US$8 500 000. The (relatively) socially liberal centers in the Gulf, such as Dubai, Qatar, Abu Dhabi and Kuwait have begun to offer visual arts exhibition spaces and higher education programs for women—as well as developing their own biennial events, such as that at Sharjah, in the UAE, begun in 1993.[34]

The overwhelming basis of the Gulf states' enormous wealth remains the revenue gained from export sales of oil. In India, however, it is tax revenue raised from its working population—in a country where, despite growing affluence for a substantial minority, 400 million people out of a population of 1.21 billion earned less than US$1.25 dollars per day and where wage inequalities are growing.[35] In the Gulf territories with developing markets for modern and contemporary art, the vast bulk of the profits are still made by and for the US–British auctioneers Christie's and Sotheby's, who maintain a slowly diminishing but still majority control over the global market for art as a whole.[36] India's often-celebrated status as the "world's largest democracy" jars with the authoritarian, monarchic and theocratic Gulf regimes lying to its northwest which are reliant for their growth and reproduction on very low-paid south Asian migrant workers who are allowed very few rights. The "political legitimation" troubles that beset elected leaders in Delhi and Kochi do not generally press on these rulers, such as the royal family of Saudi Arabia, where, for instance, the King Abdulaziz Center for World Culture (badged insouciantly as the Wahabi kingdom's "home for knowledge, creativity and cross-cultural engagement"), offers what has been called a multidisciplinary "platform for creative cultural development in the nation."[37]

Another artist from South Africa took part in the Kochi Biennale, though not as part of the BRICS video art project. Clifford Charles's also low-key, understated installation work, *Five Cloud Rooms,* housed in a small building in the grounds of Aspinwall House, suggestively recreated aspects of the history of Kochi, including its now fading socialist activism. Charles's first of five interconnected mini-environments, *The Communist Party Reading Room,* modeled his experience of visiting such dusty spaces in the city where popular affiliation to the local Communist Party was once very strong—its supporters had for several decades controlled the Kerala state assembly. This work implied a broader foregrounding and consideration of India's national development since independence, the fate of its democracy given the embrace of neoliberal capitalism in the 1990s and the record on social development and human rights—in the Indian subcontinent and region as a whole.[38] Can contemporary art have a significant voice within discussion of these matters?

The Highs and Lows of Art, Media and Kochi Biennale Capital

What might be termed the high theory of the purpose and value of contemporary art world biennials emphasizes their claimed radical "transnational" aesthetic, cultural and political potential. These ideas have been proposed by influential curators such as Nigerian, Okwui Enwesor, and Cuban, Gerardo Mosquera, who have between them developed and "guest edited" many of the "periphery" or "non-Western" recurrent exhibitions now in the contemporary art world calendar. These sociocritical concerns have not usually been set alongside but neither set explicitly against the instrumental "cultural tourism" role of biennials—although this putative socioeconomic regenerative function has certainly been far less foregrounded, to the point of virtual invisibility, in what have become the canonical essays.[39] While the first Kochi Biennale in 2012 foregrounded the latter role in its promotional materials, it also made some space for one of its invited artists, Delhi-born Amar Kanwar, to comment on the revolutionary–emancipatory discourse enunciated by global contemporary art world curator-stars such as Enwesor and Mosquera. This centered on the ability of biennials, Kanwar noted, to "break or redefine the notions of nationalism [...] and democracy" in their choice of artists, themes and exhibition formats.

Kanwar decided, however, mostly to sidestep this issue, especially as it related to Kochi, and instead advocated pragmatism. What he called the utopic "burden of hope" carried by biennials arose, he noted, from the "traps" of "fixed ambition and notion[s] of success."[40] Kanwar's own contribution to the Biennale, a multimedia and interactive work, *The Sovereign Forest* (2012–), dealt with the compulsory acquisition of land in Orissa, India, by the government and mining corporations. The moving image component of this project, "The Scene of the Crime," offered a record of the land and its flora and fauna prior to its planned destruction. Crime, politics, human rights and ecology were thus at the center of Kanwar's work, which directly implicated the interests and actions of Indian national and regional governments, and asked fundamental questions about the state's commitment to democracy and the real costs of neoliberal modernization. According to Kanwar, India's vaunted regional community diversity, in ethno-religious, caste and class terms, had suffered great strain and antagonism, as the Gujurat riots in 2002–2003 indicated. The sources of these conflicts had intensified and were more likely to recur because of the increasing exploitation of labor, land and environmental resources by the forces of global capitalism with the connivance of government.[41]

In an earlier historical moment, in the second half of the twentieth century, sociocultural change in India had registered more as a popular, positive advance, toward a national, or even "pan-Asian," identity, away from what had been perceived as constricting traditional regional mores. It is interesting that the term "other" in India can be used to refer both to foreign (that is, external-to-India) influences, but also to national rather than prevailing regional, small "c" conservative, values and habits. An example would be the modernization of women's dress in the Gujurati and Bengali communities that had started to occur in the 1980s and 1990s. I will return briefly to questions of fashion and dress in India later. The 2012 Kochi Biennale's commitment to showing films, both as part of the main exhibition and in its "collateral program," reflected the national and "pan-Asian" progressivism particularly associated with film—of both documentary and fictional kinds—since the days of the Independence movement when Indian democracy had been a force mobilized against British imperial rule. The Netpac organization ("Network for the Promotion of Asian Cinema," founded in 1996), for example, continues to support new film-making and celebrates film as a socially progressive force inside India, though it also works for greater Asian cooperation understood as a necessary form of continental cultural–intellectual Decolonization.[42] Screening and discussing films symbolized the pluralism of the Kochi Biennale in its earnest wish to attract many different groups—local, regional, national and international—to the exhibition.

Netpac, like the Kochi Biennale, works with a similar range of national and international organizations, as well as with the Confederation of Indian Industry on health, education, livelihood, "diversity management", development of skills and environment projects. (The neoliberal coinage of "entrepreneurship" and "Business for Livelihood" has steadily crept into advertisements by Netpac's sponsors in its in-house magazine.) The organization's 2013 conference, "Roots, Identity, Modernity: Asian Voices on Culture and Creativity" set out to examine the intra-Asian dimensions to the arts and culture broadly understood. Film itself was conceived, as several of the speakers indicated, to be the developed techno-cultural outcome of a number of premodern Asian "precinematic" visual forms and social rituals, including drawings on paper, shadow play and puppetry.

Film-making across many Asian societies since the 1980s has achieved a social and aesthetic status that the Kochi Biennial organizers desired for contemporary visual art in India. The film critic Latika Padgaonkar remarked that this confidence:

> mirrored the resurgence of Asia, or at least of large swathes of the continent, as an economic powerhouse and as a major stakeholder in the emerging world order. Filmmakers showed both the talent and the willingness to exploit new opportunities of globalization without forsaking their engagement with the turmoil in their societies [...] Some make oblique comments on the prevailing moods and social tensions in their countries; others tackle them head-on.[43]

Kanwar's "The Scene of the Crime" could certainly fit into this last category. I've noted in earlier chapters that film and video artists in Hong Kong and South Korea have mobilized the moving image in this direct manner as a means of sociopolitical critique. In a way similar to the call by contemporary art curator Johnson Chang for people in Asian countries to understand and share the extent of their "self-colonization," veteran Netpac activists Aruna Vasudev and Wong Tuck-Cheong explain that film is a popular and effective means through which to articulate and understand the colonial experiences of India's and China's Asian neighbors. This recognition of a "common heritage" was delayed or blocked as the people in these postcolonial countries turned their attention to "urgent internal reconstruction" and consolidating the "gains" from their "colonial masters." Through film, Vasudev and Tuck-Cheong observe, a facility exists to "examine Orientalism and National Identity as well as the cinema's evolving identity in the age of globalism and the development of new technologies."[44] This process is intimately tied up with all aspects of pan-Asian modernity and modernization as well as with the development of contemporary visual art in India (of which film and video art is a part) and the first edition of the Kochi Biennale.

The "Roots, Identity, Modernity" conference also sought to bring together discussion of film with that of design, fashion, craft, literature and the visual arts. (In a telling contrast with the Kochi Biennale, the Ministry of Culture of the central Indian Government financially supported the conference, indicating that film has a sociocultural significance and popularity in India that contemporary visual art currently lacks.) Had modernity been a "Western-centric" Enlightenment notion and process, Vasudev and Tuck-Cheong ask; an external reality based on the dissemination of supposed "universal ideas" brought to the colonized world in the form of "the streamlined precincts of the mechanised technology modes"? If so, then perhaps this domination, and the worship of Western modernization by some colonized groups that grew up around it, might help to explain why "historical contacts between Asian countries" themselves have been long overshadowed. Full recognition of these intra-cultural roots had been at the core of anti-imperialist writer Rabindranath Tagore's vision of "an Asian connect in the early twentieth century." Examples of this pan-Asian cultural integration included, according to Vasudev and Tuck-Cheong, the influence of Japanese art on the work of Indian artists such as Nandlal Bose, that of Chinese embroideries on the Parsis in India, the recent "iconic following of Tamil film-superstar Rajneekanth in Japan," and in music collaborations between Pakistan and India.[45]

These innovations constituted a living legacy of transnational Asian cosmopolitanism, a "commonality" "in the celebration of the multitudes of technologies including the erraticism of the hand-made, in the imagination of the arts to transform a troubled world, and in the exploration of new cultural paradigms as the foundation for new global conversations"[46]

Such intra-Asian connections also extended beyond Asia—as part of "global Asia"—back and forward into the metropolitan post-imperial centers of the West. Design critic Jahnvi Dameron Nandan has related how Jawaharlal Nehru (India's first prime minister after Independence in 1947), on a trip back from Beijing in the early 1960s, purchased a Mandarin-collared women's jacket and asked his tailor to replicate one for him. Nehru had this jacket made in numerous lengths, added a rose in the buttonhole and paired it with white *Churidaar* pants. The Beatles famously adopted the item and turned it into a day coat. James Bond villains wore versions of it in the films *Dr No* and *Tomorrow Never Dies*. It re-emerged in *The Matrix*, worn by hacker Neo, and more recently in the *Harry Potter* films worn by the magician Severus Snape.

Installations, or films, or jackets can thus become influential and powerfully symbolic. The "Nehru jacket" carried with it something of the optimism of 1950s and 1960s India when the country began to become influential globally as the superpowers' stand-off got complicated by the rise of the "Third World" Non-Aligned movement and regional disputes distanced the hitherto allies China, the Soviet Union and India. Like Vasudev and Tuck-Cheong, Nandan points to a number of intra-Asian style innovations in design and fashion, what she calls a "fusion of Indian and non-Indian concepts" that had "always been an Indian strength." These had included Indian *Parsigara* and *Tanchoi* textiles influenced in their design and manufacture by Chinese embroidery and weaving, Japanese-art inspired tea Calico textiles and Burma teak ceilings.[47]

The ubiquitous "Ambassador" car was another example of a customized import, subject to what Nandan terms "Indian-isation." This model was introduced into the Indian market in 1957, based on the British 1948 Morris Oxford series. Like other artefacts subject to innumerably varied popular, anonymous adaptations—such as the *lota*, the small handle-less brass or copper vessel in everyday use in India—the Ambassador, Nandan says, "was considered efficient, all terrain, and its roomy interiors carried everything from poultry chicken to up to ten human passengers at a time."[48] Subodh Gupta made two oil paintings of the car, both of which he entitled *Doot* ("messenger"), as well as a full-size aluminum cast of the car, in 2003. Many thousands of Ambassadors still choke India's roads and it wasn't until the mid-1970s that smaller, more efficient Japanese cars, such as the 800 cc Maruti Suzuki, became popular. That model's arrival indicated the continuing demise of British influence in India since decolonization and the rise of globalized automobile production that was rendering British-made cars and the workers responsible for them redundant. The "message" had changed, Gupta's use of the car-as-symbol in 2003 suggests, and India's neoliberal turn a decade earlier would be decisive in producing societal transformations at all levels in the country. Emblematic of this turn is the history and role of the biggest corporate supporter of the Kochi Biennale.

The Weiden + Kennedy global advertising agency—key sponsors as well as involved in the practical organization of the exhibition—relocated their Indian offices and purpose-built gallery to a space within a newly opened shopping center in south Delhi in 2010. These buildings were part of a vast development complex owned by the DLF (Delhi, Land and Finance) corporation, and one of the largest retail spaces in the city. DLF's ownership effectively superseded the city government's own control of urban space in the city that had been previously overseen by the DDA (Delhi Development Authority). DLF is owned by Kushal Pal Singh, rated the 98th richest man in the world by Forbes magazine in 2009 and the world's wealthiest property developer. Another weather-beaten Ambassador car, this time a crashed, broken and graffiti-clad specimen, was positioned outside the shopping center entrance as an evidently graphic symbol—not clearly not an "artwork"—of pre-globalized India, suggesting a sharp contrast with the values of neoliberalism, consumerism and advertising culture that the shopping center itself represents.[49]

The South Court of the DLF center also houses KNMA, the first private art museum in India and home to Gupta's mushroom cloud tower of stainless steel pots and pans, *Line of Control*. The shopping center has been called "design generic." According to one commentator, it is "hyper-ordinary in appearance" and one capable of being built anywhere in the globalized world. In the case of Delhi's iteration, however, the poor and homeless of the city began to use its public toilets and other spaces for their daily living activities. The retail complex rapidly became itself a poignant index of the extremes of mass poverty and minority affluence that Delhi and neoliberal India as a whole manifests. The shift from DDA to DLF represents another kind of border or "line of control" crossed. From, that is, a residual post-Independence state-socialist paternalism based on nominal public control of India's environment and resources to an economic and sociocultural neoliberalization—part of an ongoing global process—with its "trickle down" theory of wealth redistribution and actual chaotic societal upheaval.

Utopian Rhetoric in Contemporary Art at the Kochi Biennale

A report issued in 2008 claimed that 65% of all luxury consumption in India occurred in just five neighborhoods—four located in Mumbai and Delhi, and one in Punjab. Since then, affluence has, it seems, been spread a bit further afield. By 2012, for instance, over half of all India's luxury car dealerships were located outside the country's five biggest cities.[50] An article in *Jetwings* inflight magazine which referred to this report itself comprised a kind of "info-ad" for luxury branding and its role in the economic and social development of Indian society. It raised the interesting questions of (1) whether Indian contemporary visual art is also a kind of luxury brand, or could be; and (2) whether the Kochi Biennale organizers would do better or worse if they characterized their own product and its packaging as such.

The equivocating, "pluralist" rhetoric displayed in this article—aimed at airborne managers of luxury brand designs as much as at their consumers—sounds rather similar to the Biennale line. "Luxury in India," it intoned:

> will always celebrate the core values of Indian heritage [...] The challenge for international luxury brands is to create a fine balance that integrates global brand values with Indian meaning. The strategy to incorporate Indianness across all relevant touch points is key to ensuring brand relevance [...] International brands should view the need to instill Indianness as an opportunity to resonate with the Indian sentiment [beyond mere] transactional relationships [...] Montblanc came under intense pressure when it launched a pen containing images of Mahatma Ghandi that was seen as bad taste.[51]

A vision of the apparently incompatible bedfellows now sharing the global contemporary art world duvet floats once more into consciousness. Its constituent groupings, as noted earlier, are divided amongst, sometimes fighting over, the biennial's triple, overlapping social functions. These may be characterized roughly as (1) the marginal-dissident art/criticism role; (2) the "cultural tourism"/regeneration role; and (3) the investment-for-"High Net Worth"-individuals and corporate organizations role. Professional artists in India, of course, as in all countries (those, that is, that are able to make a full living purely from selling works) comprise an infinitesimally tiny proportion of the working population. The private KNMA, along with the "not-for-profit" Devi Art Foundation, also situated close to Delhi, have been created by extremely wealthy individuals following their personal tastes and social-philanthropic hobby horses. They have invented quasi-public missions for these new visual arts organizations, while the resources provided by the state for cultural funding projects in India declined after the Crash in 2008, although the recession was not as deep as in Europe and the United States.[52]

The Devi Foundation's international historical and contemporary collection includes regional folk and tribal artefacts—thus representing something of the productivity of India's mass of craft producers, past and present. Delhi-based designer and critic Mayank Mansingh Kaul has observed that historical knowledge of the work and lives of the country's artisan masses is indispensable to an adequate understanding of Indian senses of the terms "ancient," "traditional," "modern" and "contemporary"—in the contexts of art (*kalo*), design and craft (*karigari*—"workmanship") and in their complex interrelations. It was in the 1980s in Jawaja, in the province of Rajasthan, Mansingh notes, that an "entire community of leather scavengers [were] transformed into skilled craftspeople, giving India its first iconic bag" (the Jawaja bag). This was a real advance upon the simple mass imitation of imported product designs, a typical practice across many Asian countries in earlier decades after the Second World War.

India's Independence and postcolonial development had been bound up with upheaval at all levels, including the cultural. This "kind of destruction and renewal after 1947 belonged to a longer history of European colonization and social transformation," Mansingh explained:

> M.K. Ghandhi's struggle for political freedom from colonial rule was linked to the dissolution of feudal divisions in Indian society itself. And even while India's first Prime Minister Jawaharlal Nehru's ideas of development may seem directly opposed [...] they cannot be divorced from those of Ghandhi's, which influenced state policy until much later. This led to institutions like the National Institute of Design ultimately performing towards rural upliftment, and state patronage for craft and design continuing til the 1980s.[53]

The eruption of neoliberal globalizing forces within India in the early 1990s brought back, for Mansingh, the same fundamental questions about societal identity. What does it mean to be "Indian"? What, if anything, is "Indian art and design"? If received senses and embodiments of Indian nationality were in retreat before the forces of globalization, then what interests or affiliations might replace them—resurgent or new regionalisms, alternate globalisms, ultra-nationalisms, ethnic and religious fundamentalisms? In many respects, the artists who took part in the first Kochi Biennale were also asking these questions and offering some kinds of answers. Equally, the publicity materials generated by the organizers sometimes dealt seriously with the same questions and attempted to juggle a range of what they believed or hoped were not irreconcilable answers.

Business entrepreneurship, export/import agencies, new technologies, digital communications and the internet have all become watchwords of global neoliberalism's development framework. They are also key elements now in the familiar mantra of state organizations in India and everywhere else (e.g., see my account of ARCO's role in Spain in Chapter 2) set with the task of "facilitating" these forces for supposed common economic and social good. One of Mansingh's anxieties concerns the ability of Indian designers and craftspeople to forge a truly successful global brand, and he asks what agencies exist in the country to support such a development. Will India remain simply a base for the manufacture of goods of all kinds conceived and branded elsewhere? As an inspiring Indian model of the creative and anti-imperialist synthesis of "East" and "West," Mansingh cites Gyanonandini Tagore's traditional dress fashioned in the moments after she was initially refused entry to a British social club in Bombay before Independence in 1947. Indian clothes were not allowed. So Tagore "tweaked it by pushing the pallu [the fold of additional material then worn at the front] at the back, simulating a western dress, and that's how The English *Sari* came to be!" It's also how it's often worn in India today.[54]

The moral of this story is that political resistance and innovative design may go hand in hand—that, in fact, they might actually sometimes require each other. Knowledge of the brutal social conditions of much design industry in contemporary urban India, however, can help to sabotage the optimistic "high theory" produced by globally influential art critics and curators of the likes of Enwesor and Mosquera. Consider Dharavi, for instance, a coastal area of 1.7 kilometers in Mumbai where over 5000 types of so-called "informal" design production take place. This is a massive manufacturing center, in some accounts the most densely populated place on Earth and commonly referred to as "Asia's biggest slum." Everything appears to be made there, from *papads* (crisp breads) to high-end leather goods. Dharavi, called by one critic a "purgatory of consumerism," distils the rigid social division of labor that characterizes craft and design cycles of production and consumption in India. The actual makers are always the poor, the designers are middle class and the consumers the elite.

Much of the work done in Dharavi encapsulates the squalor of the global economy and its division of labor. According to graphic designer Ishan Khosla, the "brunt of this is borne by the workers of Plot 13, who, in reincarnating "our" junk into diced, reusable plastic pellets, which are then China-bound—unknowingly—breathe in noxious, cancer-causing fumes. The environmental damage is also palpable: the Koli fishermen don't fish near Dharavi since all the fish are poisoned."[55] Nehru had introduced modern design education into India in the early 1960s—an innovative decision for the whole world then—in an attempt to rejuvenate small and cottage industries after Independence, and "rescue India from the shambles of colonialism." Nehru commissioned a report by the US designers Charles and Ray Eames that articulated a vision for design based on developing indigenous Indian practices, not on the Western model of industrialization that presumed an historical development (originating in Enlightenment modernization) that had never occurred in that manner in the colonized countries.[56]

Arguments proposing the social value of contemporary art in India that the Kochi Biennale organizers couched mostly in terms of projected economic and social betterment for the Kerala region might have hoped to match the tangible success of the educational card games mobilized in the 2006 *Campaign To End Violence Against Women*. This South Asian anti-violence coalition of groups designed a series of graphic card packs, aimed at illiterate and uneducated men and women, which were later used in 15 countries, along with other media tools including games, models, films and audio tools. The cards were pictorial and interactive, intended to develop knowledge and embed the rights of women and girls to personal freedom and security. Other card sets were developed to inform poor people about family planning provision and to help illiterate urban street children—the shoe shine boys, *coolies* (porters) and rag pickers. One of the tools was a set of 36 brightly colored picture cards showing a series of moments, emotions, choices and milestones in the life of the children. They were used to discuss "actions and their consequences, social problems relevant to the children's lives."

Once created, these cards could be used effectively by the populous ranks of so-called "barefoot facilitators" and "peer educators" rather than relying on a sparse cadre of literate specialists to conduct education and information activities with the rural and urban poor of India.[57] Natasha De Betak's photographs for her project *Nightshade*, exhibited at the Experimenter gallery in Kolkata in 2012, show some of the urban poor sleeping, in haunting—perhaps even rather aestheticized—images that reveal yet another kind of border. Two *Nightshade* (from the series) photographs show in close up, for instance, the faces of children, seemingly in a state of peace that might be that of death as much as deep sleep. As the text in the book of these photographs put it, this time is "the thin line between death and dream [...] when the city sleeps, in a state of trance."[58] Biennials have nearly always been staged in or identified with a particular city, carrying the implication that the event is, in some meaningful way, specifically and irreducibly "of" that place. (The roving European "Manifesta" event staged every five years was set up in order to challenge the various complacencies thought to be latent in this convention.) Kochi Biennale's arguments for its "cultural tourism" role also relied on acceptance of the necessity of this rootedness. The names of its Board of Trustees confirm the prevalence of government and commercial stakeholders based in the city and contiguous region.[59]

Enwesor has claimed that it is the "global city," with its social, political and cultural "diasporic public sphere," that has inspired the creativity and challenge of the so-called "periphery" biennials. The dualisms (more borders here) and dialectics of globalization compact within the spatial and human density of such cities—"center and periphery," "local and global," "national and regional," "enlightened and backward," "mobility and stasis," "citizens and subjects," "the cosmopolitan and the provincial." Enwesor's rhetoric is high-flown. The "diasporic public sphere," he announces

> becomes the space where the problems of translation for culture arises. Avid for the critical incarnation of new forms of experimental production, cultural translation in the global present confronts us with a way to begin again, whereby the past is neither a foreign country nor simply the authentic name of origin [...] the recent phenomenon of biennials in the periphery should not be bemoaned as a readymade example of the biennial syndrome [...] there is a need to see in the biennial phenomenon the possibility of a paradigm shift in which we as spectators are able to encounter many experimental cultures without wholly possessing them.'[60]

While Mumbai and Delhi might both qualify as examples of such a "global city," the Kochi Biennale organizers wanted to project the admittedly geographically distant regional capital of Kerala as a past, and/or incipient, one. The first edition's dual themes of cosmopolitanism and inclusion and its intent to build a "sustainable platform for contemporary art in India" would be the grounds for this.[61]

Ever hedging their bets, the organizers of the Kochi exhibition claimed that its inauguration could also be seen as a practical, almost ad hoc, device offering what they called "a natural gateway for a biennale [...] to get into the Indian subcontinent," especially now that some contemporary Indian artists "have of late wowed international pundits."[62]This assertion begged the question of the fate of what had initially been called the "Triennial of Contemporary World Art," established in 1968 by the Indian National Academy of Art. The Triennial, a Delhi-based, central state-funded operation from the pre-globalization and neoliberal era, had, nevertheless, also been initiated in order to address, though in markedly different (perhaps even opposed) ways, the "peripheral" status of the subcontinent and Asia as a whole within a world dominated by art, artists, markets and art institutions in the West. Dating from its third edition held in 1978 the Triennial's organizers had taken the fateful decision only to invite the participation of artists from countries that had signed "cultural agreements" with the Indian government. This resolution publicly politicized the selection process for the Triennial and terminally sabotaged the event's international artistic credibility with most Western critics and curators. The underlying principle (and shibboleth) was, and remains, that the realm of aesthetic experience and value is held to be in crucial respects autonomous from the social order as a whole, and that exhibitions of all kinds, if they are to be taken seriously by the global art world dominated by Western interests, must always respect this.[63]

Contemporaneity, however, was perhaps as much of an issue for the Indian Triennial organizers in the last third of the twentieth century as it has become for biennials and art fairs in the twenty-first. The difference, or one of the differences, was that the socialist states and Non-Aligned movements in Asia, Africa and Latin America then were significant forces both within, and, to a degree, against the two superpower Cold War blocs situated to the north. Mulk Raj Anand, chair of the Indian National Academy had noted at the time of the inaugural Triennial:

> Many Asian, African, and socialist countries have not been able to establish a platform where the desired images of the oldest and youngest continents (youngest in the sense of secular achievement in the arts) may be seen together with the achievement of the dynamic west."[64]

As the Triennial organized its exhibitions on the basis of national "delegations," it was inevitable that the widely perceived anachronistic conservatism of this method would eventually lead to or hasten the demise of its already limited credibility—in Western countries and elsewhere, especially as neoliberalism became increasingly powerful in the 1990s, after the end of the Soviet Union. Though the Triennial had only followed historical practice at the longest and then most prestigious established biennales in grouping artists in terms of their putative national belonging—that is, those exhibitions at Venice, Pittsburg and São Paolo—the changes within "post-national" means of selection and presentation of contemporary art at biennials around the world had begun.[65]

These issues of the origins and representativeness of contemporaneity throughout the whole world, in terms of what is identified and exhibited as "contemporary art" in all biennials—necessarily a quantitative as well as a qualitative matter—remains prominent, and has become, if anything, even more of an urgent historical, critical and philosophical concern.[66] Probing examination of this problem could really test the too easily repeated use of the term "inclusivity" by Kochi Biennale organizers in their promotional material for the event's first edition. The seminar topics discussed at the exhibition's opening symposium could all be construed to have posed acutely this question and the matter of its economic, social, cultural, political and intellectual ramifications: (1) "The Biennale in the Indian Context: Perceptions of Change and Realities of Exposition"; (2) "Artist as Social Commentator: Generating Discourse"; (3) "Knocking Down Roadblocks"; (4) "Biennale as Imaginary: An Artist Prepares"; and (5) "Biennale as a Cultural Exercise." This latter discussion posed the uber-question of "inclusion"—what was or might be the place of Asian and African art and exhibitions within the "Euro-American discourse"?[67] The Kochi Biennale's stated commitment to a radical political questioning of the meanings of "inclusion" was perhaps meant to be symbolized by the inclusion of a work by Netherlands "relational-aesthetic"/"interventionist" artist Jonas Stahl, called the "New World Summit."

This piece consisted of an installation of 44 billboards depicting the flags of banned political organizations: 23 within India and 21 in other countries. These were all ideologically left wing, or claimed to be, which in itself indicated something of the limits of Stahl's own rhetoric. It had been his intention to invite people from five of these organizations to a planned Biennale discussion. His work was designed, he told *The Hindu* newspaper, to "expose the limits of democracy" and to work towards something he called "a limitless democracy."[68] The leaden weight of antagonistic interests (if not contradictions) is easy to see and in one sense afflicted the Kochi Biennale as much as Stahl's installation. The term "progressive," for both, was required to do far too much rhetorical work. Nevertheless it could be argued that, despite the nuts and bolts of developing "cultural tourism" in Kerala and garnering support from global capitalist corporations to extend the economy of the city, the organizers themselves held, at least in spirit, to Stahl's utopian definition of the potential of contemporary art and the biennial form.

This constituted a model, a veritable contemporary Tatlin's Tower, of wishful thinking. According to Stahl

> The imagination of alternative political spheres starts in the field of progressive art. Not in that of the mass media, which is one of the worst architects of the monopolies of information and representation that we need to deal with [...] Art has evolved, wriggling its way out of the clutches of authority, through individual mediums and bold blending of them, and contemporary art is in an exciting phase.[69]

Has contemporary art, and one of its paradigmatic expository forms, the biennial exhibition, really escaped from the control of the state and the bourgeoisie, as Stahl goes on to claim? (Enwesor seems to share at least some of this optimism): "The international democratisation movement is in need of tools to help shape the horizon of a fundamental democracy, and that's what's next."[70] The history and form of the Kochi Biennale's first edition in 2012 suggests not. What follows here is an account of how the "state and the bourgeoisie" are faring in the development of contemporary art and its higher education institutions in one of India's neighboring states—mainland China, the PRC, forty years on since the death of Chairman Mao and "the great leap forward" taken by his successors into the global capitalist neoliberal world order/disorder.

Notes

1 *The Times of India*, December 17, 2012: Section A: 16; "India's First Biennale," *Jetwings* December 2012: 216; "Non-Stop Shopping, Non-Stop Surprises," *The Hindu*, December 15, 2012: Section A: 1. The full title of the biannual

exhibition is The Kochi–Muziris Biennale. Note this preference for the Italian "biennale": at once an emulation of Venice and a subtle rejection of the English.

2 "The Desert Gem," *Alef*, December 2012–January 2013: 98–103 (100). *Alef* (the name of the first letter in the Arabic alphabet) was launched in London at the Serpentine Galleries to mark the 2013 Qatar–London "Year of Culture" partnership.

3 "Relics," *UK–Qatar UK 2013* brochure, included in same *Alef* edition: 10–11 (10). Several Gulf States have begun to build art museums and house collections purchased by their royal families, governments, corporations and super-rich individuals, but remain almost wholly reliant on Western contemporary art world institutional and professional expertise. See, e.g., "Abu Dhabi and Qatar," in Don Thompson, *The Supermodel and the Brillo Box* (Palgrave Macmillan: Palgrave Macmillan, 2014): 207–214.

4 "10,000 Visitors in First 3 Days," *The Hindu*, December 15, 2012: Section A: 4 and Hormis Tharakan, "Kochi and Venice: A Tale of Two Cities," *Biennale Leaf*, 1 (21), November 21, 2012: 6 (the event's own publicity vehicle). The Wikipedia entry on the first Kochi Biennale indicates that 400 000 people had visited the exhibition by the end of February 2013 (accessed March 28, 2017). *The Hindu* article on which these numbers are based reported that, with "one month to go, the highly publicised but beleaguered Kochi-Muziris Biennale may finally get the much-needed funding that the Ministry for Cultural Affairs withdrew, prior to its opening. Just a month ago, it was rumored that they might have to close early," February 24, 2013 http://www.thehindu.com/todays-paper/tp-features/tp-sundaymagazine/kochis-gift-to-the-world/article4448003.ece.

5 "Muziris Heritage Project," *India's First Biennale 12/12/12* (information leaflet published by Kochi Biennale Foundation): np.

6 P. J. Cherian, "Kerala's Cosmopolitanism in Antiquity: Material Evidence from the Pattanam Port Site," *India's First Biennale 12/12/12* (information leaflet published by Kochi Biennale Foundation): np.

7 "Muziris Heritage Project," *India's First Biennale 12/12/12*: np and Cherian, "Kerala's cosmopolitanism in antiquity": np.

8 On "settler colonialism," also characteristic of Israeli domination of Palestinian lands and peoples since 1948, discussed in Chapter 5, see Lorenzo Veracini, *Settler Colonialism: A Theoretical Overview* (Palgrave Macmillan: Basingstoke: 2010).

9 See *India's First Biennale 12/12/12.*

10 *India's First Biennale 12/12/12.*

11 The two-day opening program included lectures by critics, artists and academics Geeta Kapur, Sarat Maharaj, Ranjit Hoskote, Gayatri Sinha, Pooja Sood and Nancy Adajania. The "Let's Talk" daily program included additional talks, discussions and performances. Ten international films were selected by

filmmaker Adoor Gopalakrishnan. See "Welcome," unpublished, unpaginated Kochi Biennale information distributed at the venues.

12 See "Welcome Kochi–Muziris Biennale 2012," unpublished leaflet, np. W + K is a global advertising agency based in the United States with offices in Brazil, the United Kingdom, the Netherlands, PRC, India and Japan. The development of contemporary art has been closely bound up with advertising, its corporate agencies and, paradigmatically, with Charles Saatchi who opened his first gallery in 1985, which moved to its central London premises in 2008. See Julian Stallabrass, *High Art Lite: The Rise and Fall Young British Art* (Verso: London, 2006).

13 For valuable archive material on the Indian Triennial exhibitions, see the holdings made available by Asia Art Archive at http://www.aaa.org.hk/Collection/Details/16465 (accessed March 28, 2017).

14 For details of these cultural activities, see "Engaging Culture, Reinforcing Values," *Biennale Leaf*, 1 (1): 8.

15 "Biennale a Catalyst," *Biennale Leaf*, 1 (1): 6.

16 "Kochi and Venice: A Tale of Two Cities," *Biennale Leaf*, 1 (1): 6.

17 "Kochi and Venice: A Tale of Two Cities."

18 For a critique of the meaning and claims within the rhetoric of regeneration through the arts and architecture, see the range of essays in Jonathan Harris and Richard Williams (eds.), *Regenerating Culture and Society: Architecture, Art and Urban Style within the Global Politics of City-Branding* (Liverpool University Press/Tate Liverpool: Liverpool, 2011). Aid and development agencies within the State of Palestine are a focus in Chapter 5.

19 The organizers judiciously decided to include some finally dismissive discussion of local resistance to the exhibition in the event's *Biennale Leaf*, 1, (1): "'Indian Biennale' excites artists": 3. Artist "Paris" Vishwanathan, for instance, was quoted saying "I know that there has been some resistance to the Biennale. It's not difficult to see the reason. Who brought the Biennale? Some artists who have gone out of Kerala. Who is opposing? Those who have not gone anywhere."

20 See, for example, Neil Padukone, *Beyond South Asia: India's Strategic Evolution and the Reintegration of the Subcontinent* (Bloomsbury: London, 2014).

21 "Kochi and Venice: A Tale of Two Cities."

22 *India's First Biennale 12/12/12.*

23 For positioning of the artworks and a virtual walk around the sites, see https://www.google.com/maps/d/viewer?mid=zsHtymhWw_Qs.kW9RRJopYz-A&hl=en (accessed January 15, 2016). On artists who made site visits, see "Kochi Thumps in Artist's Heart," *Biennale Leaf*, 1 (1): 2.

24 New York/Dhakar (Bangladesh)-based artist Naeem Mohaiemen has made several multimedia installations on the specificities of Bangladeshi

entanglements with India, Pakistan and Cold War regional geopolitics since 1971. These include *I Have Killed Pharaoh* (2010), a set of paired texts and image panels dealing with the assassination of Bangladesh's "founding father" Sheikh Mujib in 1975. See "The Young Man Was…Naeem Mohaiemen," exhibition at Experimenter gallery, Kolkata April 8–June 9, 2011, and gallery publication *Experimenter 2011–2012* (Kolkata, 2012): 7–22.

25 See John Pijnappel, "Moving Images in the 21st Century in Indian Video Art and Beyond," *Moving On Asia*: 430. On poverty in Asia and globally, see Mike Davis, *Planet of Slums* (Verso: London, 2007).

26 Nalini Malani's single-channel video work *Unity in Diversity* (2003) also dealt with sectarian conflict in India, posing paintings and moving image portraits within a collage framework. See *Moving On Asia*: 186–187.

27 Kashmir was awarded to India as part of the British division in 1947 but was dominantly Pashtun in ethnic terms (along with the rest of what was then Western Pakistan). It was later divided between the two states. See Iftikhar Dadi and Hammad Nasar (eds.), *Lines of Control: Partition as a Productive Space* (Green Cardamon/Herbert F. Johnson Museum of Art, Cornell University: Ithica, NY, 2012).

28 See *Nalini Malani: Cassandra's Gift* (Vadehra Art Gallery: Delhi, 2014). Exhibition catalogue for show held January18–February 27, 2014).

29 See "Video Exhibits on Show," *The Hindu*, December 14, 2012: 3.

30 On violence against women in India as an index of rapid social and cultural change, see, e.g., Svati P. Shah, *Street Corner Secrets: Sex, Work, and Migration in the City of Mumbai* (Duke University Press: Durham, NC, 2014).

31 See Michael Hardt and Antonio Negri, *Multitude: War and Democracy in the Age of Empire* (Penguin: New York, 2004). For their earlier account of capitalism and globalization, particularly relevant to Asian social development since 1945, see *Empire* (Harvard University Press: Cambridge, MA, 2000).

32 "Economy to See a Fillip," *Biennale Leaf*, 1 (1): 8.

33 "Supporting Kochi–Muziris Biennale, 2012," *India's First Biennale 12/12/12* np.

34 On the Christie's sale, see *Alef*, December 2012–January 2013: 24.

35 See http://borgenproject.org/10-facts-poverty-india/and, on growth in inequalities, see http://profit.ndtv.com/news/global-economy/article-income-inequality-increasing-globally-including-india-lagarde-379540 (accessed January 22, 2016).

36 On the almost complete dependence of Gulf States' contemporary art world development on Western expertise, see Don Thompson "Abu Dhabi and Qatar," in *The Supermodel and the Brillo Box*: 207–214.

37 On the center, see the wholly celebratory account "A Space for Culture," *Alef*, December 2012–January 2013: 83–88. The "Arab Spring" uprisings of 2011–2012 interrupted the rule of despots, kings, functionaries and plenipotentiaries across the region. See the wide range of relevant essays and illustrations of related artworks in Anthony Downey (ed.), *Uncommon Grounds: New Media and Critical Practices in North Africa and the Middle East* (IB Tauris: London, 2014).

38 "Painting with Fluidity, Painting with Water," *The Hindu*, December 15, 2012: 4.

39 Enwesor lives in New York and Munich, while Mosquera, now based in Havana and Madrid, was adjunct curator at the New Museum of Contemporary Art in New York between 1995 and 2009. For essays by these and many other influential curators and critics, see the selection and copious bibliographic references in Elena Filipovic, Marieke Van Hal and Solveig Ovstebo (eds.), *The Biennial Reader* (Bergen Kunsthall: Bergen, 2010). This book has helped to form the canon.

40 "Face off with Amar Kanwar," *Biennale Leaf*, 1 (1): 5.

41 "Face off with Amar Kanwar."

42 See, e.g., the multievent festival publication *2010: Imagining Asia* (Netpac in association with Goethe Institut, Max Mueller Bhavan: Delhi, 2010); the conference publication *Roots, Identity, Modernity: Asian Voices on Culture and Creativity* (Netpac: New Delhi, 2013) and film/conference publication *The Many Lives of Indian Cinema: 1913–2013 and Beyond. Disciplines, Histories, Technologies, Futures* (BioScope/Centre for the Study of Developing Societies: Delhi, 2014).

43 Latika Padgaonkar "The Films," in *2010: Imagining Asia*: 8. Two Indian films examining the violence bound up in this turmoil are *Barbed Wire* (2005, directed by Bappaditya Bandopadhyay), which deals with illegal immigration, communal politics and terrorism in a border zone village and *Mr and Mrs Iyer* (2002, directed by Aparna Sen, whose narrative concerns intergenerational Muslim–Sikh violence). See *2010: Imagining Asia*: 18 and 24.

44 Aruna Vasudev and Wong Tuck-Cheong, "The Conference," *2010: Imagining Asia*: 43.

45 Mayank Mansingh Kaul, "Towards Asian Modernities," *Roots, Identity, Modernity: Asian Voices on Culture and Creativity*: np.

46 Mayank Mansingh Kaul "Towards Asian Modernities."

47 Jahnvi Dameron Nandan "Objects of Desire," *Take* 2 (7): 2012: 104–107 (106).

48 Jahnvi Dameron Nandan "Objects of Desire," 106.

49 See Hemant Sreekumar, "DDA to DLF," in Robert E. D'Souza (ed.), *Outside In: Dialogues and Documents of Art and Social Change* (W+K Publishing: New Delhi, 2012): 24–31 (30).

50 Glyn Atwal, "Rise and Shine in India," *Jetwings*, 12 (12), December 2012: 212–214 (212).

51 Glyn Atwal, "Rise and Shine in India," 13–14.

52 Maria Lind developed a similar argument in relation to the role given by the European Union to the private Frieze Foundation—on the basis of its presumed "expertise and credibility" in contemporary art—which it charged with the task of allocating public funding for visual arts organizations via the EU's

"Culture 2000" fund. See Lind (ed.), *European Cultural Policies: 2015: A Report with Scenarios on the Future of Public Funding for Contemporary Art in Europe*: 6–8. On the impact of the Crash in India, see "Global Meltdown and its Impact on the Indian Economy," *Mainstream*, XLVII (15), March 28, 2009 http://www.mainstreamweekly.net/article1261.html (accessed January 29, 2016). See the Devi Foundation's web site at www.deviartfoundation.org/

53 Mayank Mansingh Kaul, "Design in India: Towards an Agenda?" *TAKE*, 2 (7): 2012: 18–21.

54 Mayank Mansingh Kaul, "Design in India: Towards an Agenda?"

55 Ishola Khosla, "A Future for Design: Improvisation through the Informal Economy," *TAKE*, 2 (7): 100–102 (102). On Dharavi, see Mike Davis, *Planet of Slums*: 92–93.

56 Suchitra Balasubrahmanyan, "The India Report: The Search for Culturally Relevant Roots. Towards a History of Design in India," *TAKE*, 2 (7): 26–28.

57 Thoughtshop Foundation, "A for Amitabh: Games and Tools for Empowerment," *TAKE*, 2 (7): 22–25.

58 Aveek Sen, "Natasha De Batak—*Nightshade*," in *Experimenter: 2011–2012* (Contemporary Art Centre: Kolkata, 2012): 102–113 (images on pp. 108–109).

59 "Supporting Kochi–Muzuris Biennale 2012." On Manifesta origins and activities, see Barbara Vinderlinden and Elena Filipovic (eds.), *The Manifesta Decade: Debates on Contemporary Art Exhibitions and Biennials* (MIT Press: Cambridge, MA: 2005).

60 Okwui Enwesor, "Mega-Exhibitions and the Antinomies of a Transnational Global Form," in Elena Filipovic, Marieke Van Hal and Solveig Ovstebo (eds.), *The Biennial Reader*: 426–445 (440–441). See the important critical response by Chin-tao-Wu, "Biennials without Borders?" *New Left Review*, 57, May–June 2009: 107–115.

61 *India's First Biennale 12/12/12*. Text in a pamphlet on seminar discussions accompanying the opening of the Biennale expanded upon this theme, making a virtue out of necessity, given Kochi's diminutive magnitude: "The location of India's first biennale in Kochi marks a seismic [sic] in the way art will be seen in the subcontinent [...] replacing the model of a state supported metropolitan exposition [...] Located outside the metropolitan, heavily mediatized industrial cities of India, the KMB [Kochi Biennale] opens a new chapter of political and cultural realization in the arts," *Kochi-Muziris Biennale Symposium—Site Imaginaries*: np.

62 "Gung-ho for Game Changer." *Biennale Leaf*, 1 (1): 1.

63 The last edition of the Triennial, given no theme, took place in 2005, seven years before the first Kochi Biennial. See Joan Kee, "Contemporary Southeast Asian Art: The Right Kind of Trouble," *Third Text* (special issue on Contemporaneity and Art in Southeast Asia), 25 (4), July 2011: 371–381 (373).

64 See Mulk Raj Anand, "Chairman's Welcome Address," *Lalit Kala Contemporary*, 36, September 1990: 12. For an interesting implicit comparison of the Triennial's and Netpac's interests in exploring and representing Indian cultural modernities through the visual arts, including film, see Mayank Mansingh Kaul, "Towards Asian Modernities," *Roots, Identity, Modernity*: np.

65 The "breakout" from national models of modern and contemporary art production is addressed in many essays included in Elena Filipovic, Marieke Van Hal and Solveig Ovstebo (eds.), *The Biennial Reader.* See also the stringent critique of orthodox histories of biennials centered on national pavilions offered by Vittoria Martini, "The Era of the Histories of Biennials has Begun," *The Biennial Reader: The Bergen Conference* (Bergen Kunsthall: Bergen, 2010): 9–13.

66 See, e.g., Peter Osborne, *Anywhere or Not At All: Philosophy of Contemporary Art* (Verso: London, 2013).

67 See *Kochi–Muziris Biennale Symposium—Site Imaginaries*: np.

68 *The Hindu*, December 14, 2012: 9.

69 *Biennial Leaf*, 1 (1): 9.

70 *Biennial Leaf*, 1 (1): 9.

4

Social Reproduction of Contemporary Art in the People's Republic of China: Higher Education and the Branding of "Contemporary Chinese Art"

As the plane taxis along the runway in to the terminal at Beijing Capital Airport I stare uncomprehendingly at my diary, trying to force myself into morning's usual wakefulness. It's 8.30 a.m. here but 12.30 a.m. last night back in England... Asia has got ahead of me, again... A note in my diary says "lecture on globalization and contemporary art" at Tsinghua University—12 noon today. But surely it is tomorrow? No. It is today ... And tomorrow we push on to Dalian Polytechnic University, five hundred miles to the east, where my university operates a joint campus for art and design students—another lecture to do there, and a faculty meeting to review the development of our programs in fashion and design. English language ability is a concern—always an issue for Chinese students in England and in China too, now, as our 400 students (planned to double in two years) are taught and assessed only in English. "Transnational" higher education has become a big business for UK universities and several now operate campuses in the PRC. How does this education translate? ... I remember my lecture, today, in fact in only 3 hours or so, or 4 a.m. British time—globalization's "time–space compression," they call this... The looming terminal building blots out the light from my little iced-up window on the world: "Welcome to China. HSBC, The Global Bank," say the signs...

Art and Design Education as a Globalization Process

Higher education provision for art and design in China has expanded enormously since the early 1960s when 12 art schools were originally designated as the basis for national provision in the PRC. The country's first journal in the area, *Art and Design Magazine*, had been founded in 1958. One of the first 12 schools, the Central Academy of Arts and Design (also founded that year, in Beijing) began to enroll students on four-year undergraduate degree programs in 1977, just after Chairman Mao's death and, with it, the end of the Cultural Revolution (during which college entrance examinations had been banned).

The Global Contemporary Art World, First Edition. Jonathan Harris.
© 2017 John Wiley & Sons, Inc. Published 2017 by John Wiley & Sons, Inc.

The Central Academy of Arts and Design should not be confused with the Central Academy of Fine Arts (CAFA, also in Beijing), one of the most prestigious specialist universities in the PRC. CAFA was founded in 1950 and its curriculum and research areas include what Western universities usually call the "arts and humanities"—that is, literature, music, historical and cultural studies, along with visual art and design.[1]

In 1999 the Central Academy of Arts and Design merged with Tsinghua University, becoming its Academy of Arts and Design. Important art and design program developments had occurred at the Central Academy of Arts and Design between 1977 and the merger 22 years later. These reflected and embodied national change as the PRC began to open up to the world and the academy assimilated fields of teaching and research already common in Western universities. In 1980 the Central Academy of Arts and Design set up its Design Centre (which merged with Environmental Art Studies five years later). In 1982 it established the PRC's first fashion design undergraduate program. The following year it created its history of arts and crafts department and began to award PhD degrees. In 1984 it inaugurated its industrial design and fashion departments and began to organize partnerships with overseas universities. And, after joining with Tsinghua University, the Academy of Arts and Design began to run MFA (Master of Fine Arts) programs in 2005 and award doctorates the following year.[2]

Early in the twenty-first century the PRC's central government, that of the Chinese Communist Party (CCP), in what is effectively a one-party state, began to instigate developments radically to improve the quality of research and postgraduate training in selected universities—including at Tsinghua in Beijing. In doing this, the government emulated plans carried out in national higher education systems around the world, as it became clear that the forces of globalization were fundamentally changing and challenging national economies, and transforming the character of knowledge production in all areas.[3] By 2000, within a global capitalist neoliberalizing economy, apparently ceaseless technological innovation—particularly in digital, media, internet, bioscientific and material sciences areas—presented nation-states with opportunities for huge new wealth creation and societal development.

At the same time, however, this transforming change threatened the quality of life of their peoples: nation-states were obliged not to fail to interact and compete in this new world order/disorder of production, trade and consumption. The PRC, like Russia in 1991 after the end of the Soviet Union (though there are very significant differences), substantially—but never conclusively—turned its back on the Maoist-era "command economy." China joined the key global capitalist network institutions, the International Monetary Fund and World Bank, in 1980 and started extensive privatization programs within some sectors of the country's economy. In 2001 the PRC negotiated entry to the World Trade Organization. China also began to encourage unprecedented social, cultural and intellectual contact with Western—though also African and Latin American—countries (China, as I have noted, was one of the founding so-called BRIC nations).[4]

The ostensible material contradictions of and ideological conflicts between a commitment to "free enterprise" on the one hand and a political state still nominally faithful to a Communist path on the other pervade the official, institutional discourse of China's art and design higher education and research, as in other academic areas. Tsinghua University's department of art history required, for instance, according to a 2011 prospectus, that its students should "build systematic theoretical knowledge of history of Chinese and foreign art and that of Chinese and foreign arts and design [...] with basic theory of Marxism–Leninism as guideline." What this might actually mean (and require in terms of the assessment of essays) was not elaborated.[5] However, a statement in a document produced by another PRC university makes the Tsinghua statement more intelligible. A postgraduate studies and research bulletin entitled *Brands*, published by the "Brands Research and Development Institute" at Dalian Polytechnic University, informs the reader that all teaching and research takes within, and as part of, the Chinese "national economy and social development 12th 5-year plan." This plan is continuous with, that is, the central planning process instituted in China in 1950 just after the revolution inspired by Marxism–Leninism which brought the Communist Party and Chairman Mao to power.[6]

In 2008, however, when the Brands Research and Development Institute was created, led by academic Jingyang Lin, the PRC's national plan included the aim further to privatize certain "soft" areas of the country's economy. The *Brands* bulletin recognized the significance of the powerful commercial forces at work once such a process got under way. The language here replicates that of Western companies. The onus was placed on what Jingyang Lin called "brand innovation capability" and the consolidation of "brand asset" following the Crash that year and resulting slump. The rhetoric of "market absolutism" here ironically mirrors the PRC's previous commitment to doctrinal "Marxism–Leninism." For instance, "the market," according to the *Brands* statement, "is always right"—though what the market actually is isn't defined at all. Further, Jingyang Lin declares that "the market is the foundation of success" and that constant innovation of new and successful brands is necessary "because the market is cruel."[7] The very broadest definition of the field of design—now including many areas of "services" and "experience-generating products," as well as material goods of all kinds—has facilitated a vast growth area for higher education and research throughout the world. Dalian Polytechnic University's Brands Research and Development Institute carried out work concerned with, for example, cosmetics, building materials and what are called "environmental systems."[8]

The Institute is part of the School of Art and Design at Dalian Polytechnic University, and perusal of its interests and language suggest that a self-conscious and systematic "branding" of student artists' and designers' identities and roles has also taken place. This development has occurred in China and throughout the world as the labor of professional artists and designers has become represented as an elite authored/bespoke product made for a niche or luxury market. I showed in Chapter 3 how the organizers of the 2012 Kochi Biennale worked, in effect, to brand their first exhibition and the artists it featured as a particular kind of regional and national collective product. Artworks and curation programs are increasingly presented—by artists and curators or by their dealers and agents—as expert forms of "service" and "experience" product delivered to consumers, especially, for example, in the art fair environment such as at Art Basel Hong Kong. This emphasis on the meaning, purpose and value of contemporary art production and consumption is now solidly embodied in the social forms of the contemporary art biennial and art fair "event." It has also become central to the "relational-aesthetic" dimension of participatory art practices, regarded by many critics and commentators, along with installation art, as quintessential globalized art forms.[9]

Glossy catalogues of work produced by graduate students at Tsinghua University in the areas of ceramics, visual communication, industrial, environmental and information design, as well as in painting and sculpture, indicate efforts to brand students' identities as future professionals. The pages in these catalogues set aside for each student include some English language text and make recurrent reference to Western art, artists and wider cultural figures. Many Chinese students adopt what appear to be English names/identities, but because of the arrangement of page layouts these tend to become conflated dreamily with titles for the illustrations of their design work. Such hybrid author/product brand-names include, for instance, "Soul Taker," "Diffuse Nicotine," "Curve," "Falling Stone," "Hitchcock's Girl," "Call from the Last Day," "The Metamorphosis," and "Seeking Mondrian." These ambiguously meaningful textual elements raise a series of important questions regarding the use of English by Chinese students. These centrally concern the status of the language within the curriculum of higher education art and design programs in the PRC and elsewhere in Asia where English has become a central pedagogic medium.[10]

Beyond that issue, however, these questions highlight the much broader one of the status of Western socioeconomic power and cultural influence in "global Asia" and especially in the world of Asian contemporary art. My own involvement with these issues has had a strong institutional element to it. For several years it was connected directly to the matter of the quality of learning experiences facilitated by my then university in educating our Chinese students based both in England and at the shared campus in Dalian. Chinese government openness to foreign education systems has taken a number of forms since the beginnings of the PRC's "Open Door" policy in the 1980s. Allowing Chinese students to travel abroad and study at universities in Europe and North America was a big initial step which essentially—at first anyway—required these students, if they were to succeed institutionally, to assume as competently as they could the behavior patterns, standards and values of the host institutions, their staff and students. A great deal of accumulated evidence indicates that this was (and remains) a "hit and miss" experience, for all parties involved.[11]

Two issues are particularly significant within discussion of this experience of transnational education. These are (1) its role in what's called "independent learning" and (2) its technical or practical uses in specific curriculum areas. Both raise questions about the Western character of globalization processes in general and the specific Asian (including Chinese) experience of decolonization in the twentieth century, along with the continuing legacies of colonialism. Insofar as the vast majority of now practicing professional artists and designers have been through a university education process, and given that since the 1990s many from Asia have travelled to Western countries for this education's postgraduate or research element, the status of English as the world's lingua franca is a critical concern for this book as a whole. Within a formal education process—one of the key mechanisms for social reproduction in all modern societies—the use of English is inevitably tied to specific forms and processes of understanding, specific senses of self and of others, specific conventions of naming and classification, and a deep historical legacy of specific cultural references, priorities, emphases and exclusions. To "learn" all that as what is sometimes breezily called a "second language" in a formal education situation over a three- or four-year period would be a very tall order for the most scholarly, open and able students. To gain a sufficient "working knowledge" of it simply in order to pass assessments remains a challenge for nearly everyone.[12]

The PRC's decision to allow some Western universities to operate campuses and programs in China pushed the globalization of higher education an important stage further. On the one hand, this development occurred through an initial (though necessarily continuing) bilateral negotiation between respective governments and universities about many aspects of institutional education processes. This was necessary because these campuses in China, such as the Winchester School of Art–University of Southampton programs run with Dalian Polytechnic University, had to "bed down" with the host organization in terms of teaching faculty and resources, student recruitment and assessment processes, along with the whole gamut of the PRC's universities' regulatory regime. One condition for this to be possible had to be the existence of mutual goodwill and willingness on both sides to look at their own systems and that of their partners and agree to be flexible. The novel program and campus created in Dalian (out of renovated buildings) was a genuine hybrid, drawing on elements from both countries' systems but characteristic of neither's usual higher education institutional arrangement.[13]

In the case of Dalian, one of the senior academic managers was a professional artist and architectural designer who decided to allow an experiment. This was that the art and design program run with Winchester School of Art would substantially reproduce the same degree programs as those conceived, validated, operated and assessed in England. This meant that all the teaching, learning, assessment and "quality assurance" processes had to be conducted in English, although they also had to meet the specifications of Dalian Polytechnic University's own regulatory framework. The Chinese students recruited to the programs would spend half of their first two years on the degree program studying English, after having passed initial entry-level tests. The challenge, for students and staff, became that of using English language learning as an active tool in the students' education, rather than it being imposed as a necessary formality of study, as it is for Chinese students registered in UK-based universities. Was English, taught as the students' education language and medium of communication—as, that is, a resource of forms and processes of understanding, with specific senses of self and of others, specific conventions of naming and classification, and a deep historical legacy of specific references, priorities, emphases and exclusions—likely, then, to be in continuity or contradiction with the Chinese students' first language?[14]

Changing Identifications in Art and Design Education in China

An important experiential aspect to this complex of issues, especially in relation to contemporary art discourse where particularly heightened assumptions and senses of subjectivity remain pivotal, concerns the differential character and significance of states of individuality and interiority within Western and Chinese cultures. Insofar as languages are commonly held to "reflect" the forms of behavior and norms of their native speakers, it is the case that Chinese Communist-era values created, reproduced and emphasized powerful senses of collectivist, in distinction from, individualist identities. It is also well to remember, though, that Chinese Communism built on earlier, complementary societal traditions and social norms, for instance, those of Confucianism.[15] Prevalence of "ists" and "isms" indicates the active propagation of ideological belief systems in the examples of both Chinese communism and Western individualism.

By noting this I mean to suggest that one cannot separate the experience, and understanding, of what it is to be a person—literally a single individual—from the experience and knowledge of the ways in which a specific society and its practices may work to reinforce particular ways of seeing and experiencing oneself both as an individual and as a member of a group or whole society. Simplistic assertions of the existence of a border or dualism, for example, between being "English" (or "Western") and "Chinese" (or "Eastern") should be avoided. In both cultures—a phrase that already presupposes, of course, some kinds of actual separation and difference, if not a border—there have been traditions and experiences of being both distinctly individual and distinctly part of a group, and the whole society. These forms of identity and identification have been, for instance, tribal, ethnic, caste, class, gender, regional, religious, civic and politico-ideological in nature, as well as relatively mainstream or marginal at different historical times. But statist discourses and doctrines of individualism and collectivism gathered pace rapidly in the mid-twentieth century and by the late 1950s a dualistic opposition characterized the Cold War ideological standoff between the putative "democratic" (US capitalist) and "egalitarian" (Soviet/Sino communist) world powers. As these terms with their parenthetical referents should indicate, there remains no neutral, non-contested or uniform way to describe these positions and worldviews, or to account for how their proponents characterized their own, and their Cold War opponents', identities and identifications.[16]

In the visual arts this moment in the Cold War coincided closely with what is usually still portrayed as the apogee (for ideological good or bad) of "capitalist individualism" in the West. This was embodied in the "high modernist" works and adduced philosophical perspectives of the American Abstract Expressionist painters. It is worth noting, however, that several of these most celebrated artists—particularly, holding the anarchist views that they did, Mark Rothko and Barnett Newman—were actually as hostile to the US capitalist political–economic system as they were to the authoritarian Eastern communist states. This detail, however, was generally downplayed or omitted altogether in the way their paintings were exhibited and celebrated by major US and European museums at the time, during and because of, the Cold War itself.[17]

The "Open Door" policy and "modernizing" reforms of Mao's successor, Deng Xiaoping, indicated the beginnings of a significant loosening of the key ideological positions which had underpinned communism in the PRC—especially during the Cultural Revolution, against which the CCP turned decisively on Mao's death. This development certainly did not, ever, constitute anything like an official embrace of Western ideological individualism. But one of the consequences of the reform process that began then to extend privatization and encourage business entrepreneurship was the onset of a social transformation in people's experience and experiential knowledge of self and senses of interiority, away from the previous stronghold of Chinese Communist collectivist values. Deng Xiaoping's reforms certainly were meant to embody and represent a profound official reaction against the newly acknowledged horrors and egregious errors of the Cultural Revolution. During the 1980s, for instance, a key Chinese government slogan was "practice is the sole criterion of testing truth." Practice here was code for the extension of "free market" activities and implied a positive evaluative contrast with the barren "theory" of discredited Maoism.[18]

In this broader historical sense, then, Dalian Polytechnic University's decision to embrace Winchester School of Art's art and design program implied a preparedness to negotiate the entailed symbolic and sociocultural weight of "English" (and "Western"). For this was a language, culture and social order in which increasingly strong senses of individual, individual*ity*, individu*ation*, as well as individual*ism*, had begun to develop from the late sixteenth century onwards. This was when these novel terms and nuances of meaning began to come into English from Renaissance and Enlightenment Italian, German and French, and from writers on art specifically.[19] Studying art and design "in English" meant, then, that Chinese students would be exposed—intentionally or not—to a set of historically accrued societal values embedded in the language that stressed quite different and sometimes opposing senses of self, of others as also individual and individu*ated* in specific ways, and beyond that, of the social and societal worlds beyond. Notions of artistic "creativity," "invention," and "authorship" would also be closely bound up with and emblematic of these different and sometimes disputed senses of self and individuality.

As the history of the PRC from the latter third of the twentieth century indicates, since the death of Mao and inauguration of the "Open Door" policy China's ruling groups have taken steps themselves that have helped lead to the moment when the country's people (especially the young, born after Mao's death) had begun to experience their individuality and sense of self and others in ways that were becoming closer to that of Westerners. The range of resonant yet ambiguous brand/names adopted by Chinese design students at Tsinghua University—"Soul Taker," "Diffuse Nicotine," "Curve," "Falling Stone," "Hitchcock's Girl," "Call from the Last Day," "The Metamorphosis," and "Seeking Mondrian"—indicates a familiarity with the density if also postmodern eclecticism of contemporary Western and globalizing social, cultural and artistic life and mores. Two obvious objections might be raised against these assertions. Firstly, that this Chinese experience of the West and of Western-ness is in large part a mediated, vicarious one. Secondly, that many of these brand/names are simply facile, insignificant references to Western media forms and figures. But these observations actually underline how Western identity and subjectivity itself has been, and will increasingly be, reshaped within the same now globalizing mediating-technological processes. "Western" and "Eastern" are states, experiences and means of knowing in a dialectical process of mutual transformation.

How, for example, is the acquisition and deployment of a second language linked to behavior in social situations, and specifically to that of students studying art and design in a university? These questions lead to a second issue concerning use of English as the language of learning and assessment at Dalian Polytechnic University. It had become clear early on in the history of the shared program that Chinese students, in comparison with their British counterparts, were used to a different kind of education experience. This was one based largely on so-called "rote learning" in lecture rooms: a one-way process or transmission focused on a teacher whose assumed expertise and authority was at the center of the institutional definition and reproduction of what counted as significant knowledge. That mode, however, had started to become less significant in British higher education by the 1980s. In particular, art students in Western education institutions, often with the support of some of their teachers, had rebelled against such methods, which had been seen as intrinsically authoritarian and reactionary (and boring) since the late-1960s.[20]

New, "student-centered learning" and "independent learning" forms began to be implemented, along with focus on developing for individual students a research process suited to their different needs. Within theories of student-centered learning individuals would find specific answers to problems and ways to complete tasks that they themselves asked and set, though still within a largely predefined program, curriculum and assessment format. For instance, the introduction of a "sketchbook diary" for first year students' daily use at Dalian was encouraged in order to engender a valuable habit of systematic self-scrutiny and self-development long used in Western art schools but new to China. Transnational education, "contrastive rhetoric" studies and translation studies—three emergent subgenres within cultural globalization studies—assess teaching and learning modes in different institutional contexts worldwide. The topic's significance indicates the various investments at stake in what is now a multi-billion dollar global higher education business.[21] Millions of students, and tens of thousands of academic staff, relocate around the world regularly now as part of what might be called the global "knowledge acquisition, transfer and exchange economy." Its social, cultural and political implications are vast, as this discussion of art and design higher education in the PRC indicates. The transformations in contemporary Chinese society and culture, as its economy, people and institutions become increasingly interconnected with economies, people and institutions (including universities) around the world have been profound, with wide ramifications within the global contemporary art world.[22]

Higher education and research in the design fields in China (and in India as we saw in the previous chapter) is similarly in a process of globalization. Again, there is evidence to suggest that the PRC has started to move towards its own kinds of "independent learning" focus as much as it has been prepared to allow some of its students to experience Western versions—those both offered overseas and at campuses set up with partner institutions in the PRC. The establishment of independent research protocols are discernible, for example, in the organization of the Brands Research and Development Institute at Dalian Polytechnic University. The Institute, for instance, claimed that it "strove to enable students to have a sense of social responsibility with 'confidence and ability to challenge authority'"—this as part of a project linked to raising environmental awareness of pollution risks in building materials.[23] The authority of the teacher was, it seems, being partially decentered: "the traditional teaching model was changing. Professors and students formed a center of teaching together, professor as a director or guider, students as performers." This model had what was called an "experimental" performative element to it. Think of the terms "director" and "performer" here perhaps as developmental roles in a dynamic scenario rather than as part of a necessarily fixed and final order of things. This "teaching system" was developed in partnership with some institutions outside of the PRC—in this case, with Nanyang Technological University in Singapore.[24]

Maintenance of the contemporary art system in globalized Asia requires the production and reproduction of a professionalized workforce, at the apex of which stand the artists. As in the west, the figure of the artist remains an active and potent symbol of creativity and individuality. The global art and design higher education process helps now to fashion the identity or "branding" of proto-artists—a very limited number of whom will eventually make works for the market, sold by dealers and at art fairs like Art Basel Hong Kong. Some of these artists will get a chance to display their work at biennial exhibitions like that at Kochi and some of those perhaps will have their works bought by "global gatekeeper" institutions like Tate or the Guggenheim Museum. The catalogues produced in order to showcase Tsinghua University art and design graduates exemplify the wider significance of social individuation processes in China. PRC students, such as those enrolled at Dalian Polytechnic University on the Winchester School of Art program, have gone through a kind of "knowledge internationalization" process influenced by an English language-based inculcation into Western art and design practices, involving induction into facets of related occidental culture, history and philosophy.

Contemporary Chinese Art Marketed for Global Consumption

These higher education innovations are active productive elements now within China's global contemporary art world. Critic Huang Du, based in Beijing, has written—in English and Mandarin—reflecting on the nature of the qualitative and quantitative transformations within this world since the late 1970s.[25] According to Huang Du, a pervading ideology of rank "commercialism" came to replace that of "political propaganda art" in China after the death of Mao, and its morbid symptoms dominated contemporary art in the PRC into the beginnings of the twenty-first century. This "commercialization," he observed, had:

> crushed the "Utopian" [values] of the avant-garde artists in the past. Everything is commercialized and consumed in the name of art. In this way, art has become a "stock market" and "Vanity Fair." The impact of commercialization of art is reflected in the liberation of human beings [...]

> the confrontation between the previous avant-garde art and political ideology has been replaced by the alliance of contemporary art and commerce.[26]

This paradigm transformation in the period up to 2000 was marked by what Huang Du calls a shift from "macro narration"—exemplified by the epic propaganda painting stories of the Communist era—to a form of "micro personalization," in works that represented the apparently randomized daily experience and life of artists in post-Mao PRC. The commodification process that began to incorporate Chinese contemporary art into a global art market—a development I turn to in a moment, with discussion of specific artists and artworks—was encoded in a parallel shift from what Huang Du calls "individual creation" to "mass production, from single work to mass products." Art's earlier sacred "halo" under Communism was replaced, he notes, by a profane "daily, popular, graphic visual language."[27]

Huang Du believes, however, that after 2000 this overriding ethos of commercialization began to lose its grip on the production of new artworks in China. In its place a range of varied practices and genuinely heterogeneous interests has come to characterize the field of contemporary art. He identifies within it several broad themes. The first of these is what he calls "the expansion of media and the intervention of new concepts." He cites as an example the subdued color grid paintings in acrylic of Zhang Xuerui (born 1979), whose diminutive recent works, such as *72 Inclined Lattice (3)* (2014), resume a "cool," formal investigation of abstraction, eschewing any obvious (or commercial) symbolic or narrative content. Huang Du's second theme is "the interaction between photography and painting." For instance, consider Wang Guofeng's large-scale digital photographs of communist-era public buildings in China and Russia, and political rallies in North Korea, such as *North Korea 2012 no.2* (2039 × 208 cm, 2012).

These images both extend yet disrupt nineteenth century history painting conventions and objectives, provoking questions about the contemporary visual culture of post-revolutionary state power, ideology and political authority in a global capitalist world (Wang Guofeng's photographs are discussed in more detail in my Conclusion).

Huang Du's third theme is "the focused lens of video." Within this category he cites China's preeminent filmmaker Yang Fudong (born 1971), whose many

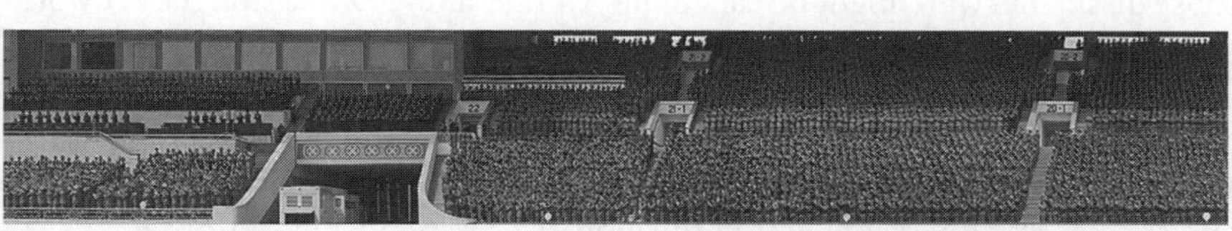

Figure 10 Wang Guofeng *North Korea 2012 no. 2* (DVD video still, 2012). *Source:* © Wang Guofeng, Courtesy de Sarthe Gallery.

black and white films have combined an interest in Western cinema genre (especially film noir) with the portrayal of contemporary life for younger people in China. Yang Fudong's 2014 five-channel digital video work *The Colored Sky: New Women II* represents a new departure, experimenting with moving-image in an installation form and format. This work, alluding to surrealist narrative imagery, is a dream-like depiction of young Chinese women in a now "global Asian" world which is simultaneously both modern and ancient. Qui Zhijie's 2013 *Playground 1* was a 1000 square meter interactive "floor map" of the world installed in a gallery in Hong Kong, upon which people were invited to roll actual spheres of different sizes and materials around a conceptual terrain linking China to a global network of place-names, ideas and objects. The artist included in his *Playground II* (the extension of this map on to the walls of the same gallery) 600 different brands of Chinese cigarette drawn from his own everyday world. Huang Du cites Qui Zhijie as one of the artists exemplifying the fourth theme, which he calls "the extension of Chinese heritage and daily life."[28]

Considering the period between the late 1970s and 2013, how might we characterize the globalizing social order within which this "transfiguration" in Chinese contemporary art occurred? As the financial crash in 2008 demonstrated and the previous chapters in this book have illustrated, globalization processes involve the creation of new conditions and systems that are inherently unstable and dangerous. That term, "system," usually understood, implies an ordering process that overrides, or that at least is intended to override, the local significance or weakness of component elements within it. Analysis of the contemporary global art world suggests, however, that this "system" (part of the globalized world order/disorder) is better understood as a kind of skewed power network whose "nodes" (that is, its key pressure points) have been controlled hitherto by a limited number of key players in financial and institutional terms.[29]

These "gatekeeper" organizations have derived their historical and present power within the global art world system, and its subsector in global Asia, from a number of sources that are sociopolitical, ideological and economic in nature. But their effective control of the system is itself limited and vulnerable to many kinds of external pressures. These notably include (1) financial crises in the global capitalist economy as a whole; (2) destabilizing local political and socio-economic conditions (in this case, those in the PRC); and (3) actions by some of those dissidents who might be called the "worker ants" comprising the art world system itself. By this perhaps provocative term I mean some artists, critics, curators, gallery owners and others who explicitly oppose—in the name of art itself—the function and character of contemporary art in the globalized art world system where they see it reduced to the status of simply another commodity, and spectacular diversion, within the globalized capitalist world-order.[30]

As Chapter 1, focused on Art Basel Hong Kong, demonstrated, over the past 20 years in particular, the market for contemporary art has become a structurally significant, if still relatively minor, part of global corporate, state and private "wealth investment management" strategies, along with, for instance, trade in commodities such as gold and securities such as US government bonds.[31] The art market's key sites of activity (its most significant auctions, dealing galleries and fairs) have expanded from New York, London, Paris and other North American and European centers, to global Asian venues, primarily Hong Kong, Singapore, Shanghai, Dubai, Beijing and Delhi. These have attached themselves in some cases to urban centers where pre-existing regular local commercial art fairs, galleries and auctioneers help to pump prime the markets and generate related media and public interest.

The art market's very rapid expansion globally in the years after 2000 was tied directly to the growth in the world economy in the early years of that decade. Its size, in fact, doubled between 2003 and 2006.[32] The subsequent rapid decline equally closely mirrored the losses and bank failures that occurred in the second half of 2008. Yet, since then, the art market has recovered quickly, in terms of volumes of sales and record individual sale prices, at a rate far more rapid than in most other parts of the world economy. This happened because art became seen as a kind of gold itself, a secure place to "park" or store capital in times of continuing uncertainty—with the assumption, or hope, that prices will not have fallen when the time comes to sell.[33] In this countervailing sense, the buoyant art market might be understood as a kind of "cracked" mirror of the stalled world economy as a whole: the rich or corporate investors in it see art as a sanctuary of sorts in continuing uncertain times.[34]

Art auctions remained illegal under Communist Party rule in China between 1956 and 1986. Chen Yifei's 1992 sumptuous "academic-style" painting of Chinese women in traditional dress *The Four Graces* (note the Western art title, referring to European Renaissance painting) was sold by Guardian Auctioneers in Beijing in 1997 for over US$275 000, then a remarkable price for a contemporary Chinese painting.[35] The sale was a "watershed" moment, indicating significant incipient change of several kinds. It was rumored that the New York and London-based dealer Marlborough Fine Art had bought the work. But Christie's attempts to sell Chinese artworks in London the following year turned out to be a failure—only 25% of the lots went under the hammer.[36] Two key developments, however, were exemplified by these events. The first of these was the intervention of Western dealers into the then just-opening Chinese art world, economy and society as a whole. The second was the marketing of works by living Chinese artists that stressed Western characteristics and references. This development signaled the creation of a branding process aiming these works at potential Western buyers. While these artworks offered an ostensibly authentic "Chinese" theme or narrative, they were simultaneously done in a familiar and unchallenging Western manner.[37]

Yifei has been termed one of the Chinese "Romantic Realist" painters. These two key terms associated with nineteenth-century European academic painting evoke portraiture by the likes of Ingres, Delacroix and Courbet. Other Chinese-born artists from the mid-twentieth century—such as San Yu and Xu Beihong—had done well at auctions overseas but they had generally lived outside China and rarely had works sold anywhere in the country's mainland.[38] Their pictures instantiated for Western buyers "traditional" Chinese styles and subjects of painting from the history of Chinese art—especially the prominence of calligraphic works combining image and text.[39]

In the early twentieth century visual and stylistic affinities developed—or, more importantly, were perceived to have developed—between paintings done by these Chinese artists living abroad and the works of the European masters, such as Picasso and Matisse. As modernist art developed in Europe and then in the United States after 1945, more affinities—assumed visual similarities read as evidence of actually shared themes or values, whatever the actual intentions or knowledge of the Chinese artists—were registered.[40] These claims were generally based on the presuppositions of some Western art critics and historians that the development of abstract painting in the West had meaningful rather than superficial parallels in kinds of work that had been produced in China and other Asian countries for hundreds of years.[41]

It is of course possible at one level to identify kinds of "visual similarity" in these works—between, for example, "drip paintings" made by Chinese painter Wu Guanzhong and American Jackson Pollock. But the conclusion that these similarities are evidence of actual thematic or authorial continuities in works produced sometimes many years or decades apart under very different historical and social conditions remains arguable. The matter is even more contentious and complicated because, by the mid-twentieth century, some Chinese and US artists actually were sometimes definitely self-consciously exploring each other's cultures, being, in the strict sense of the term, "contemporaries."[42] The still-typical Western critical assumption, however, that Chinese (and, in another important instance, Japanese) artists were "copying" or had been decisively "influenced" by Western artists, rather than the interrelation being dialectical, underlines the dominance and entailed arrogance of European and US art history and criticism, as well as its "gatekeeper" organizations.[43]

Ten years after Yifei's painting had sold for what was then a startlingly high price for a Chinese painting, Zao-Wou Ki's 1959 picture *14.12.59* was sold by Christie's Hong Kong, in May of 2007, for US$3.32 m—much more than its then estimated value. Zao-Wou Ki is termed in the sales literature a "second generation modernist."[44] This term replicates an item in the terminology developed by US art critics in the 1950s and 1960s to describe and sequence works by American Abstract Expressionist artists, who also used dates and numbers rather than conventional titles for their paintings. In the claiming of another kind of affinity or analogy here, Chinese art made in the mid-twentieth century onwards is connected explicitly to Western modernist abstract art, and, by extension, to its critical and historical understanding through aesthetic philosophies within the European tradition derived from Immanuel Kant.[45] Zao-Wou Ki's paintings can fit neatly into this capacious and accommodating terrain of understanding—they may be "abstract" or have "abstract" qualities, but they also evoke less challenging, more familiar works by earlier European landscape painters such as Turner and Caspar David Friedrich.

This question of formal resemblance exemplifies something of the complex processes of interaction that have developed between some Chinese artists and the world (and art world) outside of the PRC. Through these processes they have come to know Western artworks, to know these as emblematic of Western Art, and to associate their own activities and values with this entity, to varying degrees. Alongside the dealers Christie's and Sotheby's, Western art museums became the most powerful "gatekeeper" players in the globalizing art world after 2000. The greatest artworks of the European and American modernist era are owned and exhibited in the Museum of Modern Art, the Metropolitan museum and the Guggenheim museum in New York, at Tate Modern in London, at the Reina Sofia museum in Madrid and in the other great collections (public and private) held in Europe and its satellite centers. The related authority and once wide influence of US critics such as the Americans Clement Greenberg and Michael Fried—both associated very closely with identifying what was thought of as the best painting and sculpture of the late 1940s, 1950s and early 1960s—underpinned the museum collections of these canonical works.[46]

Chinese Art and the World Art System

The globalized Asian art world, of which the PRC is a part, is this "systemic power network" of interlinked economic, institutional and ideological–cultural relationships and interdependencies. This global system has been founded on the economic and discursive power of Western art (historical, modern and contemporary), its host societies' legal systems, art discourses and infrastructures for the buying, selling, authentication and critical validation of artworks. China and Chinese artists have become assimilated to this system within the processes of globalization over the past 20 years.[47] The Chinese government was invited to take part in some of the key events of the annual art world calendar—for example, to first allow and support the exhibition of Chinese artists' works in a national pavilion at the Venice Biennale in 2003 (their involvement was cancelled because of the outbreaks of the disease SARS). In the same year, the first large-scale exhibition of contemporary Chinese art was held in France at the Centre Georges Pompidou in Paris, also organized in association with the Chinese government. The notional guarantee of "museum quality" is a regulatory key to the workings of the art market—it is a recurrent phrase used in the sales rhetoric of auctioneers and dealers. In this respect the museums and auction houses inflect and entrench each other's roles in the globalized art world.[48]

In 2000, most market activity for modern and contemporary Chinese art remained "offshore," conducted in Hong Kong and Teipei in Taiwan. But as China began to develop its economic and social reforms, allowing private businesses to exist and grow, new markets for art on the mainland began to emerge—in Beijing, Shanghai, Hangzhou and Guangzhou, and in about six other centers.[49] Centers for art and artists emerged, too, mostly famously at "798" in Beijing, a former factory district turned mixture of galleries, cafes and bars—though this mutating entity has been more tolerated than directly encouraged or supported by the government authorities. This situation is one of the sources of local "system vulnerability" in the global power network. Since the beginnings of the "Open Door" policy, Chinese government regimes have blown hot and cold on the existence and meaning of an indigenous art world, at "798" and elsewhere.[50]

Corruption scandals and political crises in the Chinese Communist Party, and in its rule in China as a whole, have had direct and indirect effects on the activities and changing status of its artists and art discourses. A continued attempted blanket censorship of sexually explicit material in art and the wider culture is one instance.[51] The treatment and status of the most famous Chinese contemporary artist in the west, Ai Weiwei, is another—though he has had a long and complicated history of connection to and disconnection from the Communist Party, reaching back to his father's activities as a well-known poet. Ai Qing had been a Cultural Revolution dissident but was then officially rehabilitated and became a celebrated figure.[52] As I've noted, Weiwei was named "the most influential artist in the world" in 2011, by *Art Review*, a US-based Western journal and online media source. In 2016 he was still in the top ten. He has become, for some powerful agents in the West, a late-Cold War symbol of resistance to communist power in China and this development marks the perennial ambivalence of US and European political interests generally over the place of China in the world economic and sociopolitical order.[53]

China undoubtedly has become the key structural element to continued global economic growth (as part of the BRIC zone of countries), within which the art market is a small part, but there is a potentially catastrophic asymmetry between China's economic and sociopolitical character—at least as far as the US and its NATO alliance members are concerned.[54]The term "authoritarian state capitalism" may aptly name the Chinese socioeconomic system. It characterizes a nation-state ruled by a single unmovable (though not unchanging) cadre of elites that is trying to manage and dominate enormous economic forces and related, unpredictable social change more typical of the development of the capitalist–democratic societies in Europe and North America since the late nineteenth century.[55] This development, however, is by no means historically anomalous. Versions of the combination of a "free enterprise" capitalist economy with an authoritarian state occurred many times in Western Europe in the mid-twentieth century. Some of the fascist regimes that erupted there in the interwar period, in parallel and then opposition to the Soviet Union, aspired precisely to this combination. Francisco Franco's autocratic regime in Spain was, by far, the most successful of these in melding systematic repression of all kinds with "private enterprise" and big business interests through from 1939 to the mid-1970s.[56] This was possible because NATO, led by the US since the mid-1950s, supported Franco's regime as a bulwark against the Soviet Union, and, sometimes, against the PRC too.

Zhang Xiaogang's 1994 painting *Bloodlines: Three Comrades* sold for US$2.1 million at Sotheby's in New York in 2007. It represents a form of so-called "political pop art" that developed in China, made by Chinese artists, in the 1990s. The painting, depicting the curiously inert faces of a trio of CCP members, alludes to something of the internal upheavals experienced by the population as the (self) image and significance of the Communist Party itself went through crises and transformation—especially as it tried (and tries) to legitimize itself while overseeing a limited internal capitalist revolution and beginning to act as a key player on the world stage.[57] The Chinese political pop artists did learn from and partly emulate aspects of Western and particularly US recent art and mass culture. Warhol-type ambiguities and paraded banalities characterized much of Chinese political pop's own "content processing." It remained, however, a part of the wholesale commercialization of art that Huang Du attacks. Like Warhol's products, it remains unclear how "critical" rather than celebratory or neutral Chinese "political pop art" actually is of the things it depicts, though the faint/feint smell of satire and coded attack is there in many of these works. It may well be that this ambiguity was a necessity, in order for its producers to avoid censorship, and worse, from the government. (It was a necessity, also, to avoid use of the pictorial rhetoric of orthodox Chinese Communist Party socialist realist painting, except in parodic–satirical terms.)[58]

But, again in market terms, it was also a necessity for Chinese artists to meet the expectations and visual knowledge of buyers from within the recent Western era—for, since the 1960s, the "cool" ambiguities and seductive banalities of mass-cultural imagery, sometimes dressed up as "complexity" and "multi-accentuality," have been requisite elements of "serious" art in the neo-avant-garde tradition.[59] This requirement developed based on a Cold War-era rejection of both the political posturings of the Surrealists, half of whom had joined the Stalinist communist parties of Western Europe in the 1930s, and the reactive asocial individualism of the American Abstract Expressionists, whose works later became tainted by this painting's now well-known role as an insidious propaganda vehicle for US state department interests during the later 1950s and 1960s.[60]

Yue Minjun's 1993 painting *Goldfish* sold at the same New York auction as *Bloodlines* in 2007 for US$1.38 m in a sale of 300 lots that made, in total, US$25 m. This work shows a man laughing sardonically as he appears to watch

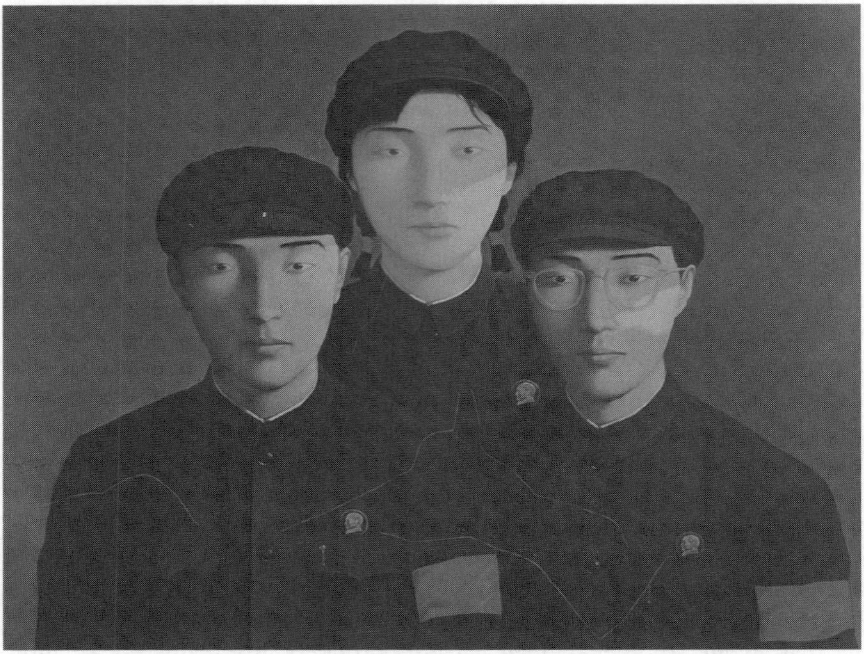

Figure 11 Zhang Xiaogang *Bloodlines: Three Comrades* (oil painting, 1994). *Source:* © 2016 Zhang Xiaogang.

a fish swim below in the moat of a castle. But his eyes are closed and his serially repeated image diminishing into the distance seems to signal a comprehensive inauthenticity of the world, vision, meaning and image itself. By that year, the market for Chinese contemporary art (sometimes branded less politically directly as "East Asian painting") had become "mainstream," with important sales also taking place in London and Hong Kong.[61] Though Christie's and Sotheby's still dominate world sales of Asian art, the number of mainland Chinese auction houses continues to grow. Taiwan-based firms, for instance, developed a specialized role in selling to mainland Chinese buyers works by Chinese artists that they acquired on the international market ten years earlier.[62]

Despite this, the majority of the global players—buyers, dealers and auction houses—are still based in the West. This reflects a continued comparative lack of interest by Chinese people themselves in buying contemporary works by Chinese artists. In 2006 and 2007, for instance, Sotheby's recorded that only 13% and 16%, respectively, of their sales of Chinese art in New York auctions in those years went to Chinese mainland buyers.[63] The massive growth in the rise of Chinese people recorded as "middle class" (upwards of 500 million by 2012) masks the important question of how they seek to express their wealth status in cultural terms, and what signs of "cultural capital" they seek out and why.

Certainly, as a group they are responsible for huge purchase of worldwide "luxury goods" such as designer clothes, bags and cars. A 2012 survey suggested, for instance, that 44% of all luxury goods sold in Britain are bought by Chinese visitors.[64] Perhaps this explains the *Goldfish* man's ambiguous and rueful smile, avoiding eye contact with the viewer. It is the smile of the artist who recognizes that, whatever high-minded principles might motivate his work, when it reaches the market it, too, must meet the requirements of this niche luxury goods territory. And the smile indicates that the creative artist's supposed singularity and unrepeatability is finally another advertising and branding gambit, as internally contradictory as the idea of the Citroen "Picasso" signature range of mass-produced cars.[65]

Sotheby's business is also an industrial concern, setting aside the rhetoric of its luxury art and antique sector interests. It has a global workforce of about 1500 staff, two-thirds based in New York and London. It sells shares in itself on the New York stock exchange, under the symbol "BID," and April 2017 had a market capitalization of US$2.4 billion. In Great Britain, Christie's, Sotheby's, Bonhams and the Fine Art Auction Group were the four biggest auction companies in 2010, while leading world dealers and dealing galleries include New York and London-based Anthony D'Offay, Richard Green, Pace-Wildenstein, White Cube and Gagosian—the so-called "powerhouse" companies.[66]

But while there will continue to be a rise in the number of mainland China-based buyers, the arts infrastructure there, as noted earlier, started out and remains comparatively weak. Because of this, the intervention of Western companies, expertise and resources was required in order to enable the internationalization and "marketization" of Chinese art to occur in the first place. However, it may be the case by 2020 that effective Western dominance of the Chinese art market could stifle and restrict the further emergence of autonomous private organizations on the mainland. The behavior of the Chinese Communist Party's national and regional government, its legitimacy in China, and changing sensitivities to the power of Western economic and sociocultural interests acting in or on Chinese territory, will also have important effects. The global art world system as a whole, then, and global Asia's sector of it, is always bordering on precariousness—as are globalization processes as a whole.

Globalization, however, as well as comprising a set of interconnected economic and social relations and institutions, is also a set of discursive claims, some amounting to a kind of intellectual "system." It is a conceptual construct and set of working hypotheses concerning how human activities across cities, countries, regions and continents have become "mutually coexistent." Ideas of "the contemporary" and "the contemporary in art" are now closely tied to this question of how people's lives, activities, meanings, products, societies and beliefs have acquired this globalized status: the appearance of what might be called timely "mutual coexistence" and "mutual coexistence" in time. These are certainly ideas fraught with analytic complexities.[67] But this mutual coexistence (which may be both socially beneficial and catastrophic, as worldwide infections such as the 2015–2016 Zika virus contagion suggest) in the case of the global art world system is still fundamentally a question of the asymmetries that condition the exercise of power and resources held by those individuals, groups and organizations located differentially in the power network. The power and resources remain held overwhelmingly by Western art world interests, although they must to some degree be prepared to share some of that power and wealth in order to extend and develop markets, in China, India and elsewhere, for contemporary art.[68]

The idea of "contemporary," did not, of course, come into existence only in the last two decades when theories of globalization became popularized and thought to be essential to an understanding of the changed nature of the world. The contrast between "modern" and "contemporary" had become significant in much earlier accounts of the history of twentieth-century art. By the early 1950s a difference, and then a partial antagonism began to emerge between modern and contemporary art and culture. "Modern" became increasingly associated with a tradition in art traceable back to the mid nineteenth century—to a set of canonical paintings and critical ideas—that had come to seem either "dated" (even clearly "out of date") or that had actually ended, as part of a concluded past.[69]

This much bigger question of "the modern" bears directly and very importantly on the world, and on the global art world, that emerged after the end of the Second World War in 1945. The end of that war unleashed a surge of "decolonization" in the still Western-controlled or dominated societies across the globe—a process that occurred in both relatively peaceful and very violent ways, especially in Asia. The creation of the nation-states India and the People's Republic of China in the first few years after the end of the Second World War instance this global transformation.[70] But this process occurred at the same time that the United States and NATO on one hand, and the Soviet Union and the Warsaw Pact countries on the other, attempted to create the totality of a single world system based on two Cold War camps. China's anti-colonial revolution, its social development and recurrent disasters and crises under Mao and the Communist Party was also conditioned by that world system's power network as it extended across the Pacific and Indian oceans, as well as by the PRC's complex and mutating relationship with the Soviet Union and Soviet Communism.

The heralding of its "Open Door" policy began when Mao famously met President Nixon in 1974—an entente designed to create a powerful ally, or potential ally, for China and the United States against the Soviet Union. Since then, China's political and economic relations with the Western powers have been under permanent redefinition and reconfiguration, and their future form remains hard to anticipate.[71] The PRC's internal political and legal structures, still permanently managed by the Communist Party attempting to dominate the global capitalist forces it has unleashed and welcomed, remain a key source of potential destabilization. In relation to the growth of the indigenous art market in particular, discussed in Chapter 1, China suffers from a highly complex tax structure restricting the export of artworks—even to Hong Kong.[72] This structure works to undermine the confidence and ability of Western companies wishing and trying to do business in China. The ambivalence of the Chinese government authorities on the question of the meaning and value of contemporary Chinese art—its place in China, for the Chinese people, and in the world—is mirrored arguably by the ambivalence Chinese artists and critics themselves feel about the meaning of their own labors and products in a global context.

Weiwei's sculpture/installation *Fountain of Light*, exhibited in the dock at Tate Liverpool, England, in 2007 as part of its exhibition "The Real Thing: Contemporary Art from China," reconstructed one of the great utopian modern monuments of the early twentieth century.[73] This was Vladimir Tatlin's 1919 "Model for a Monument to the Third International," planned to be a colossal combined sculpture and building that was to house and symbolize the institutions fighting for global communism based in Russia, the center of world revolution in 1917. A 7-meter chandelier of light, Weiwei's work was a kind of late "political pop" item from China—a satire, a joke, even a celebration, perhaps, of a revolutionary and egalitarian spirit that was supposed to have also infused the peasants' uprising in China.

This work might itself be read as a fetish, or as a critique of a fetish, of revolutionary art in our deeply counter-revolutionary times. Its "pop" credentials might be underlined in its own evident, ambiguous processing of an image. Tatlin's model was lost in the 1920s and survives only in reproduced grainy black and white photographs. But Weiwei's *Fountain of Light* was itself rendered into image. By placing the sculpture at some distance on the water, meters from the quay and away from close contact or touch, this tangible object lost most of its three-dimensionality and was experienced by viewers in Liverpool as an ethereal sign or beacon, a shining on of a light that represents a socialist transformation unaccomplished in Russia and China.

Fountain of Light might be interpreted to offer a sardonic critique of the lack of freedoms in China that are assumed to be normal in the West, for artists, and everyone else, under capitalist-democratic systems. But Chinese "political pop" crudely but clearly indicates that what were thought of or claimed to be irreconcilable systems can and have, in fact, often been reconciled and normalized everywhere: neoliberal global capitalism equals consumerism shackled to an eroding or absent democratic accountability. The globalized art world, and the place within it for global Asian countries and artists, encapsulates these reconciled if permanently unstable combinations, but perhaps also represents aspects of the likely future for all of us, everywhere or not at all.

The next and final chapter considers the status of contemporary art on global Asia's far western periphery, in the Palestinian Authority or State of Palestine. Could anything reasonably describable as an art world system exist here, given the extremities of the societal and political antagonisms active in this territory since the State of Israel came into existence, along with China and India, in the late 1940s? Or might the specific crises in Palestine–Israel relations, often fought out across the myriad borders that divide and connect their peoples, actually reveal some of the deepest structural characteristics of the global world order/disorder?

Notes

1 *Academy of Arts and Design, Tsinghua University*: 2 (information brochure, no publication details provided but c. 2011). On the impact of the Cultural Revolution on visual arts and culture in China, see Jiang Jiehong, *Red: The Chinese Cultural Revolution* (Jonathan Cape: London, 2010). For CAFA's range of research and teaching, see web site details at http://www.cafa.edu.cn/aboutcafa/lan/?c=1101.
2 *Academy of Arts and Design, Tsinghua University*: 2–4.
3 For discussion of the PRC "Project 211" and "Project 985"initiatives, see "Developing First-Rate Universities and Key Academic Fields," in Zhou Ji, *Higher Education in China* (Thomson: Singapore, 2006): 35–43.The transformation in the nature and purpose of universities within globalization is the focus of the analysis in Peter Jarvis, *Universities and Corporate Universities: The Higher Learning Industry in Global Society* (Kogan Page: London, 2001).
4 For a valuable overview of the historic changes in China since the death of Mao, and the effects on and limits to the privatization of the country's economy under the CCP, see Wang Chaohua, "The Party and its Success Story," *New Left Review*: 91, Jan–Feb 2015: 5–37. On the detail of China's economic development within the global economy, see "The Integration of China," in Leo Panitch and Sam Gindin, *The Making of Global Capitalism: The Political Economy of American Empire* (Verso, London: 2012): 292–300. For discussion of the PRC's interests outside the West, see, e.g., Howard French *China's Second Continent: How a Million Migrants are Building a New Empire in Africa* (Knopf: New York, 2015).
5 *Academy of Arts and Design, Tsinghua University*: 19.
6 Jingyang Lin, *Brands Research and Development Institute* (Dalian Polytechnic Institute, School of Art and Design: no date): 1. The PRC's government identifies what it calls a "socialist market economy" in China; about 50% of national economic activity remains state-controlled. If perhaps 40–50% of the PRC's economy is now privately owned—though accounting procedures remain highly unreliable—the state remains firmly in "command," wishing to direct the

growth and character of the social order of China as a whole. See, e.g., "The Rise of State Capitalism," *The Economist*, January 21, 2012: http://www.economist.com/node/21543160 (accessed March 28, 2017).

7 Jingyang Lin, *Brands Research and Development Institute*: 1 and 4.

8 Jingyang Lin, *Brands Research and Development Institute:* 5, 7 and 8. For an illustration of the rise of "service design" discourse, see Tim Brown, *Change by Design: How Design Thinking Challenges Organizations and Inspires Innovation* (Harper Business: London, 2009).

9 For sharply contrasting views on this mode, see Grant Kester, *The One and the Many: Contemporary Collaborative Art in a Global Context* (Duke University Press: Durham, NC, 2011) and Claire Bishop, *Artificial Hells: Participatory Art and the Politics of Spectatorship* (Verso: London, 2012).

10 See *2011: Collection of Graduate Works* (Academy of Arts and Design, Tsinghua University, 2011), Textile and Fashion design: 21, 22, 27, 28, 30, 32, 34. See also David Crystal, *English as a Global Language* (Cambridge University Press: Cambridge, 2012).

11 See, e.g., John Cross and Richard Hitchcock, "Chinese Students" (Or Students from China's) Views of UK H.E.: Differences, Difficulties and Benefits, and Suggestions for Facilitating Transition," *The East Asian Learner*, 3 (2), November 2007: 1–31.

12 See, e.g., "Translation," edited transcript of a discussion between Shigemi Inaga, Bhaskar Mukhopadhyay, Pedro Erber, James Elkins, Shelly Errington, Thomas Dacosta Kaufmann, Michael Holly, Keith Moxey, Michele Greet and Harry Harootunian, in James Elkins, Zhivka Valiavisharska and Alice Kim (eds.), *Art and Globalization* (Pennsylvania State University Press: University Park, 2010): 22–35.

13 See Part 1, "Internationalisation and reform of China's higher education: Structures and policies," in Janette Ryan (ed.) *China's Higher Education Reform and Internationalisation* (Routledge: Abingdon, 2011): 7–63.

14 See Phiona Stanley, "The Hidden Curriculum: A Critical Analysis of Tertiary English Teaching in China," in Janette Ryan (ed.), *China's Higher Education Reform and Internationalisation*: 193–210.

15 For a set of documents mapping this ideological shift in contemporary Chinese art in the 1980s, see Wu Hung "From Collectivity to Individual Creativity: 1987–89," in Wu Hung (ed.), *Contemporary Chinese Art: Primary Documents* (Museum of Modern Art: New York, 2010): 99–152.

16 See "Capitalism and Communism as (Failed) Utopian Totalities," and "Spectacular Cold War Communisms and Capitalisms," in Jonathan Harris, *The Utopian Globalists: Artists of Worldwide Revolution, 1919–2009* (Wiley-Blackwell: Oxford, 2013): 16–22 and 35–43.

17 Serge Guilbaut, *How New York Stole the Idea of Modern Art: Abstract Expressionism, Freedom and the Cold War* (University of Chicago Press: Chicago, 1983). The consequent literature on this topic is vast, but Guilbaut's

study—which built on insights in several essays published in the 1970s—remains the fullest historical account. See also Francis Frascina (ed.), *Pollock and After: The Critical Debate* (Harper and Row: London, 1985).

18 "Chinese Students' (Or Students from China's) Views of UK H.E.": 9. Accounts of the rise, character and future of capitalism in the PRC vary as much as their authors' perspectives, but see, e.g., Linda Yueh, *China's Growth: The Making of an Economic Superpower* (Oxford University Press: Oxford, 2013); Stephen Bell and Hui Feng, *The Rise of the People's Bank of China: The Politics of Institutional Change* (Harvard University Press: Cambridge MA, 2013); You-tien Hsing, *The Great Urban Transformation: Politics of Land and Prosperity in China* (Oxford University Press: Oxford, 2016); and Daniel Buck, *Constructing China's Capitalism: Shanghai and the Nexus of Urban–Rural Industries* (Macmillan: London, 2012).

19 On the rise of Western individualism in cultural history, see "Individuals and Societies," in Raymond Williams, *The Long Revolution* (Parthian: Cardigan, 2011(1961)): 95–126.

20 See, e.g., Lisa Tickner, *Hornsey 1968: The Art School Revolution* (Frances Lincoln: London, 2008).

21 See Peter Jarvis, "Globalization and its Implications," in *Universities and Corporate Universities*: 20–36.

22 For an early discussion of some of the implications of this, see Hou Hanru, "Entropy, Chinese Artists, Western Art Institutions: A New Internationalism," (1994), in Wu Hung (ed.), *Contemporary Chinese Art: Primary Documents* (249–251).

23 Jingyang Lin, *Brands Research and Development Institute*: 11.

24 Jingyang Lin, *Brands Research and Development Institute*: 12–14.

25 See, e.g., Huang Du, "The Implosion of Urbanization in China," in *China Contemporary: Architecture, Art, Visual Culture* (exhibition catalogue, Netherlands Museum/NAi Uitgevers: Rotterdam: 2006), and "Art in Negotiations," in Zhang Zikang and Huang Du (eds.), *Negotiations: The Second Today's Documents 2010* (Culture and Art Publishing House/Today Art Museum: Beijing, 2010): 16–35.

26 Huang Du, "Status of Chinese Contemporary Art: The Transformation in Concept and Language" (transcript of talk given at "Asian Maps" seminar at ARCO Art Fair, Madrid, 2013): np.

27 Huang Du, "Status of Chinese Contemporary Art": np. On Chinese Communist Mao-era epic propaganda painting, see Chen Lusheng, *Revolutionary Art since the Yan'an Era: Extended Edition* (Long Museum: Shanghai, 2014).

28 Huang Du, "Status of Chinese Contemporary Art": np. There is no space to include discussion here of the other artists Huang Du associates with each of these themes, and a fifth, which he calls "new generation painting," with which he identifies the artists Yuan Yuan and Chen Wei.

29 See my critical anatomy of the global art world system in Jonathan Harris (ed.), *Globalization and Contemporary Art* (Wiley-Blackwell, Oxford: 2011).

30 See, e.g., Sections I, II and III in Zoya Kocur and Simon Leung (eds.), *Theory in Contemporary Art since 1985* (Blackwell: Oxford: 2005).

31 See, e.g., Part I in Iain Robertson and Derrick Chong (eds.), *The Art Business* (Routledge: Abingdon, 2008) and, specifically, "Investing in Art: Art as an Asset Class," Jeremy Eckstein, *The Art Business* (Routledge: London, 2008, 69–81).

32 See Iain Robertson, "The Art Market in Transition, the Global Economic Crisis and the Rise of Asia," in Harris (ed.), *Globalization and Contemporary Art*: 449–463 (453).

33 "There is every indication that in the future buying will be dominated by state-backed cultural funds, part of the sovereign wealth management funds [especially] from East Asia and the Middle East, when the many new museums and cultural zones are opened." Robertson, "The Art Market in Transition": 451.

34 See Michael Silverstein and Neil Fiske, *Trading Up: The New American Luxury* (Boston Consulting Group: Boston, 2004).

35 Iain Robertson, Victoria L. Tseng and Sonal Singh, "'Chindia' as Art Market Opportunity," in Robertson and Chong (eds.), *The Art Business*: 82–96 (83).

36 Iain Robertson et al., "'Chindia' as Art Market Opportunity": 83.

37 See Michael Hue Williams, "The Auction Houses are Distorting Our Understanding of Chinese Art," *The Art Newspaper* (January 25, 2008): 24.

38 Iain Robertson et al., "'Chindia' as Art Market Opportunity": 83.

39 For a sophisticated empirical critique of this notion of "traditional," see John Clark, *Modern Asian Art* (University of Hawai'i Press: Honolulu, 1998).

40 On this issue, see James Elkins, "Afterword," in Elkins, Zhivka Valiavicharska and Alice Kim (eds.), *Art and Globalization* (Pennsylvania State University Press: University Park, 2011): 251–283 (267–269) and the essays that Elkins discusses here, published in the same volume.

41 On philosophical and pictorial problems of notions such as "similarity," "affinity" and "analogy," see the useful range of essays included in Charles Harrison and Fred Orton (eds.), *Modernism, Criticism, Realism: Alternative Contexts for Art* (Harper and Row: London, 1984).

42 See, e.g., Wu Guanzhong, "Formalist Aesthetics in Painting" (1979), reprinted in Wu Hung (ed.), *Contemporary Chinese Art: Primary Documents*: 14–17, and Gao Minglu, "The '85 Art Movement" (1986), *Contemporary Chinese Art: Primary Documents*: 52–63.

43 See, e.g., Ming Tiampo, "Cultural Mercantilism: Modernism's Means of Production: The Gutai Group as Case Study" (212–224), and

Reiko Tomii, "The Discourse of (L)imitation: A Case Study with Hole-Digging in 1960s Japan" (344–356), both in Harris (ed.), *Globalization and Contemporary Art*.

44 Iain Robertson et al., "'Chindia' as Art Market Opportunity": 83.

45 See my account of this art-historical and critical–philosophical lineage in Jonathan Harris, *Writing Back to Modern Art: After Greenberg, Fried and Clark* (Routledge: Abingdon, 2005).

46 See, in particular, "Pure Formality: 1960s Abstract Painting," in Harris, *Writing Back to Modern Art*: 63–90.

47 See "Chronicle 1976–2006," in Wu Hung, *Contemporary Chinese Art: Primary Documents*: 408–436.

48 The *Alors, la Chine?* exhibition opened at the Centre Georges Pompidou in June 2003.

49 Iain Robertsonet al., "'Chindia' as Art Market Opportunity": 83–86.

50 See, e.g., Huang Rui (ed.), *Beijing 798: Reflections on Art, Architecture, and Society in China* (*Timezone* 8, Hong Kong, 2004/Thinking Hands: Beijing, 2004).

51 See, e.g., Li Xianting, "Confessions of a *China/Avant Garde* Curator" (1989), reprinted in Wu Hung, *Contemporary Chinese Art: Primary Documents*: 116–120. The exhibition of 1980s "new wave" performance art, *China/Avant Garde*, took place in Beijing in 1989 following years of difficulties with National Art Gallery authorities over its planned contents.

52 See, e.g., Hans Ulrich Obrist, *Ai Wei Wei Speaks* (Penguin: London, 2011): 48–50.

53 See https://artreview.com/power_100/2011//(accessed April 6, 2017).

54 See, e.g, Robert Terrill, *The New Chinese Empire and What it Means for the United States* (Basic Books, New York, 2003) and, from a very different perspective, Leo Panitch and Sam Gindin, *The Making of Global Capitalism*.

55 The concept of "authoritarian populism" was developed by Stuart Hall in the 1980s in his work on the nature of then emergent British neoliberalism; see *The Hard Road to Renewal: Thatcherism and the Crisis of the Left* (Verso, London: 1988). Neoliberalism under Thatcher was, that is, economically liberal (evangelizing "free trade"/privatization) but socially and politically reactionary—though in fact this may have been neoliberalism's default form globally in that decade.

56 See, e.g., Paul Preston, *The Spanish Holocaust: Inquisition and Extermination in Twentieth-Century Spain* (Harper Press: London, 2012).

57 Iain Robertson et al., "'Chindia" as Art Market Opportunity," in Robertson and Chong (eds.), *The Art Business*: 86.

58 See, e.g., Li Xianting, "Apathy and Deconstruction in Post '89 Art: Analysing the Trends of 'Cynical Realism' and 'Political Pop'" (1992), reprinted in Wu Hung, *Contemporary Chinese Art: Primary Documents*: 157–166.

59 See Robert Hughes, "The Rise of Andy Warhol," *The New York Review of Books*, February 18, 1982, reprinted in Brian Wallis (ed.), *Art after Representation: Rethinking Representation* (New Museum of Contemporary Art: New York, 1988): 45–58.

60 See, e.g., Francis Frascina (ed.), *Pollock and After: The Critical Debate* (Harper and Row: London, 1985).

61 Iain Robertson et al., "'Chindia' as Art Market Opportunity" 86.

62 Iain Robertson et al., ""Chindia" as art market opportunity": 86–90, and Robertson "The Art Market in Transition, the Global Economic Crisis and the Rise of Asia": 457–462.

63 Iain Robertson et al., ""Chindia" as art market opportunity"~: 86.

64 See Yuval Atsmon, et al., *Luxury Without Borders: China's New Class of Shoppers Take on the World* (Mckinzie Consumer and Shopper Insights, 2012): 83.

65 See also, on art and its relations to the conditions and relations of industrial production, Robert Morris, "Notes on Art as/and Land Reclamation," *October* 12, Spring 1980: 97–102.

66 Robertson and Chong, "Introduction to Studies in Art Business," in *The Art Business*: 6–7, and see Derrick Chong, "The Emergence of Powerhouse Dealers in Contemporary Art," in Harris (ed.), *Globalization and Contemporary Art*: 431–448.

67 See, e.g., Terry Smith, *What is Contemporary Art?* (University of Chicago Press: Chicago, 2009), *Contemporary Art: World Currents* (Laurence King: London, 2011), Daniel Birnbaum, et al., *Defining Contemporary Art: 25 Years in 200 Pivotal Artworks* (Phaidon: London, 2011), Marsha Meskimmon, *Contemporary Art and the Cosmopolitan Imagination* (Routledge: London, 2010) and Peter Osborne *Anywhere or Not At All: Philosophy of Contemporary Art* (Verso: London, 2013).

68 The term "market" has become an abstracted, ideologically highly partial representation of social activities and relationships—a very loaded way of perceiving the order and purpose of human relations and interests. The claim, for instance, that health or education provision is essentially a matter of "markets" indicates this clearly. But what if anything is truly outside of "the market," once the full range of factors influencing or conditioning "buyers" and "sellers" is truly taken into account? "Market" has thus become the preferred name—a reductive, partial abstraction generated within neoliberal discourse—for what used to be called "society" or "social formation," holistic and imaginative terms drawn from Enlightenment sociology and social theory. See Jonathan Harris, *The Myth of the Art Market* (IB Tauris: London, forthcoming).

69 For an early register of this distinction, see Harold Rosenberg, *The Tradition of the New* (New York: Horizon Press, 1959) and, for a theoretical discussion of the contrast, Raymond Williams, "When Was Modernism?" in Williams, *The Politics of Modernism: Against the New Conformists* (Verso: London, 1989): 31–35.

70 See, e.g., David Smith, *The Dragon and the Elephant: China, India and the New World Order* (Profile Books: London, 2008).

71 See, e.g., Ted Fischman, *China Inc.: How the Rise of the Next Superpower Challenges America and the World* (Scribners: New York, 2005).

72 Iain Robertson et al., "'Chindia' as Art Market Opportunity": 87

73 Christoph Grunenberg, *The Real Thing: Contemporary Art from China* (Tate Publishing: London, 2007), exhibition catalogue.

5

Contemporary Art and Post-National Identities in the State of Palestine

We fly into Ben Gurion airport, a few miles east of the suburbs of Tel Aviv, on the same day that the pope arrives in Bethlehem from Jordan, the first time a pope hasn't entered the West Bank from the State of Israel. The Jerusalem Post article I've just been reading insinuates that the pope had been effectively hijacked by Palestinian Authority officials and made to "pay an unscheduled visit to the security barrier just outside Bethlehem"– the matter of propriety is a pervasive and corrosive preoccupation here. Travelling with a Palestinian who also has Israeli and British citizenship can be disorienting. Bashir Makhoul, an artist who relocated to England in 1989, never really gets to arrive "home" wherever he lands up. We fiddle with the seat belts and I think ahead to our talks about contemporary Palestinian video art in Jerusalem and Ramallah. "Welcome to Israel" the air stewardess pontificates over the intercom, as if it was her country. But the real Pope, praying at the "security barrier," has just blessed what he called the "State of Palestine." No place like home?

"Palestine is Open for Business"![1]

The Palestinian Authority was constituted following the signing of the Oslo Peace Accords of 1993 and 1995 by representatives of the State of Israel and the PLO (Palestine Liberation Organization), in a deal brokered by the United States and the then Russian Federation. While it was generally assumed to be agreed that the objective of these accords was to enable "self-determination" of the Palestinian people, senior Israeli politicians did not believe, and said so at the time, that this would or should require the creation of a Palestinian state. Out of these accords, however, did develop a process of attempted "normalization" of relations between Palestinians, their official representatives and the State of Israel. For "normalization" understand absorption of Palestinians—their fragmented economies, lands and resources—into the neoliberal global

The Global Contemporary Art World, First Edition. Jonathan Harris.
© 2017 John Wiley & Sons, Inc. Published 2017 by John Wiley & Sons, Inc.

capitalist world order/disorder (the world's "normal" now, as my earlier chapters have shown). The global contemporary art world in Palestine could only emerge, if at all, as a creature intelligible within this broader system as it took root in the local conditions.[2]

This process was and is facilitated primarily via three determining conduits: (1) Israel's political–economic security state; (2) international aid provided mostly through "non-government organizations" (NGOs); and (3) resources of the *shatat*, the diaspora of Palestinians, along with others, who've wished to invest in the "era of peace" putatively ushered in by the Oslo agreements. In November 2012 the United Nations organization officially recognized the PA as a non-voting "observer member" state of the UN General Assembly. By September 2015, 136 of the 193 member states of the United Nations had recognized the existence of an entity called the State of Palestine. I shall use this name when referring to events after November 2012. Pope Francis incurred the annoyance of the Israeli government because he recognized this new status, explicitly using the term "State of Palestine" in his visit in the summer of 2014.[3]

NGOs and the dissemination of aid for which they are responsible worldwide now constitute a variant of the globalizing development business. At the same time, most of these agencies, which are US- or Europe-based and get their funding from governments and private charitable sources, provide a means through which the donor states and private donor organizations are able to pursue their political interests overseas. The "aid" and "development" help offered is a mixture of money, material resources and training for local people in establishing and running public services and commercial activities.[4] The United States, for instance, has given US$400m in aid to the PA/State of Palestine since the death of Yasser Arafat, Leader of the PLO, in 2004. Total external financial support to the PA/State of Palestine since 1994 has been in the order of US$18 billion.

In 2006 the PA was ranked the 11th "most aided" territory in the world, with over 60% of the money it received going to security, health and education areas. More than 130 NGOs work in the State of Palestine on "civil development" areas, including some specifically dedicated to the inculcation of democracy, culture and the arts. Khalil Nakhleh, a Palestinian commentator who previously ran an NGO, has observed that since the end of the Second Intifada—the Palestinian popular uprising against Israeli occupation in 1999–2001—an "almost total dependency on external (primarily Western) sources of aid" has come about. Nakhleh describes the Palestinian aid regime as a form of "cultural re-engineering of a new crop of depoliticized and managerial NGOs." These work closely, he notes, with their counterparts in the new private commercial sectors hatched since the Oslo agreements were signed.[5]

The Israeli company "Better Place Israel," for instance, was engaged in 2011 by the PA to provide electric cars for the territory. Its investors include US-based multinational financial services corporation Morgan Stanley and the former World Bank president James Wolfensohn. Its CEO is the former Israel Defense Forces (IDF) commander Moshe Kaplinksi, who was in charge of repulsing the Second Intifada and oversaw the Israel Defense Force's re-invasion of the West Bank. The Portland Trust, another private sector corporate developer active in Israel and the State of Palestine includes as one of its executives Lord Freud—a former vice-chairman of the Swiss UBS Investment Banking organization, one of the main sponsors, as I discussed in Chapter 1, of Art Basel's fairs and now also a provider of mortgage loans for Palestinians.[6]

Aid supplied by Western nation-states through NGOs essentially constitutes a form of reward handed out in the State of Palestine to those who are deemed to continue to acquiesce to the terms of the Oslo peace agreement. Conversely, aid has been withdrawn—for instance, from school-building and other projects in Gaza—as soon as armed resistance recurs, or when, for example, the US government designates certain organizations in receipt of aid, directly or indirectly, to be "terrorist" in nature.[7] In one sense, civil society in the State of Palestine is this network of activities and social relations that the NGOs have largely created and maintain. The system has produced a hybrid class system, with distinct political and bureaucratic layers overseen by the State of Palestine's "Development Center." This is formally known as The Palestinian Coalition for Integrity and Accountability, or AMAN (which is itself an NGO).

In another sense, the NGO system has effectively supplanted the Palestinian organized mass movement against the illegal Israeli occupation of Palestinian territory, as set out in UN resolutions 242 and 338 (following the regional wars in 1967 and 1973). There are now 170 000 people working for NGOs in the State of Palestine and their salaries go to support 1.5 million dependents out of a population of 4.5 million. These jobs do not belong to a substantive productive local economy; according to Nakhleh they could actually be seen as a kind of "hidden unemployment." Though many of the NGOs do conduct important work on issues to do with human rights and the empowerment of women, jobs and activities in others are allocated, Nakhleh claims, on the basis of factional loyalties tied to the Fatah government administration. The gross domestic product of NGO aid is largely what he calls a "non-productive industry" of conferences, workshops, seminars and forums that proliferate towards the end of each fiscal year by which the annual budgets have to be spent.[8]

Through the NGO system the State of Palestine has been allowed to become part of the global corporate capitalist political economy. As such, this system has become the substitute for any genuine liberation that the Oslo agreement might have been thought to promise the Palestinians—although its critics were numerous, fierce, articulate and comprehensive long before the deal was signed.[9] From their perspective, the PA/State of Palestine has done nothing more than conform as well as it can—given the chronic history of violence and occupation in the region—to the development of global capitalism everywhere since the early 1990s. This has involved, as previous chapters have noted, a combination of targeted state interventions, the privatization of public assets and extension of "free markets."

Both complementing and contrasting with the NGO system in the State of Palestine has been the emergence of a "public sector" economy, especially in and around the commercial center of Ramallah. This "public sector" consists of state monopolies in, for example, telecoms, electricity, cement, petroleum, cigarettes and flour. Although these industries and services appear to be run by the Fatah government they are basically state holdings in commercial companies that distribute goods overwhelmingly made in Israel. The State of Palestine has also been opened up to regional and global corporate penetration. This is based on open and sometimes disguised Israeli and *shatat* capital investment. It has led to the eruption of the same kinds of private debt-based consumerism that fueled the US and European banks' collapse in 2008. Conversely, there has been virtually no development of an indigenous agricultural sector or strong local industry for the Palestinians.[10]

The PA's economy since 1995 has come to constitute a part of what the historian Carroll Quigley in 1968 called the world capitalist system. This was built by the dominant Western nation-states and its key transnational financial institutions, such as the Bank of International Settlements, originally formed in 1919 and based in Basel (the home of Art Basel since 1970). This entity was, and remains, as Quigley characterized it then:

> a world system of financial control in private hands able to dominate the political system of each country and the economy of the world as a whole [with] central banks acting in concert by secret agreements arrived at in frequent private meetings and conferences. The apex of the system was [...] the Bank of International Settlements [...] a private bank owned and controlled by the world's central banks which were themselves private corporations.

The Palestinian capitalist class, as Nakhleh terms it, operates through a network linking Egypt, often-blitzed Gaza and Israel itself. The Arab Bank, run from Jordan, is the other main player channeling and controlling the *shatat* stake in the State of Palestine.[11]

Grounding the Culture Industry in Palestine

Remember the qualifying plurals I inserted at the beginning of this chapter: Palestine's lands and economies. These are necessary because the geospatial and sociopolitical reality on the ground is that the Palestinian territories are chronically fragmented across the complex and interwoven "Security Areas" designated A, B, and C created as part of the Oslo agreement. These areas have dictated which military, police and civil forces control territory, resources and development of all kinds inside Israel "proper," the PA/State of Palestine, and the West Bank zone. The latter includes Jerusalem, Israel's self-declared "eternal" capital, occupied illegally, according to UN resolutions, since the war in 1967. Gaza, meanwhile, is a wholly geographically non-contiguous Palestinian territory—run by Fatah's rival, Hamas, until 2014 when the two organizations entered into what was termed a "unity government."

Israel withdrew all its citizens from Gaza in 2005 but the territory's borders, communications, and in/outflow of resources remain controlled entirely by Israel, except for secret tunnels dug under Gaza's southern border with Egypt, a country which has signed numerous security and other agreements with Israel over several decades.[12] The Oslo agreement naming conventions and security responsibility allocations loosely disguise the basic reality that the State of Palestine, despite the latter's self-declarations of autonomy, remains a "dependent state" tied to Israel for virtually all basic amenities and services, including access to water and energy, TV, radio and phone communications signals, airspace, all border controls and its currency. Even most of its tax revenues are collected directly by Israel from the Palestinians who live and work in State of Palestine territories.[13]

Attempts at societal "normalization," despite and yet dependent on these conditions, have enabled the erection of a façade of Palestine's entry into the neoliberal global world order/disorder. Quite literally, in that this is what, for example, the Grand Park Hotel in Ramallah—with its counterpart in Bethlehem, proclaiming that it is "proud to be the first Palestinian hotel chain"—really stands for. From the open-air restaurant and swimming pool area high above Ramallah's burgeoning skyline of office buildings and apartment blocks, there is a very good view of the extent of the Israeli "security fence." This is what the Israelis call what is in fact a towering concrete wall that has been erected on the Palestinian side of the border, annexing massive areas of land for reasons of "security" that always favor Israeli settlements, businesses and communications. Nine kilometers to the north of Ramallah is the site for the proposed new town of Al-Rawabi, a risky corporate investment development plan entirely dependent on Israeli permission to build an artery road between it and Ramallah, over "Area C" land which the State of Israel controls.[14]

The Grand Park Hotel is part-owned by a government company of the State of Palestine. It recommends itself as a "5 star" luxury venue to its clients, many of whom are Arab and Gulf states businessmen doing deals in Ramallah. The hotel is another link in the apparently secure chain of high-quality hotels now stretching across greater, globalized Asia. *Layalina Palestine*, a glossy magazine provided free in all the rooms at the hotel, visualizes the aspirations and character of the "5 star occupation" that the State of Palestine is able to offer its wealthier citizens, investors and visitors.[15] *Layalina Palestine* is intensely Westernized and secular—full of sexy Arab women dressed in couture, with big hair, big nails, cosmetics and bling. The adverts and info-ads exemplify the commodification and spectacle that the neoliberal image-economy promises and which this State of Palestine attempts to emulate.

Layalina Palestine has adverts for Hublot watches and "Big Bang Ferrari," but also for the "Palestine Motors Co Ltd.," offering a "New Space Star Economic but Quality Compact." This might be read as a kind of unintended satire on the Oslo agreement that left the PA with little actual land but a lot of hot air above it (only 2.7 % of the total land mass was given over to sole PA control). Almost every page features Palestinians represented as carefree consumers, enjoying their new wealth and freedoms at weddings, parties and business events. There are ads for whitening cosmetics, Italian food, baby milk powder and breast cancer awareness. Photo-stories feature groups of friends dancing and singing, camping holidays (no refugee camps, but "Refutrees"—a feel-good story about tree planting to improve the urban environment), tourism experiences at the Dead Sea, in Jordan and sepia photos of Old Palestine and old Palestinians. "New Revolution no more frustration—just Wash and Go," says a shampoo advert, and a kind of symmetrical consciousness washing seems to be at work in the pages here too.[16]

Layalina Palestine doesn't omit direct discussion of the political situation entirely. This edition included an essay on the Israeli separation wall along with documentary photographs and reports on a State of Palestine Ministry of Tourism and Antiquities "Universal Peace Day." At this event, as the photographs demonstrate, volunteers wore T-shirts emblazoned with the ambiguous slogan "Palestine Volunteers." But if the magazine washes or bleaches out the historical knowledge and symbols of Palestinian political struggle from contemporary consciousness in favor of spectacular consumerism, body narcissism and a standard neoliberal worship of material affluence—achieved or desired—then the deeper, repressed realities seem to emerge in the language and imagery of spectacle itself. Fantasies of space, power, control, luxury, corruption and potency spout copiously forth in the ads already mentioned. These seem to be lurking and implicit somehow even in the contingent names of the Hollywood films selected for Palestinian movie multiplex consumption: *Planes, Gangster Squad, Jobs.* The first multiplex cinema in Ramallah, the Palestine Tower Cinemas, which opened in 2011, is located at the "Palestine Trade Tower" in Al Ersal Street, part of the city's growing business district.[17]

Across the separation wall, on the eastern side, now "Palestinian side," of Jerusalem in the West Bank, where Israel continues to encourage Jews to settle and to appropriate land, against repeated UN petitions, there is Palestinian Art Court—al Hoash. "Al Hoash" is Arabic for courtyard. This is a visual arts gallery and cultural center dedicated to the history and future development of Palestinian art and society.[18]Formed originally in order to work to provide a museum home which could become the focus for appreciation and study of the Qupty Art Collection of over 250 works by Palestinian artists, Al Hoash has since radically reconceived and expanded its objectives. This has partly occurred through its supportive dialogue with European institutions such as the Herning Art Museum in Denmark and Tate Liverpool in England.

Al Hoash has defined its mission as seeking to explore the historical and contemporary relationship between Palestinian art and the globe, utilizing its collection, but also organizing talks, symposia, new art commissions and publications in order "to connect to the world."[19] Given the history of British mandate rule in Palestine after 1919, the creation of the State of Israel in 1948, the subsequent *Nahkbah* (the Arabic term for "catastrophe") when about one million Palestinians were displaced and dispossessed by Israeli occupation and settlement, and the continuous wars, invasions and collective violence up to and since the signing of the Oslo Peace Accords in 1993, it might be reasonable to assume that Al Hoash's local conditions and perspective bears little comparison to the work of most of the other art galleries, museums, art fairs and biennials in greater Asia discussed in earlier chapters.

But, to the contrary, the evidence is actually that the history of this part of the "Middle East"—far western global Asia—has significant parallels with the sociopolitical circumstances out of which contemporary art worlds have developed in Hong Kong, South Korea, India and the PRC. In all these states or substate territories, Western imperial regimes had been imposed and were all finally ended through popular struggle against the colonizers. Liberation came about through a mixture of organized armed mass resistance to imperial power by "proto-state" forces, as in, for instance, the PRC and Korea; decolonization process agreements, as in, for example, India (although the history of 1948 Partition with the co-creation of the state of Pakistan (and later Bangladesh, in 1971) was extremely violent); and through "terrorist" insurgency, in, for example, British Mandate Palestine, as various then-illegal Jewish paramilitary organizations sought to destabilize and end British rule. The situation in contemporary Israel/State of Palestine in many ways constitutes a radical continuity in this long history, with some anachronistic novelty lying rather in the persistence of the occupation of one colonized people (the Palestinians) and territory by another (Israeli Jews, including some Jews also colonized alongside the Palestinians under Ottoman and then British mandate rule). The State of Israel continues to refuse to negotiate a final settlement with the Palestinians it has colonized since 1948.

Given the continued military and settler occupations in Israel/State of Palestine territories, in the West Bank and in Gaza, the broad questions Al Hoash has asked about the context, meaning and purpose of historic, modern and contemporary art made by Palestinians are intrinsically and inveterately political. These include what was described in one statement as:

> The question of Public (social) space, what is it? [...] How to act in the public space? Is it a (manifestation of) Power over the space and over the

> groups? A question of representation and memory of landscape? A place for the community? [...] We seek the development and elevation of art in recognition of its role in development, free will and expression of people and also as a constituent and representative of national and cultural identity through innovative approaches.[20]

Al Hoash, in a manner similar to Seoul Museum of Art (discussed in Chapter 2), has had to subject its own character and role to such critical, and self-critical, considerations. What, for example, should be the function of a contemporary visual arts institution that supports the struggle for the achievement of an autonomous Palestinian state within the State of Palestine as it present exists, following the Oslo Accords and the neoliberalization of Palestinian territories under the tutelage of Israel?

Al Hoash's recent answers to this question sound in many ways like the ambitious claims made on behalf of the organizers of Kochi's first biennial. Al Hoash will, one of its position papers explained, undertake a range of activities—curatorial, educational, research, community-centered—that will create what are called "synergies between visual culture, economy and the [Palestinian] society." These activities, defined as "research-based," "critically driven, community linked, educational, collaborative and open to the public" aim "to engage and integrate cultural work with the community as a vector for urban development, economic growth and social enhancement."[21] But Al Hoash's stress on the relationship between Palestinians and the whole world—on, that is, "Palestinian" understood as a now globalized condition and experience—marks a fundamental departure from long-standing Fatah policies based on an assumed PA "nationhood" and "sovereignty" which remains conditional on the Oslo agreements, and therefore on a State of Palestine dependent on Israel for its existence and future development.

Palestinian Museums-of-art-in-waiting

Al Hoash, in fact, asks the radical questions that now face all nation-states and peoples living under the conditions of our globalized world order/disorder—though the specificity of the Palestinian situation adds some extremities of definitional complexity and existential danger. The key questions include the following.

> (1) What does it mean and what is it to be Palestinian, or to want to be Palestinian, if you happen to live in Jerusalem, or Ramallah, or in Gaza, or in Tel Aviv? In each case quite different politico-legal and geospatial relations to the State of Israel exist.

(2) What constitutes "Palestinian culture" or "Palestinian art" in each of these places, if anything, and what might or should? In the latter case, the situation is perhaps the most problematic. This is because within the State of Israel "Palestinian" is not recognized as a legally possible identity—Palestinians living in Israel are dis/identified generically by that state as "Arabs."

(3) How have these questions of identity, origin and meaning been answered historically, while the unending crises of colonial occupations, wars, dispossessions, settlements and intifada have continually reformed and transformed and deformed the lives and lands of Palestinians since 1948?[22]

Michael Hardt and Antonio Negri, influential commentators on the processes and consequences of globalization, believe that the whole world has become newly precarious because of the impact of those forces that have undermined the autonomy, identity and powers of nation-states and their citizens. Nevertheless, for Hardt and Negri, it is only through more globalization that a future possible liberation of all peoples, those they call the "multitudes," may occur, in their final freeing from both the still powerful nation-state system and the global capitalist world order.[23]In particular relation to Palestinian struggles for independence, Hardt and Negri laid down a kind of gauntlet.

"As soon as the nation begins to form as a sovereign state," they claim,

> its progressive functions all but vanish. Jean Genet was enchanted by the revolutionary desire of the Black Panthers and the Palestinians, but he recognized that becoming a sovereign nation would be the end of their revolutionary qualities. "The day when the Palestinians are institutionalized," he said, "I will no longer be at their side. The day the Palestinians become a nation like the other nations, I will no longer be there." With national "liberation" and the construction of the nation state, all of the oppressive functions of modern sovereignty inevitably blossom in full force.[24]

While it's not entirely clear if Hardt and Negri concur completely with Genet here, it is certainly productive to consider the latter's comments in relation to the specific Palestinian form of "institutionalized [...] nation like the other nations" which the Oslo agreements, in the circumstances of global neoliberal capitalism, have produced. Likewise, all the case-studies in this book have raised diverse questions germane to what Genet calls "the oppressive functions of modern sovereignty"—in Hong Kong, South Korea, India and the PRC—which the neoliberalized, NGO-dependent State of Palestine shackled to Israel has now taken on. This is true especially given precisely how "modern sovereignty" has been reconfigured in these disputed territories through the processes of state capitalist-led globalization since the 1990s.

Formed in 2004, Al Hoash initially embodied what appears to have been a conjoined "conservationist" cultural and sociopolitical objective. In art-museological terms, the organization was created in order to secure an appropriate physical home for the Mazen and Yvette Qupty collection of over 200 works (mainly paintings) that constituted what was seen by many as the basis for a Palestinian "national collection" of art. The Qupty collection was described, for instance, in a statement published by Al Hoash entitled *The Palestinian Art Museum Jerusalem* as containing artworks embodying "the human cultural image of a nation with roots engraved in history."[25]This museum-in-waiting was presented as a kind of evidence for the authentic national statehood that the Palestinian people both already embodied in spirit and to which they also aspired in reality.

This incipient State of Palestine aspired to emulate the way that authentic nation-state building, from the nineteenth century onwards, had included Western countries (e.g., Great Britain, Germany, the United States) building and filling national museums of culture and national galleries of art, housed in capital-city based, purpose-built neoclassical structures designed to suggest favorable continuities with their image of Roman and Greek civilizations.[26] Decolonization in the late 1940s had led to the newly emerged nation-states of India and Israel itself (along with several others) moving to create their own versions of such state museums and galleries—precisely in order, their statist cultural elites believed, to entrench and validate their position in the world of formally autonomous nation states that the United Nations organization, itself established in 1945, explicitly sought to recognize and bring together.[27]

In sociopolitical terms, *The Palestinian Art Museum Jerusalem* project was intended to entrench and validate the assumed proto-nation state created by, and as, the PA, following the Oslo agreements. The Al Hoash document goes on to outline key aspects of the intended museum. This building was to be located in Jerusalem (the Palestinian nation's de facto capital, irrespective of Israeli occupation) and would be what was called "the medium through which the Palestinian national cultural memory is preserved and maintained, thus allowing it to take its rightful place within the global and historical narrative of national museums."[28] This definitive statement was followed by another explaining that the museum-in-waiting would serve all Palestinians, including those living in the State of Israel created in 1948, as part of what was called "the creative endeavours of Palestinian artists in the West Bank, Gaza and Jerusalem, as well as Diaspora artists."

This suggests that the deliberately disaggregated areas created by the Oslo accords comprising "Palestine" were nevertheless being ratified by some Palestinians as a kind of normal, or at least "normalized," condition of contemporary Palestinian life. These fragments were not seen, that is, as the chaotic and contingent historical product of all the wars, occupations, resistance, subsequent reprisals and further colonization visited upon Palestinians across the territories that, since 1995, had come to constitute the Security Areas designated A, B and C. An actual Palestinian Museum under construction on land in Birzeit, sixteen miles north of Jerusalem and within Security Area A, built on land controlled wholly by Palestinians, was due to open in May 2016. Statements on the web site explaining the genesis of this institution suggest a critical understanding of the purpose of museums similar to the intellectual perspective of Al Hoash. This Palestinian Museum is funded by the Welfare Association, an amalgam of wealthy *shatat* Palestinian individuals and groups founded in 1983.[29]

But given the "Israelification" of Palestinians living in the State of Israel, the effective sequestration of Gaza by the IDF when its people voted for a Hamas government in 2007, and continued Israeli occupation and extension of settlements in the West Bank, including in east Jerusalem, the material substance of the State of Palestine has melted into air, to paraphrase Marx. With Oslo agreement Area A territories wholly controlled by the PNA constituting only about 3% of the land, Area B territories operated with mixed Israeli/PNA control comprising about 27% and Area C, where Israel operates all civil and security control save that over Palestinians at 70%, it is not surprising that the demographic integrity of the nascent State of Palestine—in political and social, as well as cultural and artistic, terms—comes to seem almost wholly impracticable, if not simply a product of wishful thinking.[30]

Conversely, the global population of Palestinians—that is, all those peoples and their descendants living in the rest of the world outside of Security Areas A, B and C, including all those living or born in Israel proper, as well as in sequestered Gaza—comprises an overwhelming majority, thus vitiating both the idea, and the ideal, of a "State of Palestine" constituting a specific, actual single national place and time of being.[31]Remember, too, that in the State of Israel a law was passed in 2011 preventing any government funding of activities organized to mark the *Nahkbah* (the catastrophe of dispossession of Palestinians during and after the Israel–Palestinian war of 1947-49). The State of Israel, indeed, celebrates what Palestinians call the *Nahkbah* as its triumphant "War of Independence" from British rule. The "Present-Absentee" law passed in 1950 entitles the State of Israel to continue to accumulate the property and assets of Palestinians who remained in the country after 1948.[32]

In one sense Al Hoash's plan in its *Palestinian Art Museum Jerusalem* statement seems to envisage the role of Palestinian artists to be that of imagining and depicting this integral nation-that-does-not-yet-exist and which really could not, given the conditions set by the Oslo agreements that effectively ratified the Israeli occupation and division of the West Bank and Gaza territories. In that "conservatory" sense, then, as the Al Hoash statement notes, "Palestinian artists play an essential role in the preservation of their heritage, culture, and historical past." In Jerusalem, since its occupation in 1967, it notes, "Israel has been implementing a systemized policy against the eastern part of the city and its residents, aiming at eliminating its Palestinian Arab identity." Given these conditions, Palestinian Jerusalem has only been able to develop a poor "under-developed cultural infrastructure" and one under increasing threat as Israel attempts to take over more and more of its land.[33]

So, as Israel expands its settlements into eastern Jerusalem and areas in the West Bank, it might be assumed that the potential for the creation of a material, real, viable State of Palestine continues to contract. Nevertheless, as I've noted, the Welfare Association inaugurated the building of the "Palestinian Museum" in 2013. This institution might be thought to constitute a kind of cultural "Higgs boson particle" of teleological statist historicization—though its financial, political and administrative relationship with the Fatah government is undoubtedly complex. The museum's theoretical, though soon to be actual, existence is intended, that is, to offer a "proof" of the reality and authenticity of the State of Palestine, in the face of all the facts on the ground.[34] (I do not intend to suggest that this museum should not be built or will not be a useful thing to have been built; I am interested here rather in its symbolic significance.)

Al Hoash had become aware of the mutating meanings and purposes of museums under globalized conditions. The organization had sent its staff to study new "mission statements" and experimental practices at the Whitworth Art Gallery in Manchester, at Tate Liverpool and other influential institutions in Europe and elsewhere.[35]Al Hoash noted what it called "the continuous changes in the meaning of the museum and its transformation from a static space into a more interactive space that serves both local and international audiences."[36] In the case of the Palestinian diaspora, this meant that the vast majority of Palestinians themselves were already part of these "international audiences," already effectively part of the global multitudes.

But if the State of Palestine had originally been constituted after the Oslo agreements with financial support from the troika of Israeli state and commercial backers, *shatat* capitalists and external NGOs, then Al Hoash, too, had been offered and accepted funding from a range of partisan international donors. These included the Welfare Association, the United Nations Development Programme of Assistance to the Palestinian People, the EU, some European states and private supporters including Price Water House Coopers, which describes itself as a "multinational professional services network" company.[37] This accountancy and audit global combine, operating in over 150 countries, is the fifth-largest privately owned company in the world and works to support the privatization of state-owned and state-run organizations including industries, hospitals and universities. In 2012 it was fined £1.4m by the British government for falsely reporting that the J. P. Morgan investment bank had complied with rules regarding the protection of its clients' own funds. Five years earlier, before the financial Crash, Price Water House Coopers was criticized by the UK Treasury Select Committee for malpractice in its dealings with the British building society Northern Rock, just before it went bust.[38]

The "NGO-ization" of the Contemporary Art World in the State of Palestine

The State of Palestine's Grand Park Hotel chain is another expression of this neoliberal globalized world, with its promise of seamlessly available "luxury with pride"—providing the "modern standards" and "superior facilities" that the weary world business traveler now expects to find at the end of his or her busy day, be it one that ends in London, Delhi, Beijing, Tel Aviv and now also Bethlehem or Ramallah. The global contemporary art world has a minor but constitutive role in this totality too. It provides the possibility of more luxury in the form of high-quality cultural experiences (via the biennial exhibition and the art fair), a potential means of financial investment for High Net and Ultra-High Net Worth individuals and corporations (via the art market and dealing galleries), or simply an aesthetic means for the suitably cultivated or broad-minded to relax and enjoy some precious recreational time away from their business meetings appreciating contemporary art.

Or, as the Grand Park Hotel brochure puts it, this businessman, when he can, should enjoy his moment of "glory, success, and creativity." And Ramallah, the State of Palestine's burgeoning commercial and government center, now offers what one commentator has called its own highly "localized cosmopolitanism" (also known as "the Ramallah syndrome"). The Grand Park's sister hotel, meanwhile, is located in "downtown Bethlehem"—like Ramallah, in Security Area A, where it is illegal for Israeli citizens to enter, although the Israeli army sometimes operates there in order to arrest suspected militants. The Bethlehem Grand Park provides what the brochure describes as "outstanding service in the spirit of the city of peace [...] where Magis and Kings from the East have followed the star to where Jesus was born." Surely this is the epitome of the State of Palestine's "Five Star Occupation" experience: what Susaina Maira calls the surviving "colonial present" within neoliberal capitalism.[39]

How have other visual arts and cultural organizations operating in this State of Palestine been shaped by the Oslo agreements and their consequences? Sounding disconcertingly like President George W. Bush when he infamously declared that victory had been achieved after the US invasion of Saddam Hussain's Iraq in 2003, the then Palestinian prime minister, Salam Fayyad, announced in Ramallah in 2011 that another "mission had been accomplished." The Palestinians, he declared, had succeeded in creating the conditions necessary for the State of Palestine to exist.[40] It was no coincidence that Fayyad had previously worked for the World Bank and that this State of Palestine would be constructed along global neoliberal principles tailored to the specific conditions of continued occupation by Israel, Oslo agreement security and control protocols, and Palestine's consequent "dependent state" position. Fayyad's state building project derived from the 2008 "Palestinian Reform and Development Plan," an apparent blueprint for "free market" neoliberalism.

But while capital, industrial and commercial developments led by Israeli state and private business sectors along with *shatat* interests began to flow into the PA during the mid-1990s and continued in the new millennium, what might be called the sociopolitical gestation of the Palestinian territories has effectively been managed through "NGO-ization." This is the work done by a veritable "industrial-complex" of international aid and development agencies, linked to key donor states such as the US and Norway, and to organizations of states such as the United Nations and the EU that fund, channel, direct, monitor and review the activities of the Palestinian state apparatuses and other civil society institutions.[41]

NGOs have also been created by, and work for, corporate transnational agencies, such as the World Bank and the Ford Foundation, as well as for Arab/Islamic corporate and transnational agencies, and for UK charities. The Welfare Association operates its own group of limited companies which have been established as monopoly businesses in the PNA, and are effectively run as tax-exempt charities following the American model developed by corporations such as Ford, Rockefeller and the George Soros Open Society Foundations. What might be described as a too-happy symmetry of business and "sociocultural development" interests has characterized the Welfare Association's activities, according to Khalil Nakhleh. For example: given the continued Israeli building of settlements in eastern Jerusalem, the Welfare Association valuably raised US$28m from the Arab Fund, the EU and UNESCO ostensibly in order to purchase land and fund building renovation specifically for Palestinian projects. But it contributed no money itself and instead channeled the sums it had raised into the investment funds of the Welfare Association's own commercial corporate backers.[42]

To take another example, Nakhleh shows that the Welfare Association's 1997–2011 NGO project organized directly with the World Bank—focused on the West Bank, Jerusalem and Gaza—converted what had been radical political objectives centered on land reclamation, opposition to Israeli land confiscation, housing and income generation into depoliticized healthcare, education and legal services provision.[43] The NGO run by the EU's European Commission Technical Assistance Office in Jerusalem funds all EU education in the State of Palestine, part of what Nakhleh calls an "absolute dependence" culture in which the Fatah leadership has entered: an alliance of regional politico-financial interests superintended by the NGO's managerial culture, all "under Israeli occupation and the overall consent of the USA."[44]

Cultural NGOs working in the State of Palestine include the Sharek Youth Forum, based in Ramallah but also active—erratically, given the intermittent high levels of violence—in Gaza, funded by USAID. My focus here, however, is on visual arts organizations rather than on these more socially influential NGOs concerned with the lives of younger generations of Palestinians. Sunaina Maira has compellingly written about these in her study of music, performance and youth subcultures, *Jil Oslo* ("jil" is Arabic for "generation").[45] The language of NGOs operating in the State of Palestine is highly significant and embodies the international governmental effort above all to manage the Palestinians living in Security Areas A, B and C into a form of administered peace and co-habitation, under a neoliberal capitalist social order superintended by Israel. This is the apparently benign argot of "development needs," "human rights enhancement," "democratization" and "conflict resolution." Palestinian curator and critic Rawan Sharaf has noted, however, that the social system encouraged by such foreign nation-based aid has replaced the building of indigenous livelihoods and autonomous political capacity by Palestinians (highly limited by Israeli occupation and military power) with the imperative of what she calls the "vicious circle of securing funding."[46]

The intended, if still only partial, result of NGO-ization has thus been a radical depoliticization of Palestinian society under a Fatah-dominated state apparatus subservient to Israel and its key international allies. Nevertheless, the work of the NGOs, in helping to "professionalize" artists and other groups of cultural workers has had, Sharaf observes, positive as well as negative effects. In the mid-1990s, immediately following the Oslo agreements, the upbeat "peace," "tolerance," "coexistence" and "reconciliation" agenda led to some Palestinian artists and groups working with Israeli cultural organizations. New, and hybrid, Palestinian arts organizations emerged. These included Al Wasiti, the first art archive (closed in 2000), the Al Mamal Foundation for Contemporary Art, founded in 1998 and the still extant Sakakini Cultural Center in Ramallah, connected to the *shatat* A. M. Qattan Foundation (registered as a UK and Palestinian charitable organization).

Post-Oslo, these organizations tried to begin to foster a kind of indigenous Palestinian Authority "contemporary art"—based in performance, installation, video and multimedia. These are the forms of global art, discussed in previous chapters, popular with biennial exhibition curators around the world though not, according to Sharaf, with most local Palestinians, with whom the new visual arts agencies in the main failed to engage. Along with and utilizing the globalized idioms of contemporary art production, a number of Palestinian artists living both inside and outside of the State of Palestine have become renowned on the global biennial and museum circuit, joining the pantheon of Asia's global contemporary artists. It is not my purpose here, however, to enhance their already considerable fame and significance.[47]

Some NGO-funded art colleges opened after the Oslo agreements, such as the International Academy of Art-Palestine in Ramallah, which, along with Al Najah and Al Quds universities, are the only higher education institutions currently offering formal qualifications in art practice in the State of Palestine. Other organizations for visual arts and culture have been inaugurated since the 1990s, including Al Hoash, Art School Palestine (a residential/arts exchange project, not an education institution), the Yabous Cultural Center, Dar Annadwa and the Peace Centre based in Bethlehem.[48] But no art market could be sustained across the Palestinian territories during the 1990s as there were no commercial galleries—with the exception of Anadil, founded in Jerusalem in 1995, which later morphed into the Al Mamal Foundation. The A. M. Qattan Foundation, run with *shatat* capital from Kuwait and Lebanon, had been founded in 1993 to support Palestinian art and culture, and it continues to maintain centers in Ramallah, Gaza and London. The Foundation also organizes an annual Young Artists Award.

Gallery One, located in Ramallah and the first commercial gallery to open for many years, was started in 2014 by the director of the not-for-profit Art School Palestine.[49] Development of the Palestinian Museum has been financed, as mentioned earlier, by the Welfare Association. Some sales of contemporary artworks have been conducted by the United Nations Development Programme to support artists living in Gaza, and Al Hoash has worked to organize annual art auctions in order to raise money to support local artists. There are some avid and wealthy private collectors of Palestinian art active in the global markets across western Asia, as well as in Europe and the United States.[50]

The NGO-ization of civil society in the State of Palestine has fundamentally reformed the definition and character of the workers (of virtually all kinds, including artists, curators and administrators) who access such funding. In one direction, Sharaf notes that since the Oslo agreements their identities have been reshaped into that of "clients" rather than autonomous, self-directed producers. In another, Maira concludes that successful Palestinian artists, including musicians and dancers, have been refashioned by what she calls "neoliberal models of individualism that have detached artists from the collective spaces of cultural production" and links to popular struggle. The most promising were groomed for connection to a global arts market, its publics and the international funding structures available via participation in events such as biennials and the patronage of powerful museums. This is clearly a political and ideological as well as a cultural and social "reframing" process. The League of Palestinian Artists, established in 1974 and connected closely to the Palestinian Liberation Organization (PLO) during the 1970s and 1980s, progressively lost influence following the Oslo agreement when the Palestinian Authority took over from the PLO, became the local "ruling politico-bourgeois class" and the process of depoliticization by "NGO-ization" began.[51]

Through a combination of the ostensibly humanitarian work of NGOs and capital directed from both Israel and *shatat* interests into the State of Palestine the territories have been prepared for and penetrated by neoliberal global capitalism. "Industrial Zones," for example that at Beit Hanoun on the Gaza–Israel border, supported by NGOs and international banks, have enabled Israeli businesses to source low-paid Palestinian labor employed without reference to the labor laws of either states in order to manufacture goods for export, not to develop the State of Palestine's own societal livelihood. These workers are forbidden to join unions and they labor under military control, with security arrangements subcontracted out to the PA's own soldiers and police.

Industrial Zones have become a common feature of the global Asian neoliberal capitalist economy, operating sporadically, as noted in Chapter 2, between North and South Korea (as well as in many other countries in the region, including the PRC and the Philippines). The NGOs involved across Asia operate what Naomi Klein has called a form of "philanthropic imperialism," often also providing intelligence to the US military. Colin Powell, US secretary of state for defense during much of the 2000s, described NGOs as "an important part of our combat team," while Klein has observed that they act as "the charity wing of the military silently mopping up after wars."[52]

In the State of Palestine the NGO-led "development" environment, symbolized by the Industrial Zone, has normalized and legitimized the continued Israeli occupation and domination of Palestinian lands, resources and its people. They have become dependent upon it, as well as exploited by local and absentee Palestinian capitalists (there was actually an increase in urban poverty in the PA between the years 1993 and 2008). The result, according to Nakhleh, has created:

> exploitation, monopolies, misuse and corruption of available funds [which has secured] dealerships for non-productive consumer goods and services from regional and international companies, conducting business deals with Israeli capitalists to expand the profit base for both sides, with the support of the entire gamut of the dominant colonial structures, the control and possession of economic assets that PA bureaucrats managed and regulated earlier, through coalitions, often fabricated, by their capitalist allies.[53]

The separation wall's construction, for instance, along with that of checkpoints, terminals, settlements and roads inside the occupation, was the work of the Israeli Nesher company which has been given an effective monopoly in the State of Palestine (as well as being responsible for producing 85% of all concrete used in Israel). The Palestinian Authority government pays "rent" for the concession to dispense these Israeli goods through its holding companies directly into Israel-based banks.[54]

Concrete, however, had no role in the construction of two of the most ostentatious mansions built by wealthy Palestinians that exemplify gross inequalities within the political economy of the State of Palestine. Rashad Al-Shawwa's so-called "Pyramid," officially titled The Shawwa Cultural Center, was built in 1985, nearly a decade before the Oslo agreements. It is located in Rimal, Gaza, the town of which Al-Shawwa was mayor for eleven years, appointed then under effective Israeli tutelage. The mansion was built with Welfare Association funding disbursed from Geneva and included an extensive library facility for public use which remained empty and unused for five years. Ignoring the skills of local craftspeople and indigenous materials, the mansion was made entirely from materials imported from Europe.

Munib Al Masri's "House of Palestine" mansion was built in Nablus, a Palestinian town 30 miles north of Jerusalem. In 1994 Israel allowed Al Masri, along with PLO leader Yasser Arafat, to return to Palestine. Al Masri worked as a liaison agent between the Fatah and Hamas parties, and also acted as a messenger for the Israeli government. Al Masri's "House of Palestine"—a Palladian-style mansion overlooking the Balatta refugee camp built in 1950 which is now home to 30 000 people—was also built entirely with European materials during the Second Intifada. A kind of pseudo-monument to religious and ethnic tolerance, the mansion includes a central structure, the "Dome of Tolerance," a tribute to Islam, Christianity and Judaism. Al Masri, dubbed the "King of the West Bank," is reputedly the world's richest Palestinian, with personal holdings—including a collection of European artworks—worth, it has been estimated, a third of the value of the State of Palestine.[55]

Concrete into Dust

The Gaza-born artist Tayseer Barakat runs a café in Ramallah. Barakat's catalogue of images and texts, published as *Dust, Dialogue, Iron,* was exhibited at Ramallah's Al Mahatta Gallery Station in 2009. This composite work presents a series of imagined/imaged voices and people coupled with some photographs and artworks. The latter are a mixture of drawings and shallow-relief prints.[56] In virtually all cases the images suggest the substantially obliterated remains of people killed violently and subsequently recognizable only through abstracted silhouettes. They resemble the disturbing image-like trace outlines of incinerated bodies of those killed by the atomic explosions at Hiroshima and Nagasaki in 1945.[57]

The people depicted in Barakat's images seem wholly anonymous as well as abstract. They have themselves, in death, become abstractions, apparently twice over. The actual individuals killed have been represented, abstractly, only as facial, head or partial body silhouettes. Then, within the context of the catalogue, they have been rendered (I construe) into abstractly representing all Palestinians killed in the conflict in the Middle East. Children are often depicted in Barakat's prose, but again, although sometimes given names, these appear to be meant as abstracted representations or "typifications." One text, set alongside such images, reads "At night, I cry my mother [...] My name is Shahd the girl of fifteen years" ("I am Shahd from Palestine")". It is not clear if these short pieces of prose are based on actual individuals whom Barakat knew personally or came to know about through other sources.[58]

These images in some ways resemble ancient Egyptian painted wall depictions—abstracted profiles of heads and shoulders, like the hieroglyphics one sees on the walls of pharaohs' tombs or on coins. No identifying detail remains—the images are flat and flattening, mostly in outline, with the quality of what looks like rough sand constituting the figure with the background in roughened black, although this form also evokes a kind of sand texture. In another image (none have specific titles and there is no pagination in the catalogue) a schematic face in frontal view looks out at us—with just the dark slit of one eye, part of a nose and half a dark lip identifiable. It is as if the whole human being's form has been sucked out of the image, leaving only a kind of residual sediment of shape and former animation: "I am 12 year old Amer from Deir El-Balah. My father cried me since the deafening sound until my new colours." The latter reference might make sense in relation to the face with its life sucked out. A kind of peacefulness, or pacific release, characterizes this image.

The text "Mariam from Izbet Abd-Rabbuh in Gaza" is accompanied by a beautifully rendered profile of a woman, or young girl, almost, or apparently, in motion—flattened, reduced to schematic outline, but also seemingly at peace. Other, ordinary, color photographs interspersed with these drawn and relief images show exploding bombs, or an actual child carrying loaves of bread on his head. Others—whitened and overexposed to an almost X-ray appearance—show parts of what look like several dead bodies of children neatly lined up for inspection or burial. But no potentially identifying faces are to be seen—their individuality is withheld. A focus on limbs instead shows the bodies as if in sleep rather than, or as, death. "Are you in Somalia or do you live in a faraway Indian village?" another text asks. Some of the references suggest historical as well as contemporary events. One reads "I am Maria, the daughter of one of the Taifa Kings [...] Born in Malaga in 1218." The silhouette drawings are also like relief maps—schemata of territories, the end of land, the end of territory, its insides and outsides. A final X-ray type photograph appears to show three small children lying dead in a line or trench—again as if asleep, in a state of peacefulness, in this case their bodies and clothes apparently unblemished. An adult kneels behind them, again faceless, reduced to lower limbs.

Dust, Dialogue, Iron shows and rejects death, and the worlds that have created it. The people imaged as dead seem to live again, to transcend their deaths through "their" words or through the words of someone else—speaking a kind of testimony to the fact of their deaths and the situations in which these deaths occurred. The Gaza situation, the abject "Philistine"/Palestine view, is close by, present and depicted graphically. "The basic levels of experience that motivate art are related to those of the objective world", Theodor Adorno noted, "from which they recoil. The unsolved antagonisms of reality return in artworks as immanent problems of form."[59] Barakat struggles to show the life form of specific humans from which life has been removed but not extinguished, nor forgotten.

I am very grateful to Rawan Sharaf for her help and advice in preparing this chapter.

Notes

1 This was the announcement made at The First Palestine Investment Conference, held in Bethlehem, May 21–23, 2008, following the Paris Donor Conference in December 2007 that resolved to attract Palestinian and foreign investors into Palestinian Authority territory. See Khalil Nakhleh, *Globalized Palestine: The National Sell-Out of a Homeland* (Red Sea Press: Trenton, NJ and London, 2012): 61 and K. Nahkleh, "Oslo: Replacing Liberation with Economic Neo-Colonialism," *Al Shabaka, the Palestinian Policy Network* (April 2014) at https://al-shabaka.org/commentaries/oslo-replacing-liberation-with-economic-neo-colonialism/(accessed March 15, 2016). On the Pope's visit to Palestine, see *The Jerusalem Post*, May 26, 2014: 1–3. See Bashir Makhoul, (ed.) *Palestinian Video Art: Constellation of the Moving Image* (Palestinian Art Court–al Hoash: Jerusalem and London, 2013). The sardonic coinage "Five Star Occupation" is discussed by Sunaina Maira, *Jil Oslo: Palestinian Hip Hop, Youth Culture and the Youth Movement* (Tadween Publishing/George Mason University: Washington, DC, 2013): 33 and 189.

2 For the Declaration of Principles on Interim Self-Government Arrangements, agreed on September 13, 1993 (Oslo Accord I), see the text at https://web.archive.org/web/20021115183950/http://knesset.gov.il/process/docs/oslo_eng.htm (accessed March 31, 2017). For the Israeli–Palestinian Interim Agreement on the West Bank and the Gaza Strip (Oslo Accord II), agreed on September 28, 1995, see the text at https://web.archive.org/web/20021115180646/http://knesset.gov.il/process/docs/heskemb_eng.htm (accessed March 31, 2017).

3 On the United Nations vote in 2013 to recognize the PA's "non-voting" member "dependent state" status in its General Assembly, see http://www.un.org/press/en/2012/ga11317.doc.htm (accessed March 31, 2017). For a useful synopsis of the socioeconomic and political consequences of territorial divisions between Israeli and Palestinian areas following the Oslo Peace Accords of 1993–1995, see Perry Anderson, "The House of Zion," *New Left Review*, 96; Nov–Dec 2015 (5–37): 10–11.

4 On, for example, the operation of US NGOs in Afghanistan after 2001, see Tariq Ali, "Operation Enduring Freedom," in Tariq Ali *The Duel: Pakistan on the Flight Path of American Power* (Pocket Books: London, 2009): 227–228; on the activities of the George Soros Foundation in the Balkans, see Zhivka Valiavicharska "Culture, Neoliberal Development, and the Future of Progressive Politics in Southeastern Europe," in Harris (ed.), *Globalization and Contemporary Art*: 496–509, and H. Toukan "On Being 'The Other' in Post-Civil War Lebanon: Aid and the Politics of Art in Processes of Contemporary Cultural Production," online platform ibraaz at http://www.ibraaz.org/essays/63 (accessed March 31, 2017). See also George Yudice, *The Expediency of Culture: Uses of Culture in the Global Era* (Duke University Press: Durham, NC, 2005).

5 See Nakhleh, *Globalized Palestine*: 15, 132, 162, and his chapter "Palestinian NGOs and Transnational 'Aid' Agencies: Their Role in Impeding PCLD [People-centered Liberationist Development] Approach": 131–227.

6 See Nakhleh, *Globalized Palestine*: 88–90, 121–123, and his chapter "Palestinian Capitalist Class:" 37–129.

7 The US-based Holy Land Foundation (founded in 1988) fell foul of this "terrorist" designation made initially in 2001. Some of its senior staff were subsequently tried and imprisoned. See Francis FitzGibbon, "Low-Hanging Fruit," *London Review of Books*, January 22, 2015: 13–14.

8 See Nakhleh, *Globalized Palestine*: 26–36 and sources at http://www.palestine-studies.org/books/emergence-palestinian-globalized-elite-donors-international-organizations-and-local-ngos-1 (accessed March 31, 2016).

9 See, e.g., Edward Said, *The End of the Peace Process: Oslo and After* (Granta, London: 2003):

> Because the struggle against the repressive aspects of Jewish nationalism for non-Jews is so complex and difficult, I have always felt that what we contribute toward Palestine is synonymous with a new sense of modernity, that is, a mission for getting beyond the horrors of the past into a new relationship with the whole world, not just with Israel and the Arabs, but with India, China, Japan, Africa, Latin America, and of course with Europe and North America [...] For all sorts of reasons, we have for the time being lost that sense of confidence and worldliness, partly because we have had incapable, small leaders, and partly because we have become content with mere survival and [...] symbolic achievements. (xx)

10 For discussion of the 2008 "Palestinian Reform and Development Plan" based on the neoliberal "free market" agenda, see Nakhleh, *Globalized Palestine*: 19–25; on the lack of investment in agriculture and industry: 59. On Israel's long subsumption of Palestinian consumer demand, see "History of Israel's Power Structure," in Jonathan Nitzan and Shimshon Bichler, *The Global Political Economy of Israel* (Pluto Press: London, 2002): 84–136.

11 Nakhleh, *Globalized Palestine*: 40.

12 For an insightful comparison of the postcolonial sociopolitical orders in Egypt and Pakistan (bearing in mind my discussion of contemporary art in the subcontinent in Chapter 3), see Owen Bennett Jones, "The Military and the Mullahs," *London Review of Books* 38 (5); March 3, 2016: 15–17.

13 On what Eyal Weizman calls Israel's "architecture of occupation," see his *Hollow Land* (Verso: London, 2007). Israel collects about 75% of all tax raised in Palestinian territories and has often withheld revenue that should have been turned over to the Fatah government as punishment for its actions. In January 2016, for instance, Israel withheld tax revenue as punishment for the State of Palestine joining the International Criminal Court—and the State of

Palestine then threatened to take Israel to the ICC for withholding this money. See http://www.aljazeera.com/news/2015/04/israel-palestinians-reach-accord-frozen-taxes-150418123326283.html (accessed March 31, 2017).

14 See Nakhleh, *Globalized Palestine*: 111–115, and "Rawabi: An Economic Growth Strategy for the West Bank," published by RTI International (a US-based development agency sponsoring the project) at http://www.rti.org/brochures/rawabi_west_bank_econ_growth.pdf (accessed March 16, 2016). See Lisa Taraki, "Urban Modernity on the Periphery: A New Middle Class Reinvents the Palestinian City," *Social Text* 95, 26 (2): Summer 2008: 61–81, and T. Dana, "The Palestinian Capitalists That Have Gone Too Far," *Al Shabaka, the Palestinian Policy Network*, https://al-shabaka.org/briefs/palestinian-capitalists-have-gone-too-far/(accessed March 31, 2017).

15 *Layalina Palestine*, Oct 2013, Issue 20: 2. *The Jerusalem Post* announced, alongside its coverage that day of the pope's visit, that a group of "tech hungry Chinese investors" were in Tel Aviv looking to invest in Israel's high technology business sector. This is an area in which Israel has become a global player, with its close tie-ups to Israeli Defense Forces' and US operations, surveillance and counterinsurgency programs. The newspaper also advertised a related facet of the global capitalist system: legal services to help the wealthy legally hide their money from tax collectors. The Israel Annual STEP Conference in 2014 offered a panel on "Private Clients Practice and Anti-Money Laundering Law." One lecture was called "Heads I Win, Tails You Lose: Advising the Global Super Rich in Times of Protracted and Unprecedented Political, Economic, Cultural and Scientific Change," *Jerusalem Post*, May 26, 2014: 17 and 5.

16 *Layalina Palestine*: e.g., 4–7, 21, 29, 110–111, 121, 124–125.

17 *Layalina Palestine*: 100–101, 142–143. On Ramallah's socioeconomic development, see Lisa Taraki, "Enclave Micropolis: The Paradoxical Case of Ramallah/Al-Bireh,"*Journal of Palestine Studies*, XXXVII (4); Summer 2008: 6–20.

18 On the Israeli occupation of the city since 1967, see Eyal Weizman, "Jerusalem: Petrifying the Holy City," in *Hollow Land*: 25–56. For a study of the social impact of the wall on Palestinian life in a specific town, see Safa Husni Dhaher, "Al-'Eizariyah and the Wall: From the Quasi-Capital of Palestine to an Arab Ghetto" (unpublished PhD thesis, University of Trento, Italy: 2016). I am very grateful to Safa Husni Dhaher for allowing me to read her thesis prior to its submission.

19 See "Platform," in *Palestinian Art Court – Al Hoash* (promotional literature, no date, np).

20 *Palestinian Art Court – Al Hoash* (promotional literature, no date, np) and *Al Hoash* (promotional leaflet, no date, np).

21 *Al Hoash* (promotional leaflet, no date, np).

22 The issues are tackled directly by Bashir Makhoul and Gordon Hon, *The Origins of Palestinian Art* (Liverpool University Press: Liverpool, 2013).

23 Michael Hardt and Antonio Negri, *Empire* (Harvard University Press: Harvard, MA, 2001).
24 Michael Hardt and Antonio Negri, *Empire*: 109.
25 *Palestinian Art Museum Jerusalem* (public discussion document, no date, np).
26 The most astute critique of this Euro-North American tradition remains Carol Duncan and Alan Wallach's succinct essay "The Universal Survey Museum," *Art History*, December 1980, no 3: 447–469. For a critical review of narratives of development in Palestinian art in the twentieth century, see Bashir Makhoul and Gordon Hon *The Origins of Palestinian Art*. See also Gannit Ankori, *Palestinian Art* (Reaktion: London, 2006) and Kamal Boullata *Palestinian Art: From 1850 to the Present* (Saqi Books: Beirut, 2009).
27 The Israel Museum, for example, was founded in 1965 and the National Gallery of Modern Art in Delhi, India, in 1954.
28 *Palestinian Art Museum Jerusalem*: np.
29 *Palestinian Art Museum Jerusalem*: np. The Welfare Association-funded Palestinian Museum's mission statement explains that the Museum "will act as a dynamic, innovative forum for the exchange and development of knowledge and ideas connected to Palestinian society, history and culture. Combining exhibitions with educational programs and research projects, the Museum will be a place for inspiration, dialogue, and reflection. Through its digital platforms and international partners it aims to connect with Palestinians wherever they are in the world and with all those interested in Palestine." http://www.palmuseum.org/about/the-museum- (accessed March 29, 2016).
30 See https://www.ochaopt.org/documents/ocha_opt_area_c_map_2011_02_22.pdf (accessed March 29, 2016). These proportions, not surprisingly, remain strongly contested. See UN Office for the Coordination of Humanitarian Affairs *Restricting Space: The Planning Regime Applied by Israel in Area C of the West Bank*: (OCHA, 2009): 2.
31 On the indispensability of ideas and ideologies of "national time" and "national historicity" in the construction of nation-state narratives, see Nicos Poulantzas, "The Nation," in his groundbreaking study *State, Power, Socialism* (Verso: London, 1979). I deployed these concepts in my book dealing with art and society in 1930s United States, *Federal Art and National Culture: The Politics of Identity in New Deal America* (Cambridge University Press: Cambridge, 1995).
32 See the exhibition catalogue and text *Dor Guez: 40 Days* (Mosaic Rooms: London, 2013).
33 *Palestinian Art Museum Jerusalem*: np.
34 The "Higgs boson particle" was theorized by scientists decades before experiments in 2012 proved the entity actually existed, thus confirming, it was claimed, a basic tenet of particle psychics; see http://home.cern/about/updates/2013/03/new-results-indicate-new-particle-higgs-boson (accessed March 29, 2016).

35 I took part in a research development seminar at Tate Liverpool with Al Hoash representatives in 2012. A full list of Al Hoash's partners, donors and sponsors across Europe and the Middle East is contained in *Palestinian Art Museum Jerusalem*: np.

36 *Palestinian Art Museum Jerusalem*: np.

37 http://www.pwc.co.uk/ accessed March 29, 2016). On the role of the Welfare Association in brokering aid for the State of Palestine from 25–30 international NGOs, see Nakhleh, *Globalized Palestine*: 184–201.

38 See, e.g., "American Crisis/Global Crisis," in Panitch and Gindin, *The Making of Global Capitalism*: 301–330.

39 See Maira, *Jil Oslo*: 35 and *Grand Park Hotel* brochure, np.

40 See http://www.haaretz.com/fayyad-to-haaretz-palestinians-are-prepared-for-statehood-1.361373 (accessed March 29, 2016).

41 See Nakhleh, *Globalized Palestine*: "Palestinian NGOs and Transnational 'Aid' Agencies": 131–227.

42 On the activity of the Soros Foundations in eastern Europe, see Zhivka Valiavicharska, "Culture, Neoliberal Development, and the Future of Progressive Politics in Southeastern Europe," in Harris (ed.), *Globalization and Contemporary Art*: 496–509 (501–502). On land purchases in Jerusalem by the Welfare Association on behalf of commercial interests, see Nakhleh, *Globalized Palestine*: 196–202.

43 Nakhleh, *Globalized Palestine*: 202–208. See Mike Davis's account of the broader activities of the World Bank and other transnational financial organizations in "development" work across Asia, Africa and South America since the 1970s, "Illusions of Self-Help," in Davis, *Planet of Slums* (Verso: London, 2006): 70–94. Policies of NGOs working with the Welfare Association in the State of Palestine turn out to be exemplary of what Davis calls the World Bank's objective to "impose its own theories as worldwide urban policy orthodoxy," centered on "championing privatization" since the 1980s. (70–71). See also Naomi Klein, *The Shock Doctrine: The Rise of Disaster Capitalism* (Allen Lane: London, 2007), especially Part 7 and "Losing the Peace Incentive: Israel as Warning" (423–442).

44 Nakhleh, *Globalized Palestine*: xv, xxi–xxii.

45 Sunaina Maira, *Jil Oslo: Palestinian Hip Hop, Youth Culture, and the Youth Movement*. On the Sharek Youth Foundation and NGO-ization in Palestine, see 149–151.

46 Rawan Sharaf, "The Role Played by Palestinian Cultural Institutions in the Formation and Transformation of Palestinian Visual Art/Culture" (unpublished essay: 2014): 6–7 and see Nakhleh, *Globalized Palestine*: 208–227.

47 Sharaf, "The Role Played by Palestinian Cultural Institutions in the Formation and Transformation of Palestinian Visual Art/Culture": 14–15. On the Jerusalem-based Al Mamal Foundation, started by curator Jack Persekian,

see "Art Spaces," in Hans Belting, Andrea Buddensieg and Peter Weibel (eds.), *The Global Contemporary and the Rise of New Art Worlds* (ZKM/MIT Press: Cambridge, MA, 2012): 76. For nomination and discussion of leading exiled Palestinian artists, see Makhoul and Hon, "Al-Shataat: A Coherence of Dispersion," in *The Origins of Palestinian Art* (188–245).

48 Sharaf, "The Role Played by Palestinian Cultural Institutions in the Formation and Transformation of Palestinian Visual Art/Culture": 15–17.

49 Gallery One exhibited three artists at the Art Dubai show in March 2016—Bashar Alhroub, Khaled Jarrar and Amer Shomali—indicating the Arab regional infrastructural base of which Palestinian arts organizations are a part. See www.galleryone.ps.

50 Sharaf, "The Role Played by Palestinian Cultural Institutions in the Formation and Transformation of Palestinian Visual Art/Culture": 16. Al Hoash has continued to publish groundbreaking studies of new art by Palestinians, including Reem Fadda (ed.), *Art in Palestine: Palestinian Women Artists* (Jerusalem: 2007, based on an Al Hoash exhibition curated by Fadda), August Jordan Davis and Jonathan Harris (eds.), *Bashir Makhoul* (Jerusalem: 2012), and Bashir Makhoul (ed.), *Palestinian Video Art: Constellation of the Moving Image* (Jerusalem: 2013).

51 Sharaf, "The Role Played by Palestinian Cultural Institutions in the Formation and Transformation of Palestinian Visual Art/Culture": 9; Maira, *Jil Oslo: Palestinian Hip Hop, Youth Culture, and the Youth Movement*: 144; Nakhleh, *Globalized Palestine*: "Palestinian Capitalist Class:" 37–132. On financial support to cultural organizations, see J. DeVoir and L. Boo Jespersen *Tracking Funding to the Visual and Performing Arts in the OPT* [Occupied Palestinian Territories]*: A Quantative and Qualitative Analysis* (Ramallah: A. M. Qattan Foundation, 2012).

52 Klein, *The Shock Doctrine*, quoted in Nakhleh, *Globalized Capitalism*: 222–223. On "Free Trade Zones" operating in the PRC and Latin America, see Davis, *Planet of Slums*: 158–159.

53 Nakhleh, *Globalized Palestine*: 38.

54 Nakhleh, *Globalized Palestine*: 66–68, 57–59.

55 Nakhleh, *Globalized Palestine*: 21–26. See further details of the mansion and its grounds at http://www.ft.com/cms/s/2/d208790e-b636-11e1-8ad0-00144feabdc0.html#slide0.

56 Tayseer Barakat, *Dust, Dialogue, Iron* (Al Mahatta Gallery: Ramallah, 2009). See http://www.almahattagallery.net/(accessed March 31, 2016). See Jonathan Harris, "Apodictic Autonomy and Affirmation in Contemporary Asian Art: Four Cases," in Bashir Makhoul and Alnoor Mitha (eds.), *Conflict and Compassion: A Paradox of Difference in Contemporary Asian Art* (Home: Manchester, 2016): 9531116.

57 See: http://www.fogonazos.es/2007/02/hiroshima-pictures-they-didnt-want-us_05.html (accessed March 31, 2016).

58 Barakat, *Dust, Dialogue, Iron*: n.p. There is a long history of artists' and writers' image–text depictions of extreme human suffering using book or catalogue forms to construct documentary, or pseudo-documentary, narratives and testimonies. One of the earliest is Erskine Caldwell's and Margaret Bourke-White's US Depression era *You Have Seen Their Faces* (University of Georgia Press: Athens GA, 1995 (1937)) which combined photographs of the poor in the southern United States with what appeared to be verbatim quotations from them captured during interviews (subsequently revealed to be inventions by the authors).

59 Theodor Adorno, *Aesthetic Theory* (London: Continuum, 2004 (1970)): 7.

Conclusion: Motifs of Global Fracture in the Art Of Bashir Makhoul and Wang Guofeng

7.30 a.m.... In the taxi again, back from Manchester Airport: gentle drizzle and grey skies of the English northwest. The global cities of Hong Kong, Beijing, Seoul, Delhi and Tel Aviv fade as we proceed through the small towns of Cheshire to my home in Congleton: diminutive market and commercial center in farming countryside. Medieval and now modern, relatively un-gentrified; only verging on the "contemporary" as far as the ads in the windows of the real estate agents are concerned. Safe in England?... Congleton had been a focus for Oliver Cromwell and the republicans in the Civil War—the regicide John Bradwell kept a house here: "modernization" centuries ago, English style, with its share of violent death, social chaos and rearranging the world order/disorder... The key in the door, the door closing, time to unpack.

Re-Entering the Maze

Step outside this global contemporary art world.

Back inside Makhoul's installation *Enter Ghost, Exit Ghost* I might have felt lost, but I knew that I wasn't really. For this construction was, from its beginning to its end, an artwork, an installation, in a gallery space—all familiar and quite safe things.[1] But the work-as-maze was asking me to consider the possibility of entertaining radical doubt regarding my "disposition," although that doubt was also supposed to be entertaining, a form of diversion. Consider some of the historical and current meanings of disposition: "The action of getting rid of or making over"... "power of disposing, control" ... "The action of ordering or regulating by (esp. divine) right or power" ... "The stationing of troops ready for attack or defense" ... "A frame of mind; a mood" ... "The fact of being set in order; spatial arrangement; relative position, esp. of constituent parts". *Enter Ghost, Exit Ghost* sought to divert me, but not only for the purpose of entertainment. It led me to consider my position.

The Global Contemporary Art World, First Edition. Jonathan Harris.
© 2017 John Wiley & Sons, Inc. Published 2017 by John Wiley & Sons, Inc.

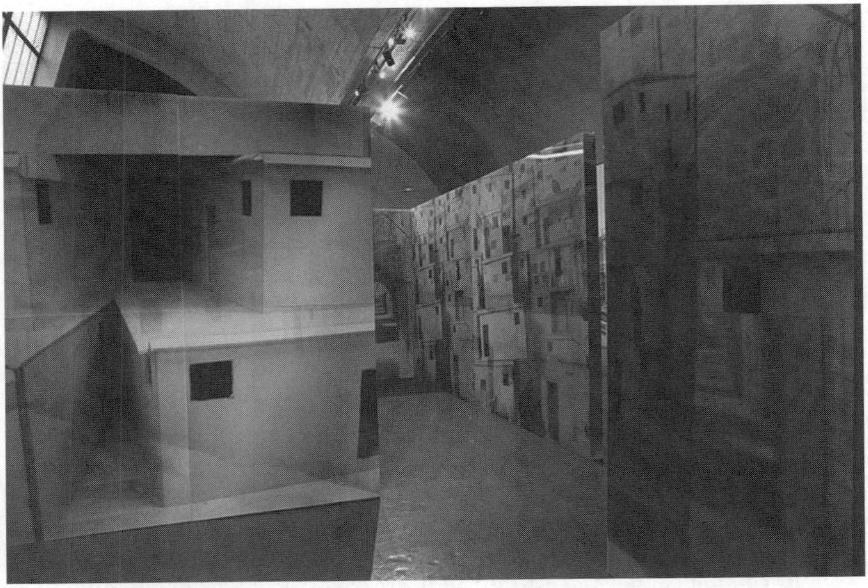

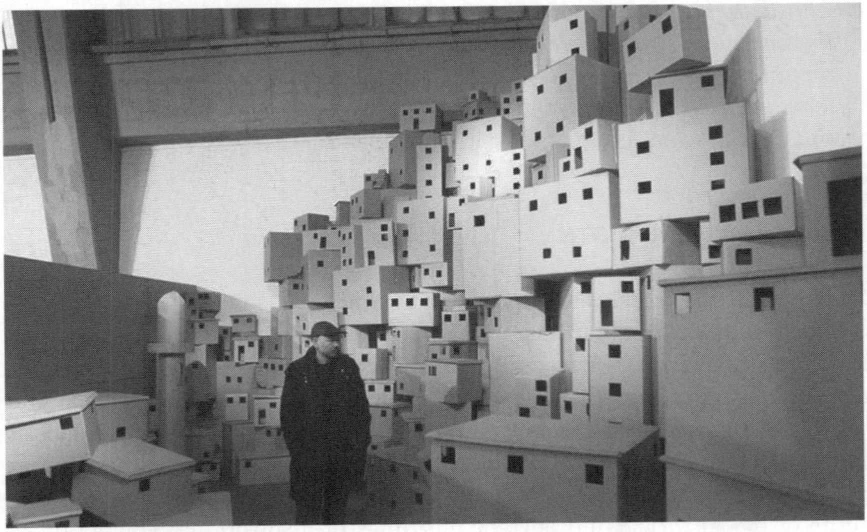

Cover image: Bashir Makhoul *Enter Ghost, Exit Ghost* (2012, mixed media installation). *Source:* © Bashir Makhoul.

The term maze in Middle English usage referred to a mental state of "delirium, delusion, disappointment"—only later did it come to mean a physical structure of paths and passages "arranged in bewildering complexity." A "maze of streets," therefore—such as an Arab Kasbah or traditional Japanese *machizukuri* warren of urban passageways—might be an unintended outcome of human construction practices, rather than one conceived from the outset as a form of diversion.[2] The psychological condition of "amazement" meant "loss of one's wits or self-possession; mental stupefaction; bewilderment, perplexity." Later it accrued the exacerbated senses of "overwhelming fear or apprehension" and, later still, "overwhelming wonder, extreme astonishment." Note these extremities of human reactions: overwhelming wonder, astonishment, fear and apprehension—suggesting a consciousness, a position, turned upside down; a world order disordered.

Human consciousness and self-consciousness is inherently situated, or seated, in material existence. Though scientific and philosophical debate on the question of the definition and location of "mind" remains intractable, it does not and cannot exist outside of the physical body and brain.[3] Without the physically situated organs of sight, touch, hearing, taste and smell, consciousness can exist—sense-deprived or sense-bereft patients are sometimes kept alive through intensive care procedures—but individual humans could not survive independently in the world. Perception abilities and consciousness, therefore, are bound up together in practical life. The information gained through these senses informs, and helps to form, consciousness and self-consciousness: our sense of who, what, where and why we are in the world. Practical in this sense does not only mean "useful in everyday life tasks" and should not be opposed to notions of theoretical or speculative activity. Our senses of why we exist, in certain places at certain times—for instance, what the value and meaning of our lives are—are inherently bound up with the nature of those places and times; that is, with their "conjunctural" significance.[4]

The sequences of "lenticular" panels which made up the walls of the maze that was *Enter Ghost, Exit Ghost* created the sense of a consciousness, a position turned upside down. Though I knew I remained in an installation, an artwork, in a gallery, these panels—projecting a series of photographic images as I walked pass them—exhibited images that appeared, then disappeared, and sometimes seem eerily to coexist in my perception of them. Because the images changed as I moved past each panel, I became highly aware that perception, and acts of consciousness and self-consciousness sequentially related to these perceptions, are inseparable from my own physical and bodily disposition. The term "lenticular," as I explained in the Introduction, also has its origins in late Middle English usage, where it referred to a lens-like shape. The root of this term, lens, lies in the Latin for "lentil"—a small rounded seed cultivated for food in Mediterranean countries. A lens was a transparent substance, such as a piece of glass, with one or more surfaces "curved or otherwise shaped to cause regular convergence or divergence of light passing through it."

Enter Ghost, Exit Ghost, even before I began to interrogate the kinds of imagery projected through its panels, was asking me to consider the nature and "situatedness" of human perception and its relation to consciousness and self-consciousness. How do we see the world and why do we see it that way? These are two of the most basic questions ever to have been asked by philosophers. To the duality and dialectic of human mind "perception-consciousness" a third term, and problem, should be added: perspectival understanding. Having a "perspective" means to see something from a particular place or position, and implies a recognition that, from that place or position, some things will be/can be seen and other things will not/cannot be seen. Place or position in this sense, it should be clear, means not simply a physical or spatial location affording a view (thought it necessarily is that), but also a correctible hypothesis, or, alternatively, a principle or belief that is held to be axiomatically true—such as that, for example, "all humans are equally precious", or that "the Land of Israel belongs to the Jews because God gave it to them for all eternity."

In contrast, an example of a "correctible hypothesis" would be that if you moved to the left of your current position you would see something that is currently not visible, or that, for instance, lack of clean water can create the conditions for disease. These two propositions are what philosophers have called heuristic (from the Greek "to find"), meaning their claims are subject to trial and error revision based on the accumulation of further evidence which can lead to a change in perspective. Scientific research is generally thought to proceed through such empirical procedure or testing. In contrast, statements of belief are sometimes also called ineffable, from Latin, meaning "too great to be expressed in words." Note that there is a sense and motor link between human consciousness, expression through language and discovery in the world. One might have begun to find a way through the maze of *Enter Ghost, Exit Ghost* by making heuristic claims about where one is and has been—to avoid, for instance, endlessly revisiting the same place. The claims could have been tested through movement and then further reconsideration. Of course, the purpose of a maze built to confuse is precisely to confound such rational and heuristic action—to defeat consciousness and self-consciousness. The other course of action, however—movement based on ineffable principle—suggests lack of communication between those trapped in the maze and a belief that divine will is guiding them.

Seeing images mutate in *Enter Ghost, Exit Ghost* as I moved through the maze, correcting or confirming my hypotheses of where I thought I was, or had been, or wanted to be, was constantly a matter of changing perspective. Whether to turn "left" or "right"—but left or right in relation to what fixed or achieved position? Whether to turn, or to return; or to hold this position? Would a "road map" perhaps have helped with the direction I wanted to go in? We enter here the geometry of radical doubt. Have some of my thinking and moves so far seemed "obtuse"? In this maze what images could I have seen, or remembered, or thought I remembered seeing, from a plane angle greater than 90 degrees and less than 180 degrees? Would a 90-degree or less change in direction have been a good idea? Would that have been to the right or the left? The ghost of an image I glimpsed once in the maze suggested I had returned, unwittingly, to a position I'd occupied before, suggesting I hadn't found a real way forward. The route was obscured, the light was bad, although the lenticular panels projected more images, more ghosts of a past, present or even future moment in movement.

Enter Ghost, Exit Ghost alluded to Shakespeare's play *Hamlet* and the dramatic-symbolic vehicle the spectral image in the play constitutes, but it also brought to mind another of the metaphors of the eponymous character's own bewilderment. In a conversation with Polonius, Ophelia's father and servant to King Claudius—the man who Hamlet suspects has killed his own father and married his mother—Hamlet facetiously debates the shape of a cloud, which seems to resemble, they agree, a camel, then perhaps a weasel, and, yet again, rather a whale.[5] But Hamlet becomes as disoriented by this exchange as he had hoped Polonius would be; his own state of mind is fearful, full of apprehension, and possibly delirious. There is, in meteorology, the genus of the "lenticular cloud": lens-shaped, occasionally iridescent, and glittering or flashing with an array of colors which changes as the observer moves.

In Girum Imus Nocte et Consumimur Igni

The maze that was *Enter Ghost, Exit Ghost* stood some comparison with the architecture of checkpoints and border crossings that both link together and divide Israel and the State of Palestine. This shift in focus makes sense because the shifting photographic images in this artwork, this installation in the gallery space, depicted past and present moments in the cities and towns of Palestine and in the nation-state of Israel. They represented the presence, within these imbricated territories, of another people whose own home and place, Palestine, once existed, but whose images and symbols are also now a matter of ellipses, shifting shapes, places, meanings, peoples and plans.[6] Take the Qalandiya crossing between Jerusalem and Ramallah in the West Bank. This particular maze operates five stages in the circulation of its temporary occupants. These channels link iron turnstiles, X-ray gates, more turnstiles, inspection booths, and then X-ray machines for bags. Palestinians negotiating this structure are hailed by the Israeli guards and other security personnel by loudspeaker and move through its locks controlled by remote controlled gates. The glass panels enabling Israeli surveillance and operation of the crossing are so thick that they prevent the Palestinians seeing the humans responsible for their transit through or detention in it. The architecture of this structure instructively embodies the hieratic architecture of visibilities and invisibilities that the Israeli state has created, maintains and constantly refines in its dealings with the Palestinians.[7] *Enter Ghost, Exit Ghost* was both a meditation upon, and a simulation of, this structure, or "logic of the visible" in Israel, and its connections to power and Palestine.

Ariel Sharon, Israeli soldier-hero from the 1967 war, later minister for new settlements and then Likud prime minister, once indicated the conditions and relations that should pertain, he believed, between visibility and Israeli power. "Arabs," he declared, "should see Jewish lights every night from 500 meters."[8] The settlements he conceived and planned were designed to institute a visual dominance of and over the "Land of Israel"—they were to be an inveterate reminder of Jewish predominance ("dominance over") and Palestinian subordination, "under the gaze" of their rulers. This architecture of the Israeli state, its physical and legal structures, is essentially asymmetrical: rules of engagement issued to the occupying forces at the end of 2003, for instance, in the wake of the Second Intifada, or *up*rising, stipulate that soldiers may shoot to kill any Palestinian caught observing settlements with binoculars or in any other "suspicious manner."[9] The act of looking, with the implication of the licit or illicitness of what can or might be seen by a particular individual or group, has itself been deemed a crime punishable by summary death.

Looking, seeing and representing are interactive processes—in legal, political and artistic practices. *Enter Ghost, Exit Ghost* as an artefact itself articulated all these processes through its serial lenticular imagery and its bewildering maze of paths leading to the seeming opacities of the cardboard city at its termination. What can be seen or not seen is dependent on where you are, but also on who you are and how your own perspective has been formed. There are many antecedents in art's history. John Constable, the English landscape painter, depicted the working people of East Anglia as only marginally visible in his great paintings of Suffolk—their represented size, such as the mother nursing a baby in *Dedham Vale* (1828) reflected his sense of their background relative insignificance within the countryside he both loved and owned.[10] Visibility is a part-synonym for the notion of transparency: the clarity associated with candor in social and democratic political life. The glass cupola built above and into the debating chamber at the Reichstag building in Berlin after it once again became the seat of the unified German parliament after 1994 was designed literally to embody and metaphorically figure this supposed transparency to democratic discourse—as if democracy could, or should, actually be seen to be happening.

Maya Ying Lin's *Vietnam Veterans Memorial*, erected in Washington, DC in 1982 turned the rhetoric of visibility in another direction. Consisting of a long rising black marble wall containing the names of all the American soldiers killed in that conflict, this structure actually throws back at the viewer the visibility of their own image looking at the Wall, as much as they simultaneously trace the names of their loved ones carved in the stone in front of them. The wall functions as a kind of "anti-memorial" to a war of invasion and occupation that was lost in 1975, and against which a majority in the United States eventually emerged. *Enter Ghost, Exit Ghost,* though focused on Israel and the Palestinians, actually connected to this longer and broader history of regional and global conflict within which the Cold War and the Vietnam War are both implicated. The maze of these interconnections is political and ideological, but also cultural and aesthetic. I have demonstrated in this book that the development of the global contemporary art world since the 1990s is not intelligible without understanding the still active legacies of the Cold War—across the Middle East (western Asia) into the subcontinent, to "Southeast Asia," and on to China, the Korean Peninsula and Japan.

In Girum Imus Nocte et Consumimur Igni/"We Go Round and Round in the Night and are Consumed by Fire."[11] This palindromic, maze-like, sentence—in Latin the letters from both beginning to end and from end to beginning spell the same words—was a favorite of Guy Debord's, the author of *Society of the Spectacle.*[12] His book sought to describe and explain the direction society had taken in the world since the mid-1920s, when forms of spectacular diversion (in cinema—with the advent of synchronized sound-imagery—advertising, urban development, and in culture and the arts generally) began to become integral to the social orders of both the Western democratic capitalist societies and the Soviet eastern European state-communist countries. For Debord, the stand-off between these two power blocs had, by the 1950s, generated a form of deadly coexistence and mutual interdependency. Some of these Cold War dead ends and impermeable borders that were products of this interdependency have featured in my analyses here of five postcolonial societies, territories and nation-states that emerged since that conjuncture.

Though certainly in conflict and competition with each other through the alliances established by NATO and the Warsaw Pact states, these two power blocs had effectively carved up the world and its resources of people and land into competing and coexisting "spheres of interest." The Berlin Wall, erected in 1961 to prevent citizens from East Germany crossing into the zones of the city controlled by the Americans and their allies, expressed and deepened the Cold War division of Berlin and Germany within the superpower conflict. Bulgarian artist Christo erected his own *Iron Curtain—Wall of Oil Barrels,* with official permission, in the Rue Visconti in Paris a year later, in what was an early artistic commentary on the aesthetics and politics of the Berlin Wall. Seemingly ambivalent or "neutral," this practical, temporary, division of a street by a high stack of oil barrels both roughly imitated and yet might be thought to have offered a critique of the Berlin Wall itself—though the meaning of the action in blocking the Paris street for a number of hours overnight still resists any simple or singular reading. The structure the artist built, however, focused upon an act and situation elsewhere—the construction and maintenance of the Berlin Wall—which had both reflected and produced extremely powerful practical, ideological, social and emotive effects, within that city and its population, divided Germany, Western Europe and the Cold War world beyond.

Christo's *Iron Curtain* worked through a "distancing" device which both literally separated—physically dividing the street in Paris—and drew attention, metaphorically, to the action of the Berlin Wall, using its different formal materials "poetically," via a *verfremdungeffekt* ("making strange") device.[13] *Enter Ghost, Exit Ghost* performed a congruent action, suggesting a reconsideration of the sociopolitical meanings of quotidian terms and preconceptions such as "walls," "doors," "roads," "barriers," "partitions," "beginnings" and "endings"—all, in fact, different kinds and extents of borders. It did so both to entertain and to prompt critical thought, referencing and utilizing—like the "affect" (sense or mood) devices of movie spectaculars and CGI technologies—the evolved machinery of a now global spectacle to achieve its own *effect*. The so-called "making strange" devices associated with twentieth-century avant-garde artistic practice included juxtaposition and dissonance in compositional (ordering) strategies. The lenticular panels central to the experience of *Enter Ghost, Exit Ghost* materialized this principle, combining as they did historically disparate and opposed images—pasts and presents of Palestinian life held visually together within acts of vision which themselves mutated as the spectator moved along the walls that channeled their progression through the maze. The "maze" here, however, refers as much to the fate of the Middle East within the logic of the Cold War and to the history of the Palestinians since their own 1948 *Nahkbah*, as it does to the actual warrens of paths in their towns and their playful-yet-serious simulation in Makhoul's diverting installation. *We go round and round in the night and are consumed by fire*. The maze is global—that is clear now to all.

Utopian Photo-Mythologies

I saw Wang Guofeng's "North Korea 2011" digital photographs *Number 1, Part 1* and *Number 1, Part 2* in his studio in Beijing, displayed and manipulated on the artist's computer screens. Other very large-scale photographic prints had been attached to the walls. *Number 1, Part 1* shows an unidentified public building, perhaps in Pyongyang, its truncated façade directly front to the camera lens—in the style in which Walker Evans photographed sharecroppers' shacks in the United States in the 1930s. (The master print of *Number 1*, showing the building in its entirety, has a very large print size of 905 cm × 450 cm.) This view eliminates any building recession detail and has the effect of flattening—in physical but also metaphorical ways—our sense of this substantial material structure. It appears to be "all front", all façade, with no "depth".

The large portrait of a somber man in a blue suit (one "Dear Father" or another, I assume) hanging from the second floor, directly in the middle of the façade, reinforces this flatness. The frontality of the portrait sitter's pose further emphasizes the whole composition's enigmatic "out-of-time-ness": the building and people in front of it, those working digging the road and a band playing music, appear oddly "frozen" too, although this quality is hard to articulate intellectually. It's more of an amorphous feeling, or saturating tone, than anything else. The vacuous blue sky and sense of physical, environmental wintry coldness (a roadie to the right of the band has his hands dug into his pockets) underlines this.

Because Guofeng was able to increase focus within images such as this on screens in his studio—digitally enhancing detail down to extraordinary levels of sharpness apparently anywhere on the photographic image as a whole—my sense developed that he had produced not really separate, or even separable, pictures, but rather a system or ecology of visual forms: from the building shape to the workers' body shape, as those two elements enter into a symbiosis of meaning and inter-reference. Clicking back and forwards from a wider shot to a detail produces this effect/affect in this viewer. Other groups of photographs by Guofeng also produce such a system, such as his *Ideality* (2006–2007) and *Utopia* (2007) series, consisting of 12 images of public building facades in Beijing and Moscow respectively. They have the look of typology sequences, meaningful only in categorical relation, oddly frozen from other references outside the system. This quality of "frozenness"—perhaps Guofeng's chief signature in formal terms—is a kind of visual correlate of Roland Barthes's myth "syntagm," the structure of linguistic elements, drawn from his use of Saussurian linguistics theory.[14] Guofeng's photo-mythologies seem to enact a parallel formal, analytic suspension of other codes and references, and of the referent, "the world out there". Yet his photographs do seek to explain and understand the world—this situation.

But step back now from Guofeng's photographs and consider briefly the historical relationship between Western capitalism and Eastern communism, as this developed during the twentieth century. I have been concerned in this book as much with the kinds of stabilities and interdependencies that have formed within globalization in the post-1945 era as with the instabilities and aggression that threatened the future of the world during the Cold War that supposedly ended in 1991. The early 1930s saw, on the one hand, the beginnings of Western states' official recognition of the Soviet Union (by the United States in 1933, for example) and, on the other, emergence of the global geopolitical division which persisted, in varying forms and at varying levels of antagonism and danger before and after the Second World War, up until the end of the Soviet Union.[15]

Debord's account of the reduction of all social life to what he calls spectacular domination by the economy (whether this is identified ideologically as "capitalist" or "communist") is certainly bleak. Perhaps this is more understandable given his own biographical proximity both to the rise of the Nazis in Germany and the dictatorial state controlling the Soviet Union during the 1930s and 1940s that claimed to be authentically "communist". In succession to that, the era of the Cold War embodied, for Debord, the domination of two interrelated forms of spectacle enshrining the global victory of modern capitalism, prior, however, to the emergence of neoliberalism in the 1980s. These were what he called the "concentrated" variants, centered on cults of authoritarian personality, that developed in the Soviet Union and later in China and North Korea, which represented a victory over the revolutionary workers' movement, while the "diffuse" forms of spectacle in the Western societies extended capitalism's "culture industry" powers that had been honed in the fascist period in central Europe.

Capitalism's actual worldwide predominance since the 1950s—in either its Soviet/PRC/North Korean "state-bureaucratic," or in its Western "democratic," forms, in the United States and Western Europe—had been founded, according to Debord, on a practical "integration of state and economy," a trend that could certainly be traced further back in the twentieth century, but which had become "at the very least the motor of all recent economic developments." Their actual institutional combination, in whatever varieties of empirical, historical modes that Debord believed stretched from the United States to China, was, he said, in all cases a union "highly favourable to the development of spectacular domination."[16]

Two factors in particular, however, isolate recent globalization from earlier nation-state systems and related internationalization processes—though not from the history of imperialist wars and incursions instigated after 1945, including those conducted by US, European and Soviet governments in, for example, Korea, Hungary, Vietnam, Czechoslovakia, Afghanistan, Kuwait, Iraq and Libya. Firstly, the emergence of truly global, as distinct from merely regional, ambitions within the superpower political, military and corporate forces involved. Strategists from these increasingly interlocked "power-elite" groups in Western Europe and the United States have operated, since the early 1950s, within supra-national alliances (dominated by the latter, now sole though weakened, superpower) with systematic global aspirations and capacity for action.[17] Though the onset of the Cold War between the Western capitalist democracies and the Soviet Union and its allied "Eastern bloc" states might in some ways reasonably be regarded as having operated a break on globalization, from another perspective it actually created two power blocs which together, in an effectively single system of rule, were even more motivated to attempt to carve up the world and manipulate all its peoples and resources.[18] Consideration of the global system must include the status of the PRC, and that of North Korea's relation to China and the world beyond. How might Guofeng's photographs critically inform analysis of both these social orders—to a degree interdependent, because of their geophysical proximity, though not symbiotic, given China's size and power?

Aesthetic and Social Implications of Digital Photography

Guofeng's most literal "theater of the frozen" comprises images of the mega-monumental sculptures of Kim Jong-un and his father, stood together, "cheesy" smiles in raincoats, acknowledging their people's adoration. The crowd appears like giant Gulliver's lilliputian antagonists beneath their leaders' monumental trouser-legged shoes. This "North Korea 2012" series *No.3 (close-up)* is a detail of *No.3* (750 cm × 220 cm print size) which pulls back to reveal father and son flanked by two enormous sculpted red flags and representatives of the people and army.

Many in the crowd—just in front of Guofeng's lens—point their own cameras toward the pair, now in the middle distance, cultish dark snowmen in front of a snowy mountain back-drop mounted on the wall of a windowless building. An actual white, featureless sky surrounds the whole event. Guofeng's photographs picture, then, semblances of North Korean "community" and human

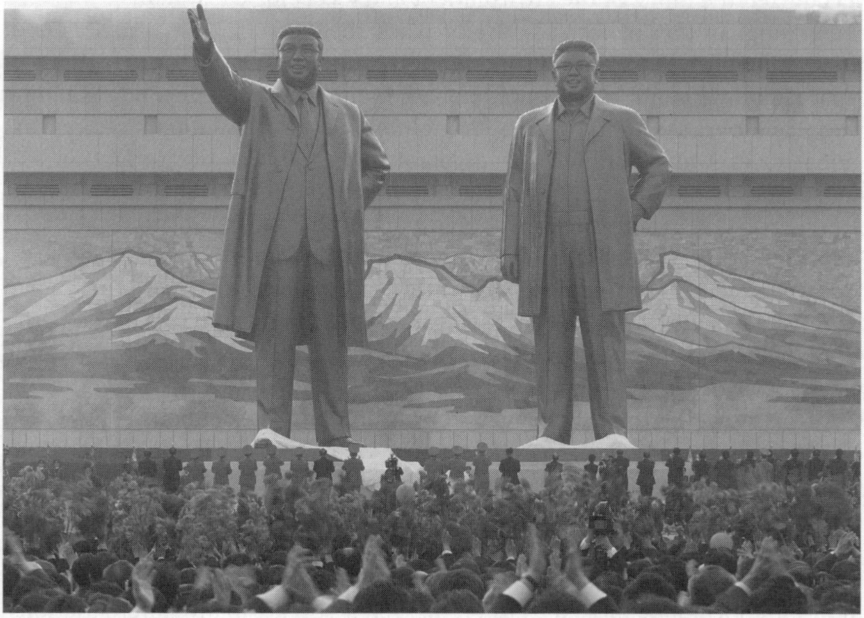

Figure 12 Wang Guofeng *Number 3 (close-up) North Korea 2012* (still from video, 2012). *Source:* © Wang Guofeng, Courtesy de Sarthe Gallery.

interrelations; they nearly all show a "coming together" of people, and of the people with, or coming near to, the Leader. They offer, in short, a visual form to this society. The question arises: what binds this society?

Though the Cold War had entrenched and sharpened antagonistic and competing economic systems, in political, ideological and military terms (think of the Korean War), those systems were nevertheless both driven by a common logic of accumulative materialism. Contemporary North Korean public propaganda painting continues to celebrate, in "Socialist Realist" mode, this drive to industrialize.[19] Any society's "mode of production" is actually comprised of its primary organization of human social relationships and activities within the physical environment. Western libertarian socialists, ecological activists and many other movements and groups from the 1960s onwards came to reject in principle, and as a basis for the practical organization of a future truly alternative society, a rapacious triumphalism in the exploitative transformation of nature that official Marxism, in China and North Korea, effectively shared with capitalism.[20] In contrast, they believed, any desirable and actually obtainable (not simply "utopian") radically alternative future would have to be, in economic, social and political terms, self-managing and self-renewing, a livelihood lived on the basis of people primarily caring for each other. Such a society would be "need-oriented," not "market-driven," offering a form of life sustained, not determined, by its material-productive capacities, and one crucially that recognized the limits of the environment and its ecological systems.

Guofeng's images of both North Korea and the PRC offer visual analogues of the totality of these societies' contemporary modes of production. Notions of "space," "image" and "representation" are as indispensable in understanding these photographs as they are, for example, to understanding capitalism's global market as a "unified space," or of the spectacles of production and consumption, or community and devotion, understood as a sphere of "image" production. In art and society, therefore, questions of the relations between "representation" (visual/cognitive) and "reality" are posed, both explicitly and tacitly. Guofeng's photographs *No.2* and *No.2 (close-up)*, also from the "North Korea 2012" series, suggest Leni Riefenstahl's well-known images of the Berlin Olympic Games in 1936, which have also been understood as an image of the Nazi social order in Germany at the time.[21] In these two photographs by Guofeng, however, the masses seem to entirely comprise soldiers.

Once again, Guofeng is able to focus in on individual heads and military hats (belonging to men and some women) seemingly anywhere in the composition when projecting these images on his computer screens. The effect is bizarre. The "social architecture" of the nation and the army is matched by the brick-by-brick construction effect in the photograph, whose print version measures in at an enormous 2039 cm × 208 cm. Detail reveals many differentiations, despite the overall appearance of uniformity and "massification." The two photographs seem "artless" in their mere quantification, or registering of bodies, but this is an effect of certain authorial decisions allied to the technical capacities of his digital camera and software. Everything, everyone, seems to be "in focus" simultaneously—which becomes a kind of metaphor of the ideological projection of equality and communal interconnection the regime claims to embody, literally, in these bodies. The sheer breadth of Guofeng's giant "landscape" picture—assembled necessarily in strips of photographic print paper for exhibition—manifests a kind of anti-compositional force as it has no compelling center or dynamic of forms, offering no particular place for the eye to settle, as it may as well settle anywhere. (Similar groups of shots show other sections of massed crowds, massed performers and stadiums, such as *North Korea 2013No.1*, 658 cm × 150 cm, which depicts an event celebrating the sixtieth anniversary of the founding of the state—Riefenstahl comparisons are obvious here too.)

Guofeng's "North Korea 2012" series *No. 20 (Traffic Policewoman)* is a sequence of five full length portraits, with the subjects placed on the road, appearing perhaps to half-smile to the camera. The code here is naturalistic, when compared with Guofeng's views of the massed ranks. These individuated women seem relaxed, even enjoying the attention of the camera, although the actual blankness of their expressions suggests this is yet another "reading in" made by this particular viewer. Barthes's famous discussion in *Mythologies* of the black colonial soldier saluting the French tricolor flag comes to mind.[22] These policewomen simply "stand for", show, the rightness of the North Korean social order: one sees immediately past their facades into their patriotic souls. Barthes's interest is in the spontaneous process, or appearing spontaneous process, wherein an image may produce this type of ideological effect. The image seems innocent of the semantic work it actually does—creating the connotation immediately jumping from a set of material signs to a naturalized meaning. Yet we know, given Guofeng's serial productivity, that he manufactures this visual syntagm while at the same time the photographs seem merely to reflect a pre-existing state of affairs. This is the constitutive contradiction embedded both in the photograph and in our understanding of it.

What are they watching? (close-up) is a detail of the broader landscape image (260 cm × 346 cm) with the same title, also part of the "North Korea 2012" series. Massed men in blue suits turn their backs to the camera, Magritte-style, while the center of the composition is taken up by a digital video camera, with a second to the right side of the image. They are both held aloft, like trophies, the first pointing down and the second up, towards the action off to the right. A third, a TV camera on a tripod, cuts through the top of the image. Guofeng's photograph pays homage to the technics of spectacular public visibility mobilized and projected by the regime and its media apparatus—a world where every gesture can and will be read as a sign of your loyalty and attentiveness towards the Leader. A group of geriatric generals stumble into view top right of the picture, their medals caught in the fading sunlight and spotlights of the cameras.

The One and the Multitude in the World Order/Disorder

Guofeng's "North Korea 2012" photographs include *No 1, Part 1* and *No. 1, Part 2,* two images that take us to the heart of this concentrated spectacular regime. *No 1, Part 1,* shows us a crowd reacting, animatedly, to an event taking place in the upper left of the composition (as if Christ might be descending to the people or revealing His stigmata). Hands and arms are raised high in joyous clapping, as if the mere sound of clapping would not be enough—the welcome and applause must somehow appear *visible* for it to be, or become, somehow authentic, verifiable. The flags above the people, yellow sickle and hammer in one, seem, improbably, to be almost clapping too, streaming and billowing dynamically towards the upper left. Another empty blue sky grounds the image. In *No.1, Part 2* we see the source of their animation. Kim Jong-un is on the edge of the concrete podium, his own arms and hands raised clapping, while he appears to look—disconcertingly—directly into Guofeng's camera lens, and so at us. Two photographers closely flank him to the right, the ubiquitous public visibility of the Supreme Leader guaranteed by their image-making, while lesser dignitaries on the podium stand back at a respectable, and safer, distance to the left, again clapping and looking at Jong-un.

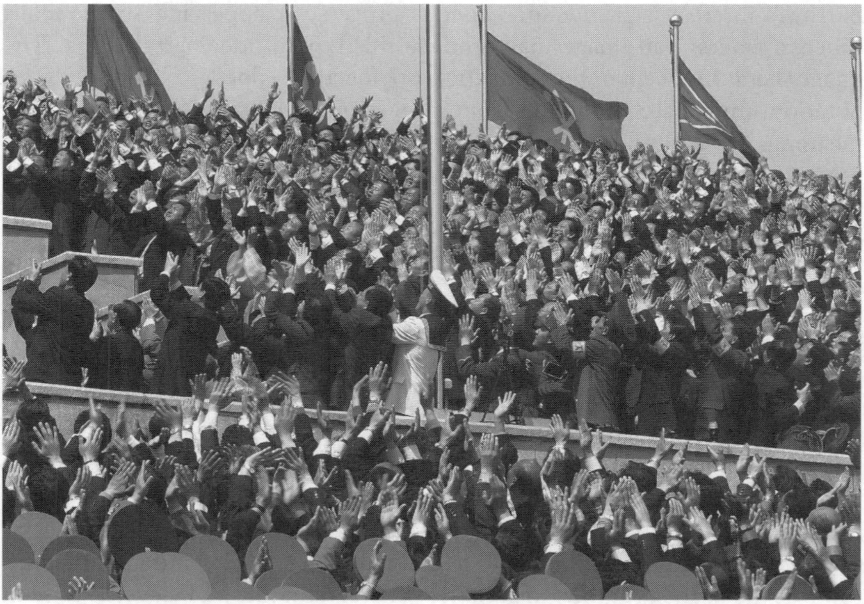

Figure 13 Wang Guofeng *Number 1, Part 1 North Korea 2012* (still from video, 2012). *Source:* © Wang Guofeng, Courtesy de Sarthe Gallery.

Jong-un's stare at the camera is disconcerting. His look, however, is fairly blank, and it is impossible to know what he might be thinking. He will no doubt turn his gaze slightly away from us in a second. But apparent contact with his furrowed brow—his eyes appear to be in darkness—is alarming: we have a reservoir of ideas, or rumors, about this man and what he has done and can do. This knowledge, or assumed knowledge, always accompanies our attention to Guofeng's photographs, but it is, in a fundamental sense, "blank" too. That is why these photographs, strangely, seem to produce whatever meaning one (wants to) brings to them, as though the images themselves are neutral, or neutralizing. There is a relativism to them which is also "freezing", leading nowhere except to another image and then—as they always belong to a system—back again. In Guofeng's broader "landscape" shot of the stadium (size given as 643 cm × 300 cm for the print) where Jong-un's appearance occurs, he attaches a slogan, reminiscent of those in Barbara Kruger's photo-text images, a kind of commentary or meta-commentary: "Abandon what you always believe; and let your brains, eyes, and mind focus on the moment of reality!" Is this Guofeng's own reading of the image, or a synoptic imagining of what Jong-un might be saying or meaning? It could be both, but neither actually carries much force. The image itself seems to me to "create" this message (or an approximation of it) automatically, somehow, between its form and my attention to it. This is Barthes's contradiction, of course. His reading of myth is clearly subjective, yet also claims truthfulness or something of the scientist's objectivity, not simply the status of one man's opinion. Likewise, Guofeng's photographs connote both, simultaneously, subjective and objective; opinion and truth.

A wider view may help, again, in how we might assess this state, this situation, of North Korea (with implications for the PRC, too). Independent, or "nonaligned," socialists and Marxists critical of the Soviet Union, both those who in some cases had had highly significant roles in the Bolshevik uprising, such as Leon Trotsky, as well as others from Russia and elsewhere, had for many decades objected, in principle, to the regime's self-designation as "communist" and, instead, characterized the Soviet Union through a variety of other names linked to particular critiques. These included "state-capitalist," "deformed workers' state," and (this sometimes intended as a condemnation, sometimes as more of a neutral description) "state-socialist."[23] The Soviet Union was certainly identified by the nonaligned left within these critiques as, in varying degrees, anti-democratic, authoritarian or totalitarian—though its parallel and usually more hostile analysis of capitalist power and the state in the Western democratic societies often operated a damaging break on both their understanding, and public statement of this critique, of "actually existing communism" in the Soviet Union and of that in the PRC.[24]

Later commentators towards the end of the Cold War stressed the interlock between the state, corporate communications technologies and the "military-industrial complex," but stressed that there were significant variations in these combinations across different countries in the Western and Eastern blocs—questioning Debord's formulations that sometimes appear to eliminate any genuine conflict or possibility of real change within these societies. It would be reckless, for instance, to claim that the end of the Soviet Union in 1991 brought about only superficial or trivial changes for people living in Eastern bloc states, or in the Germany that reunited soon afterwards. However, all the changes that did occur in the mid-1990s and since in these countries have certainly not been experienced as good or necessary, despite hubristic claims that an abstract and total Western capitalist "freedom" had finally been brought to these societies. And for the PRC now, never mind the situation in North Korea?

Guofeng's most recent photographs, taken in North Korea in 2014, pose different sized groups of workers, children, students and others in group portraits. One assumes that in each of these seventeen pictures (though this may not be the full extent of the series) the twin portraits of Jong-un and his father hang on the wall, although we don't actually see them in every picture—they are presumably sometimes located behind Guofeng as he takes the shot. So, for example, members of the *English Class at Pyongyong International Football School*—whose faces mostly look dazed and blank—themselves presumably stare at the twin Dear Fathers facing them on the front wall of the classroom. Their faces and body demeanors seem to betray a not yet fully trained sense of how they should be—how they must correctly visibly embody, themselves, the social order of which they seem to know they are a part. The room is antiseptically white and bare, save for one or two notice boards—a blankness matched by the sitters' white shirts. The picture radiates discomfort.

In *Children's Palace No.1* seventeen younger children sit at traditional musical instruments, frontally place, while Jong-un and his pater look down, or across, at us (and them) from the back wall. The children here appear not yet socialized sufficiently to worry too much about their physical dispositions and some smile unselfconsciously at the camera. *Doctors No.1*, by contrast, shows a police identification-type line-up of nine suspects, white-clad, shifting uncomfortably in a lobby area—fully aware they are participating in a group mug shot. In *Family of a People's Scientist* (though it's not entirely clear if one of these four is the People's Scientist) the back wall contains Father and Son as well as two other photographs of the massed ranks, pictures that look not dissimilar from Guofeng's own. We see what we want to see?

Five "Space" shots in the series show rooms empty of actual people but containing the disembodied images of Supreme Leaders B and C. These images are eerie: "gloomy" and "strange," shifting towards frightening. This is because the hieratic social order seems present without any actual bodies in these compositions to embody it—the representation works mechanistically, somehow, parasitically drawing on, and in, the few objects (a teddy bear, a TV aerial) that "people" these rooms in the absence of actual people. When the people return, en masse, to the same spaces and to others (remember that all these images are

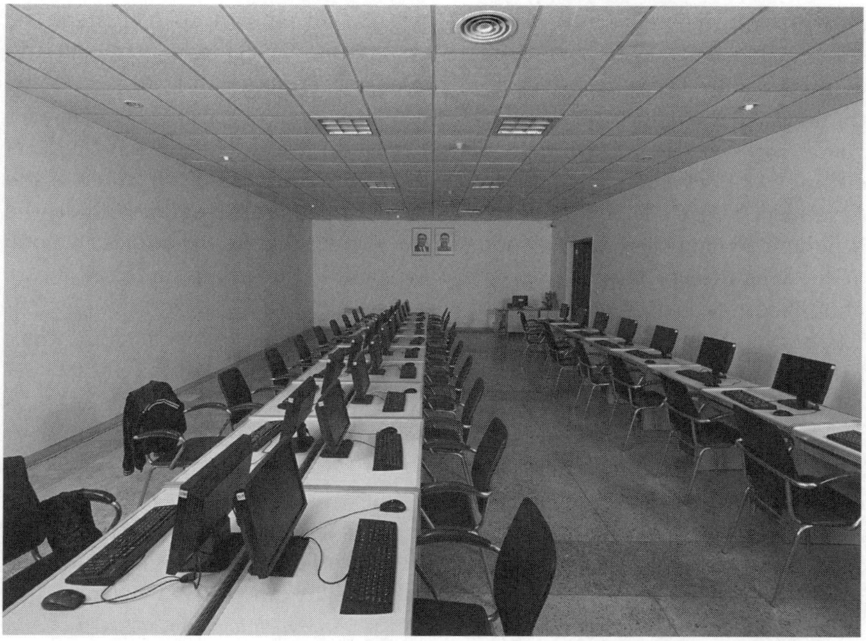

Figure 14 Wang Guofeng *Space No.1* (still from video, 2014). *Source:* © Wang Guofeng, Courtesy de Sarthe Gallery.

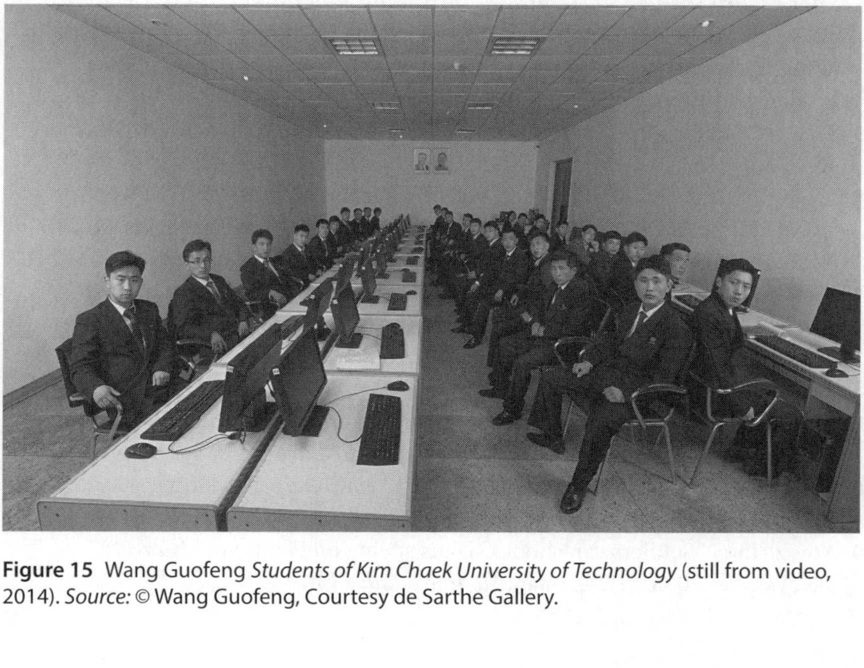

Figure 15 Wang Guofeng *Students of Kim Chaek University of Technology* (still from video, 2014). *Source:* © Wang Guofeng, Courtesy de Sarthe Gallery.

part of the system, the ecology of representation Guofeng has created) the effect remains strange. There is a surrealist "fort-da" game of throwing and taking back going on here, based on some warped Freudian image-economy trading with the cult of personality aspects of the regime.[25] Especially consider *Space No.1*—a room of computers emptied of bodies and *University Students of Kim Chaek University of Technology*, the same room filled with men at the terminals. These all look troubled—no smiles, caught metaphorically in the headlights, wondering, though apparently with no time to, which way to look or sit, what face, or façade, to project. They also look baffled, somehow aware of but not able to articulate something of the weight of the contradictions that Barthes remarked are at the heart of living. Some seem to be clenching their fists to get through this tricky situation of public and recorded visibility.

How will they seem to all the others?

Notes

1 For a discussion of literally dangerous artworks, see Anna Chave "Minimalism and the Rhetoric of Power," edited and reprinted in Francis Frascina and Jonathan Harris (eds.), *Art in Modern Culture: An Anthology of Critical Texts* (Phaidon: London, 1992): 264–281.

2 All definitions here are taken from the New Shorter Oxford English Dictionary. See Carola Hein "*Toshikeikaku* and *Machizukuri* in Japanese Urban Planning in Kobe," *Jahrbuch des DIJ (Deutsches Institut für Japanstudien)*, no. 13 (2001): 221–252. Maze-like centers constructed in Japanese cities were purpose-built to resist foreign occupation. See Yoshinobu Ashihara *The Hidden Order* (Kodansha International: New York, 1989).

3 See, e.g., Stephen Pinker *How the Mind Works* (Penguin: London, 1998), and William Lycan (ed.) *Mind and Cognition: A Reader* (Blackwell: Oxford, 1990).

4 "Con-juncture": literally "a meeting of circumstances." See W. J. T. Mitchell "World Pictures: Globalization and Visual Culture," in Jonathan Harris (ed.), *Globalization and Contemporary Art* (Wiley-Blackwell: Oxford, 2011): 253–264.

5 *Hamlet*: act 3, scene ii.

6 See, e.g., Neil Asher Silberman *Between Past and Present: Archaeology, Ideology and Nationalism in the Modern Middle East* (Holt: New York, 1989) and Nadia Abu El-Haj *Facts on the Ground: Archaeological Practice and Territorial Self-Fashioning in Israeli Society* (Chicago: University of Chicago Press: 2001).

7 See Eyal Weizman's *Hollow Land: Israel's Architecture of Occupation*: 151–152.

8 Emmanuel Sivan, "The Lights of Netzarim," *Ha'aretz*, 7 November 2003; in Weizman, *Hollow Land*: 81.

9 Amoz Harel "Soldiers can shoot Gazans spying on Netzarim," *Ha'aretz*, 5 November 2003; in Weizman, *Hollow Land*: 133.

10 See John Barrell, *The Dark Side of the Landscape: The Rural Poor in English Painting 1730–1840* (Cambridge University Press: Cambridge, 1980).

11 See Guy Debord *Panegyric* (Verso: London, 2004) and Libero Andreotti "Play-Tactics of the Internationale Situationniste," *October* 91, Winter 2000: 37–58). Note the palindrome, according to Andreotti, was an ancient "playform that, like the riddle and the conundrum, "cuts clean across any possible distinction between play and seriousness""(37).

12 Guy Debord *Society of the Spectacle*, trans. Donald Nicholson Smith (Zone: New York, 1995) and trans. Ken Knabb (Rebel Press: London, n.d.).

13 See Ernst Bloch, "Enfremdung, Verfremdung: Alienation, Estrangement," trans. Anne Halley and Darko Suvin, *The Drama Review*, 15 (1), Autumn, 1970 (1962): 120–125.

14 See Ferdinand de Saussure *Course in General Linguistics*, trans. Roy Harris (Bloomsbury: London, 2013 (1916)) and Roland Barthes, "Myth Today," in *Mythologies* (Paladin: St Albans, 1976 (1957)).

15 See ""Globalization" and "Globalism" in Theory and Practice," in Jonathan Harris, *The Utopian Globalists: Artists of Worldwide Revolution, 1919–2009* (Wiley-Blackwell: Oxford, 2013): 10–16.

16 Guy Debord, *Comments on the Society of the Spectacle*, trans. Malcolm Imrie (Verso: London, 1990): 12.

17 See, e.g., Robert Brenner, *The Boom and the Bubble: The US in the World Economy* (Verso: London, 2002) and Ted Fishman, *China Inc.: How the Rise of the Next Superpower Challenges America and the World* (Scribner: New York, 2005).

18 See, e.g., Richard Falk et al. (eds.), *The United Nations and a Just World Order* (Westview Press: Boulder, CO, 1991) and Zygmunt Bauman, *Globalization: The Human Consequences* (Columbia University Press: New York, 1998).

19 See the discussions of this art in Casa Asia *Core del Norte: el peso de la historia* (*North Korea: The Weight of History*) (Casa Asia: Madrid, 2010), based on an exhibition held in 2010 at Alhondiga Bilbao y Museu de l'Art de la Pell de Vic, Spain, curated by Menene Gras.

20 See, e.g., Raymond Williams, "Problems of Materialism," in Williams *Problems in Materialism and Culture* (Verso: London, 1980).

21 See, e.g., Rainer Rother, *Leni Riefenstahl: The Seduction of Genius* (Bloomsbury: London, 2003).

22 *Mythologies*: 116–121.

23 See, e.g., Leon Trotsky, *The Revolution Betrayed: What is the Soviet Union and Where is it Going?* (Pathfinder: New York, 2007 [1937]).

24 For an interesting account of Soviet Russian understanding of Chinese communism, see Alexander Pantsov, *The Bolsheviks and the Chinese Revolution 1917–1927* (Routledge: Abingdon, 2013).

25 See Sigmund Freud, *The Interpretation of Dreams* (Wordsworth: London, 1997) Part I, *Selected Essays*, 4: 1–338; Part II, *Selected Essays*, 5: 339–625.

Selected Bibliography

Abu El-Haj, Nadia, *Facts on the Ground: Archaeological Practice and Territorial Self-Fashioning in Israeli Society* (Chicago: University of Chicago Press, 2001).

Adorno, Theodor, *Culture Industry* (Routledge: London, 2001 [1970]).

Al Hoash Art Centre, *Palestinian Art Museum Jerusalem* (Al Hoash: Jerusalem, np).

Ali, Tariq, *The Duel: Pakistan on the Flight Path of American Power* (Pocket Books: London, 2009).

Amin, Samir, *Capitalism in the Age of Globalization: The Management of Contemporary Society* (Zed Books: London, 2014).

Anderson, Perry 'The House of Zion,' *New Left Review* 96 (Nov–Dec 2015): 5–37.

Andreotti, Libero, 'Play-tactics of the Internationale Situationniste' *October* 91(Winter 2000): 37–58.

ARCO Madrid International Contemporary Art Fair 2014, 33rd edition (catalogue).

Art Basel Hong Kong May 23–26, 2013 (catalogue).

Art Basel Miami Beach 1–4 December 2011 The 10th Edition (catalogue).

Ashihara, Yoshinobu, *The Hidden Order* (Kodansha International: New York, 1989).

Atsmon, Yuval, et al *Luxury Without Borders: China's New Class of Shoppers Take on the World* (Mckinzie Consumer and Shopper Insights: London, 2012).

Atwal, Glyn, 'Rise and Shine in India,' *Jetwings* (vol. 12, issue 12; December 2012): 2012–14.

Aveek Sen, 'Natasha De Batak – *Nightshade*,' in *Experimenter: 2011–2012* (Contemporary Art centre: Kolkata, 2012): 102–113 (catalogue).

Barakat, Tayseer, *Dust, Dialogue, Iron* (Al Mahatta Gallery: Ramallah, 2009) (catalogue).

Barthes, Roland, *Mythologies* (Paladin: St Albans, 1976 [1957]).

Barrell, John, *The Dark Side of the Landscape: The Rural Poor in English Painting 1730–1840* (Cambridge UP: Cambridge, 1980).

Bauman, Zygmunt, *Globalization: The Human Consequences* (Columbia University Press: New York, 1998).

The Global Contemporary Art World, First Edition. Jonathan Harris.
© 2017 John Wiley & Sons, Inc. Published 2017 by John Wiley & Sons, Inc.

Bell, Stephen, and Hui Feng, *The Rise of the People's Bank of China: The Politics of Institutional Change* (Harvard University Press: Cambridge Mass., 2013).

Belting, Hans, Andrea Buddensieg, and Peter Weibel (eds.), *The Global Contemporary and the Rise of New Art Worlds* (ZKM/MIT Press: Cambridge Mass., 2013).

Belting, Hans, 'The Plurality of Art Worlds and the New Museum,' in Belting, Buddensieg and Weibel (eds.) *The Global Contemporary and the Rise of New Art Worlds* (Center for Art and Media Karlsruhe/MIT Press: Cambridge Mass., 2013): 246–54.

Berardi, Franco, 'The Paradox of Media Activism: The Net is not a Tool, it's an Environment,' in Anthony Downey (ed.), *Uncommon Grounds: New Media and Critical Practices in North Africa and the Middle East* (IB Tauris: London, 2014): 39–46.

Bernal, Martin, *Black Athena. The Afroasiatic Roots of Classical Civilization: The Fabrication of Ancient Greece 1785–1985* (Vintage: London, 1991).

Bhabha, Homi, *The Location of Culture* (Routledge: London, 1994).

Bioscope, *The Many Lives of Indian Cinema: 1913–2013 and Beyond. Disciplines, Histories, Technologies, Futures* (BioScope/Centre for the Study of Developing Societies: Delhi, 2014).

Birnbaum, Daniel, Connie Butler, Suzanne Cotter, Bice Curiger, Okwui Enwesor, Massimiliano Gioni, Bob Nikas and Hans Ulrich Obrist, *Defining Contemporary Art: Twenty Five Years in Two Hundred Pivotal Artworks* (Phaidon: London, 2011).

Bishop, Claire, *Installation Art: A Critical History* (Routledge: New York, 2005).

Bishop, Claire, *Artificial Hells: Participatory Art and the Politics of Spectatorship* (Verso: London, 2012).

Bloch, Ernst, 'Enfremdung, Verfremdung: Alienation, Estrangement' trans. Anne Halley and Darko Suvin, *The Drama Review* vol. 15, no. 1 (Autumn, 1970 [1962]): 120–125.

Blum, William, *Killing Hope: US Military and CIA Interventions since World War II* (Zed Books: New York, 2003).

Blum, William, *Rogue State: A Guide to the World's Only Superpower* (Zed Books: New York, 2014).

Boullata, Kamal, *Palestinian Art: From 1850 to the Present* (Saqi Books: Beirut, 2009).

Brenner, Robert, *The Boom and the Bubble: The US in the World Economy* (Verso: London, 2002).

Breshears, Guy, *Of Papers and Protests: Hong Kong Responds to Occupy Central* (Guy Rubens Breshears: Hong Kong, 2016).

Brown, Tim, *Change by Design: How Design Thinking Challenges Organizations and Inspires Innovation* (Harper Business: London, 2009).

Brummer, Alex, *Bad Banks: Greed, Incompetence and the Next Global Crisis* (Random House: New York, 2015).

Buck, Daniel, *Constructing China's Capitalism: Shanghai and the Nexus of Urban-Rural Industries* (Macmillan: London, 2012).

Bull, Malcolm, 'The Two Economies of World Art,' in Harris (ed.), *Globalization and Contemporary Art* (Wiley-Blackwell; Malden MA: 2011):179–90.

Caldwell, Erskine and Margaret Bourke-White, *You Have Seen Their Faces* (University of Georgia Press: Athens GA, 1995 [1937]).

Casa Asia, *Core del Norte: el peso de la historia* ['North Korea: The Weight of History'] (Casa Asia: Madrid, 2010) (catalogue).

Casavecchia, Barbara 'Roman Ruins: Reflections on Italy's Decline,' *Frieze* 160 (January-February 2014):13.

Chakrabarty, Dipesh, *Provincializing Europe: Postcolonial Thought and Historical Difference* (Princeton University Press: Princeton NJ, 2000).

Chang, Johnson, 'From "Post-1989" to Asian Thought: An Interview with Johnson Chang,' *Leap: International Art Museum of Contemporary China (Art Basel Hong Kong special edition) 23/5/2013–26/5/2013*: 36–7.

Chave, Anna, 'Minimalism and the Rhetoric of Power,' in Francis Frascina and Jonathan Harris (eds.) *Art in Modern Culture: An Anthology of Critical Texts* (Phaidon: London, 1992): 264–281.

Chen Lusheng, *Revolutionary Art Since the Yan'an Era: Extended Edition* (Long Museum: Shanghai, 2014).

Cherian, P.J., 'Kerala's cosmopolitanism in antiquity: Material evidence from the Pattanam port site,' *India's First Biennale 12/12/12* (information leaflet published by Kochi Biennale Foundation, nd) np.

Chin-tao-Wu, 'Biennials without Borders?' *New Left Review* 57 (May-June 2009): 107–115.

Chiu, Melissa and Benjamin Genocchio (eds.), *Contemporary Art in Asia: A Critical Reader* (MIT Press: Cambridge MA, 2011).

Chong, Derrick, 'The Emergence of Powerhouse Dealers in Contemporary Art,' in Jonathan Harris (ed.), *Globalization and Contemporary Art* (Wiley-Blackwell: Oxford, 2011): 431–48.

Clark, T.J., *Image of the People: Gustav Courbet and the 1848 Revolution* (Thames and Hudson: London, 1974).

Clark, John, 'Modern Art in South-East Asia,' *Asia Art Pacific* (Sample Issue, 1993).

Clark, John, *Modern Asian Art* (University of Hawai'i Press: Honolulu, 1998).

Coburn, Patrick, *The Rise of Islamic State: ISIS and the New Sunni Revolution* (Verso: London, 2014).

Craggs, Ruth and Claire Wintle (eds.), *Cultures of Decolonization: Transnational Productions and Practices: 1945–1970* (Manchester University Press: Manchester, 2016).

Craven, David, '"Institutionalized Globalization," Contemporary Art, and the Corporate Gulag in Chile,' in Harris (ed.), *Globalization and Contemporary Art* (Wiley-Blackwell: Oxford, 2011): 479–495.

Cross, John and Richard Hitchcock, 'Chinese students' (or students from China) views of UK H.E.: differences, difficulties and benefits, and suggestions for facilitating transition,' *The East Asian Learner* (vol. 3, no. 2: November 2007): 1–31.

Crystal, David, *English as a Global Language* (Cambridge University Press: Cambridge, 2012).

Cummings, Basia Lewndowska, 'See Change: The Increased Visibility of Art from Africa in the UK,' *Frieze* 160 (January-February, 2014):17.

Currid, Elizabeth, *The Warhol Economy: How Fashion, Art and Music Drive New York* (Princeton University Press: Princeton NJ, 2007).

Dadi, Iftikhar and Hammad Nasar (eds.), *Lines of Control: Partition as a Productive Space* (Green Cardamon/Herbert F. Johnson Museum of Art, Cornell University: Ithica, 2012).

Davidts, Wouter, 'Art Factories, Museums of Contemporary Art and the Promise of Artistic Production from Centre Pompidou to Tate Modern,' *Fabrications: The Journal of the Society of Architectural Historians, Australia and New Zealand* 16 (1) (2006): 23–42.

Davidts, Wouter, 'The Vast and the Void: On Tate Modern's Turbine Hall' *Footprint Trans-disciplinary* (Autumn 2007):77–92.

Davis, August Jordan and Jonathan Harris (eds.), *Bashir Makhoul* (Jerusalem: Al Hoash, 2012).

Davis, Mike, 'The Urbanization of Empire: Megacities and the Laws of Chaos,' *Social Text* (vol. 22, no. 2, 2004): 9–15.

Davis, Mike, *Planet of Slums* (Verso: London, 2006).

Debord, Guy, *Comments on the Society of the Spectacle* trans. Malcolm Imrie (Verso: London, 1990).

Debord, Guy, *Society of the Spectacle* trans. Donald Nicholson Smith (Zone: New York, 1995 [1967]).

Debord, Guy, *Panegyric* (Verso: London, 2004).

DeVoir, J. and L. Boo Jespersen, *Tracking Funding to the Visual and Performing Arts in the OPT* [Occupied Palestinian Territories]*: A Quantative and Qualitative Analysis* (A.M. Qattan Foundation: Ramallah, 2012).

Dhaher, Safa Husni, *Al-'Eizariyah and the Wall: From the Quasi-Capital of Palestine to an Arab Ghetto* (unpublished PhD thesis, University of Trento, Italy: 2016).

Dooeun Choi, 'Mulling over the social role of the Korean moving image: Moving images, expecting the images that move society,' in Jinsuk Suh (ed.), *Moving on Asia* vol. 6 (Alt. Space Loop: Seoul, 2013): 340–4.

Downey, Anthony (ed.), *Uncommon Grounds: New Media and Critical Practices in North Africa and the Middle East* (IB Tauris: London, 2014).

Downey, Anthony, (ed.), *Dissonant Archives: Contemporary Visual Culture and Contested Narratives in the Middle East* (I.B. Tauris: London, 2015).

D'Souza, Robert (ed.), *Outside In: Dialogues and Documents of Art and Social Change* (W + K Publishing: New Delhi, 2012).

Duncan, Carol, *Civilizing Rituals: Inside Public Museums* (Routledge: London, 1995).

Duncan, Carol and Alan Wallach, 'The Universal Survey Museum,' *Art History* (December 1980): 447–69.

Elkins, James, 'Translation,' edited transcript of a discussion between Shigemi Inaga, Bhaskar Mukhopadhyay, Pedro Erber, James Elkins, Shelly Errington, Thomas Dacosta Kaufmann, Michael Holly, Keith Moxey, Michele Greet and Harry Harootunian, in James Elkins, Zhivka Valiavisharska and Alice Kim (eds.) *Art and Globalization* (Pennsylvania State University Press: University Park, 2010): 22–35.

Enwesor, Okwui, 'Mega-Exhibitions and the Antinomies of a Transnational Global Form,' in Elena Filipovic, Marieke Van Hal and Solveig Ovstebo (eds.), *The Biennial Reader*: 426-45 (Bergen Kunsthall: Bergen, 2010): 440–1.

Fadda, Reem, (ed.), *Art in Palestine: Palestinian Women Artists* (Jerusalem: Al Hoash, 2007) (catalogue).

Falk, Richard, et al (eds.), *The United Nations and a Just World Order* (Westview Press: Boulder, Col., 1991).

Ferguson, Charles H., *Predator Nation: Corporate Criminals, Political Corruption, and the Hijacking of America* (Crown Business: New York, 2012).

Filipovic, Elena, Marieke Van Hal and Solveig Ovstebo (eds.), *The Biennial Reader* (Bergen Kunsthall: Bergen, 2010).

Fischman, Ted, *China Inc.: How the Rise of the Next Superpower Challenges America and the World* (Scribner: New York, 2005).

FitzGibbon, Francis, 'Low-Hanging Fruit,' *London Review of Books* (22 January 2015): 13–14.

Flores, Patrick D., 'Field Notes from Artworlds: Interest and Impasse,' *Third Text* (special issue on 'Contemporaneity and Art in Southeast Asia,') ed. Patrick D. Flores and Joan Kee (no. 111, vol. 25, issue 4: July 2011): 383–94.

Foucault, Michel, *The Order of Things: An Archaeology of the Human Sciences* (Tavistock Publications: London, 1970).

Foster, Hans, 'After the White Cube' *London Review of Books*: (14 March 2015): 25–6.

Frascina, Francis and Jonathan Harris (eds.), *Art in Modern Culture: An Anthology of Critical Texts* (Phaidon: London, 1992).

Frascina, Francis (ed.), *Pollock and After: The Critical Debate* (Harper and Row: London, 1985).

French, Howard, *China's Second Continent: How a Million migrants are building a new Empire in Africa* (Knopf: New York, 2015).

Freud, Sigmund, *The Interpretation of Dreams* (Wordsworth: London, 1997).

Gannit Ankori, Gannit, *Palestinian Art* (Reaktion: London, 2006).

Gao Minglu, 'The '85 Art Movement' (1986), reprinted in Wu Hung (ed.), *Contemporary Chinese Art: Primary Documents* (Museum of Modern Art: New York, 2008):52–63.

Gaweewong, Gridthiya, 'State Ideology vs. the Rise of Small Narratives: Discourse of Moving Images on the 21st Century Thailand,' in Jinsuk Suh (ed.), *Moving on Asia* (Alt. Space Loop: Seoul, 2013): 388–93.

Goskaman, Armagan, 'Perspectives on the United Kingdom's Withdrawal from the European Union,' in Engin Sorhun, Umit Hacioglu and Hasan Dincer (eds.) *Regional Economic Integration and the Global Financial System* (IGIU Global: Hershey PA, 2015):36–48.

Graham, Stephen, 'War and the City,' *New Left Review* (44 March-April 2007):121–132.

Gras, Menene (ed.), *Corea del Norte: el peso de la historia (North Korea: The Weight of History)* (Casa Asia/Alhondiga Bilbao: Madrid, 2011).

Grunenberg, Christoph, *The Real Thing: Contemporary Art from China* (Tate Publishing: London, 2007).

Guilbaut, Serge, *How New York Stole the Idea of Modern Art: Abstract Expressionism, Freedom and the Cold War* (University of Chicago Press: Chicago, 1983).

Hall, Stuart, *The Hard Road to Renewal: Thatcherism and the Crisis of the Left* (Verso: London, 1988).

Harris, Jonathan, *Federal Art and National Culture: The Politics of Identity in New Deal America* (Cambridge University Press: New York, 1995).

Harris, Jonathan, *The New Art History: A Critical Introduction* (Routledge: London, 2001).

Harris, Jonathan, Writing Back to Modern Art: After Greenberg, Fried and Clark (Routledge: Abingdon, 2005).

Harris, Jonathan, 'Curatorial Imperialism?: From "Tate in the North" to "Capital of Culture",' in Jonathan Harris (ed.), *Identity Theft: The Cultural Colonization of Contemporary Art* (Liverpool University Press/Tate Liverpool: Liverpool, 2009): 9–27.

Harris, Jonathan (ed.), *Globalization and Contemporary Art* (Wiley-Blackwell: Malden MA, 2011).

Harris, Jonathan, and Richard Williams (eds.), *Regenerating Culture and Society: Architecture, Art and Urban Style within the Global Politics of City-Branding* (Liverpool University Press/Tate Liverpool; Liverpool, 2011).

Harris, Jonathan, *The Utopian Globalists: Artists of Worldwide Revolution, 1919–2009* (Wiley-Blackwell: Malden MA, 2013).

Harris, Jonathan (ed.), *Third Text* (special edition on 'Global Occupations of Art'): no. 123, July 2013.

Harris, Jonathan, 'To divide, to occupy: cancelled mediations in Palestinian video art,' in Bashir Makhoul (ed.), *Palestinian Video Art: Constellation of the Moving Image* (Palestinian Art Court – Al Hoash: Jerusalem, 2013):68–87.

Harris, Jonathan, 'Love Stories' (interview with Mark Boulos), *Art Monthly* November 2013; no. 371:1–4.

Harris, Jonathan, 'Apodictic Autonomy and Affirmation in Contemporary Asian Art: Four Cases,' in Bashir Makhoul and Alnoor Mitha (eds.), *Conflict and Compassion: A Paradox of Difference in Contemporary Asian Art* (Home: Manchester, 2016): 95–116.

Harrison, Charles, and Fred Orton (eds.), *Modernism, Criticism, Realism: Alternative Contexts for Art* (Harper and Row: London, 1984).

Hardt, Michael and Antonio, Negri, *Multitude: War and Democracy in the Age of Empire* (Penguin: New York, 2004).

Hardt, Michael and Antonio, Negri, *Empire* (Harvard University Press: Cambridge, Mass, 2000).

Hardt, Michael and Antonio Negri, *Multitude: War and Democracy in the Age of Empire* (Penguin: New York, 2004).

Harvey, David, *A Brief History of Neoliberalism* (Oxford University Press: Oxford, 2005).

Harvey, David, *A Companion to Marx's Capital* (Verso: London, 2010).

Harvey, David, *The Enigma of Capital and the Crisis in Capitalism* (Profile: London, 2010).

Hein, Carola, '*Toshikeikaku* and *Machizukuri* in Japanese Urban Planning in Kobe,' *Jahrbuch des DIJ (Deutsches Institut für Japanstudien)*, no. 13 (2001): 221–52.

Hlavajova, Maria, 'How to Biennial? The Biennial in relation to the art institution,' in Filipovic, van Hal and Ovstebo (eds.) *The Biennial Reader: An anthology on large scale perennial exhibitions of contemporary art* (Bergen Kunsthall: Bergen, 2010): 292–305.

Hon, Gordon, and Bashir Makhoul, *The Origins of Palestinian Art* (Liverpool University Press: Liverpool, 2013).

Hopkins, David, *After Modern Art: 1945–2000* (Oxford University Press: Oxford, 2000).

Horovich, Noah, *Art of the Deal: Contemporary Art in a Global Financial Market* (Princeton University Press: Princeton NJ, 2011).

Horst, Mariska ter (ed.), *Changing Perspectives: Dealing with Globalization in the Presentation and Collection of Contemporary Art* (KIT: Amsterdam, 2012).

Hou Hanru, 'Entropy, Chinese artists, Western art institutions: a New Internationalism,' (1994), in Wu Hung (ed.), *Contemporary Chinese Art: Primary Documents* (MOMA: New York, 2010): 249–251.

Huang Du, 'The Implosion of Urbanization in China,' in *China Contemporary: Architecture, Art, Visual Culture* (exhibition catalogue, Netherlands Museum/NAi Uitgevers: Rotterdam, 2006).

Huang Du, 'Art in Negotiations,' in Zhang Zikang and Huang Du (eds.) *Negotiations: The Second Today's Documents 2010* (Culture and Art Publishing House/Today Art Museum: Beijing, 2010):16–35.

Huang Du, 'Status of Chinese Contemporary Art: The Transformation in Concept and Language' (unpub. transcript of talk given at 'Asian Maps' seminar at ARCO Art Fair, Madrid, 2013): np.

Huang Rui (ed.), *Beijing 798: Reflections on Art, Architecture, and Society in China Timezone* 8 (Hong Kong, 2004/Thinking Hands, Beijing, 2004).

Hughes, Robert, 'The Rise of Andy Warhol,' *The New York Review of Books*, 18 February 1982, in Brian Wallis (ed.) *Art after Representation: Rethinking Representation* (New Museum of Contemporary Art: New York, 1988): 45–58.

Hyunsuk Seo, 'Digital Heterotopias: Historical 'Elsewhere' in Korean Video Art of the 2000s' (358-67), in Jinsuk Suh (ed.) *Moving on Asia* (Alt. Space Loop: Seoul, 2013).

Ishola Khosla, 'A Future for Design: Improvisation through the Informal Economy,' *TAKE* (vol. 2, issue 7):100–102.

Jahnvi Dameron Nandan, 'Objects of Desire,' *Take* (vol. 2, no. 7: 2012): 104–7.

Jarvis, Peter, *Universities and Corporate Universities: The Higher Learning Industry in Global Society* (Kogan Page: London, 2001).

Jewyo Rhii, *Jewyo Rhii: Night Studio* (Artsonje Center: Seoul, 2013).

Jewyo Rhii, *Jewyo Rhii: Walls to Talk to* (Koenig Books: London, 2013).

Jiang, Jiehong, *Burden or Legacy: From the Chinese Cultural Revolution to Contemporary Art* (Hong Kong University Press: Hong Kong, 2007).

Jiang, Jiehong, *Red: The Chinese Cultural Revolution* (Jonathan Cape: London, 2010).

Jingyang Lin, *Brands Research & Development Institute* (Dalian Polytechnic Institute: School of Art & Design, nd).

Jinsuk Suh, 'A New Sphere for Public Discourse and Media Art,' in Jinsuk Suh (ed.) *Moving on Asia* (Alt. Space Loop: Seoul, 2013): 476–9.

Jones, Caroline, 'Globalism/Globalization,' in Kim, Alice and James Elkins (eds.), *Art and Globalization* (Pennsylvania State University Press: University Park: Penn: 2010): 129–37.

Jones, Owen Bennett, 'The Military and the Mullahs,' *London Review of Books* (3 March 2016):15–17.

Jung-Sun Ni Han, *An Imperial Path to Modernity: Yoshino Sakuzo and a New Liberal Order in East Asia 1905–37* (Harvard University Press: Cambridge, Mass., 2015).

Kapur, Geeta, *When Was Modernism: Essays on Contemporary Cultural Practice in India* (Tulika Press: Delhi, 2002).

Kapur, Geeta, 'A Cultural Conjuncture in India: Art into Documentary,' in Terry Smith, Okwui Enwezor and Nancy Condee (eds.) *Antinomies of Art and Culture: Modernity, Postmodernity, Contemporaneity* (Duke University Press: Durham NC, 2008): 30–59.

Kee, Joan, 'Contemporary Southeast Asian Art: The Right Kind of Trouble, *Third Text* (special issue on 'Contemporaneity and Art in Southeast Asia') vol. 25, issue 4; July 2011: 371–81.

Kestor, Grant, *The One and the Many: Contemporary Collaborative Art in a Global Context* (Duke University Press: Durham NC, 2011).

Khoury, Tarek, 'The Art of the Written Word and New Media Dissemination: Across the Borders between Syria and Lebanon,' in Downey (ed.), *Uncommon Grounds: New Media and Critical Practices in North Africa and the Middle East* (302–17).

Kim, Alice (eds.), *Art and Globalization* (Pennsylvania State University Press: University Park: Penn, 2010).

Klein, Naomi, *The Shock Doctrine: The Rise of Disaster Capitalism* (Allen Lane: London, 2007).

Kochi Biennale, 'Muziris Heritage Project,' *India's First Biennale 12/12/12* (information leaflet published by Kochi Biennale Foundation, nd).

Kochi Biennale, *Welcome Kochi-Muziris Biennale 2012* (unpublished leaflet, nd) np.

Kocur, Zoya, and Simon Leung (eds.), *Theory in Contemporary Art since 1985* (Blackwell: Oxford, 2005).

Lankov, Andrei, *The Real North Korea* (Oxford University Press: Oxford, 2013).

Lewis, Michael, *Flash Boys: A Wall Street Revolt* (Norton: New York, 2015).

Leung, Isaac, 'Curatorial Statement: In-between Hong Kong and China – mediation as a world-making process,' *One World Exposition* (Videotage: Hong Kong, 2012): 1–3.

Li Xianting, 'Confessions of a *China/Avant Garde* Curator' (1989), reprinted in Wu Hung (ed.), *Contemporary Chinese Art: Primary Documents* (MOMA: New York, 2010):116–20.

Li Zhenhua, 'Curatorial Statement: One World Exposition: Film, Video and Integrated Media Art in Mainland China and Hong Kong,' *One World Exposition* (Videotage: Hong Kong, 2012): 6–7.

Lind, Maria and Raimund Minichbauer (eds.), *European Cultural Policies 2015: A Report with Scenarios on the Future of Public Funding for Contemporary Art in Europe* (IAPSIS: London, 2005).

Lycan, William, (ed.), *Mind and Cognition: A Reader* (Blackwell: Oxford, 1990).

Makhoul, Bashir, *Enter Ghost, Exit Ghost* (Yang Gallery: Beijing, 2012).

Makhoul, Bashir (ed.), *Palestinian Video Art: Constellation of the Moving Image* (Palestinian Art Court – al Hoash: Jerusalem and London, 2013).

Maira, Sunaina, *Jil Oslo: Palestinian Hip Hop, Youth Culture and the Youth Movement* (Tadween Publishing / George Mason University: Washington DC, 2013).

Malani, Nalini, *Nalini Malani: Cassandra's Gift* (Vadehra Art Gallery, Delhi: 2014) (catalogue).

Marchini Camia, Chiara, (ed.), *Digital Art Works: The Challenges of Conservation* (ZKM/Espace Multimedia Gantner/CEAAC: Kahlsruhe, 2012).

Martini, Vittoria, 'The Era of the Histories of Biennials has Begun,' *The Biennial Reader. The Bergen Conference* (Bergen Kunsthall: Bergen, 2010): 9–13.

Marx, Karl, *Capital: A Critique of Political Economy* vol. 1 (trans. Ben Fowkes; Penguin: London, 1990).

Mayank Mansingh Kaul, 'Towards Asian Modernities,' *Roots, Identity, Modernity: Asian Voices on Culture and Creativity* (Netpac: New Delhi, 2013) np.

Mayank Mansingh Kaul, 'Design in India: Towards an Agenda?' *TAKE* (vol. 2, issue 7: 2012):18–21.

Mereweather, Charles, *Market Forces – Erasure: from Conceptualism to Abstraction* curated by Charles Merewether (Osage Art Foundation and City University of Hong Kong, 16 May–30 June 2014) (catalogue).

Mereweather, Charles, *Poetics of Materiality*, curated by Charles Merewether 4 January–16 February 2014 (Osage Art Foundation: Hong Kong, 2014 (catalogue).

Mereweather, Charles, *Ng Joon Kiat: Towards a Horizon* (Osage Art Foundation: Hong Kong, 2013) (catalogue).

Mercer, Kobena (ed.), *Cosmopolitan Modernisms* (INIVA/MIT Press, Cambridge MA, 2005).

Meskimmon, Marsha, *Contemporary Art and the Cosmopolitan Imagination* (Routledge: Abingdon, 2011).

Ming Tiampo, 'Cultural Merchantilism: Modernism's Means of Production: The Gutai Group as Case Study' in Harris, Jonathan (ed.), *Globalization and Contemporary Art* (Wiley-Blackwell: Oxford, 2011): 212–24.

Mitchell, W.J.T., 'World Pictures: Globalization and Visual Culture,' in Jonathan Harris (ed.), *Globalization and Contemporary Art* (Wiley-Blackwell: Oxford, 2011): 253–264.

Mitchell, W.J.T., Bernard E. Harcourt and Michael Taussig, *Occupy: Three Inquiries in Disobedience* (University of Chicago Press: Chicago and London, 2013).

Morozov, Evgeny, 'Socialize the Data Centres!' *New Left Review* 91: Jan/Feb 2015, 45–66.

Morris, Robert, 'Notes on Art as/and Land Reclamation' *October* 12 (Spring 1980): 97–102.

Mulk Raj Anand, 'Chairman's Welcome Address,' *Lalit Kala Contemporary* 36, September 1990: 12 (catalogue).

Nakhleh, Khalil, *Globalized Palestine: The National Sell-Out of a Homeland* (Red Sea Press: Trenton, NJ: 2012).

Netpac, *2010: Imagining Asia* (Netpac in association with Goethe Institut, Max Mueller Bhavan: Delhi, 2010).

Netpac, *Roots, Identity, Modernity: Asian Voices on Culture and Creativity* (Netpac: New Delhi, 2013).

Nguyen Trinh, Thi 'Discourse on the Moving Image in Vietnam in the 21st Century,' in Jinsuk Suh (ed.), *Moving on Asia* (Alt. Space Loop: Seoul, 2013): 414–19.

Nitzan, Jonathan and Shimshon Bichler, *The Global Political Economy of Israel* (Pluto Press: London, 2002).

Osage Gallery, *About Osage* (Osage Art Foundation: Hong Kong, 2014).
Osage Gallery, *Works by Au Hoi Lam* (Osage Art Foundation: 2014).
Osage Gallery, *Symposium: Art and Values* (Osage Art Foundation and City University of Hong Kong: Hong Kong, 2014).
Osborne, Peter, *Anywhere or Not At All: Philosophy of Contemporary Art* (Verso: London, 2013).
Padukone, Neil, *Beyond South Asia: India's Strategic Evolution and the Reintegration of the Subcontinent* (Bloomsbury: London, 2014).
Panitch, Leo and Sam Gindin, *The Making of Global Capitalism: The Political Economy of American Empire* (Verso: London, 2013).
Pantsov, Alexander, *The Bolsheviks and the Chinese Revolution 1917-1927* (Routledge: Abingdon, 2013).
Pau, Ellen, 'The Discourse of Moving Images in Hong Kong in the 21st Century,' in Jinsuk Suh (ed.) *Moving On Asia* (Alt. Space Loop: Seoul, 2012): 420–6.
Pijnappel, John, 'Moving Images in the 21st Century in Indian Video Art and beyond,' in Jinsuk Suh (ed.) *Moving On Asia* (Alt. Space Loop: Seoul, 2012): 428–34.
Pinker, Stephen, *How the Mind Works* (Penguin: London, 1998).
Pollock, Griselda and Fred Orton, *Vincent Van Gogh: Artist of his Time* (Phaidon: London, 1978).
Poulantzas, Nicos, *State, Power, Socialism* (Verso: London, 1979).
Preston, Paul, *The Spanish Holocaust: Inquisition and Extermination in Twentieth-Century Spain* (Harper Press: London, 2012).
Reiko Tomii, 'The Discourse of (L)imitation: A Case Study with Hole-Digging in 1960s Japan,' in Jonathan Harris (ed.), *Globalization and Contemporary Art* (Wiley-Blackwell: Oxford, 2011): 344–56.
Retort Collective, *Afflicted Powers: Capital and Spectacle in a New Age of War* (Verso: London, 2005).
Robertson, Iain, Victoria L. Tseng and Sonal Singh, '"Chindia" as art market opportunity,' in Robertson and Chong (eds.), *The Art Business* (Routledge, Abingdon: 2008): 82–96.
Robertson, Iain, 'Price Before Value,' in Iain Robertson and Derrick Chong (eds.), *The Art Business* (Routledge: London and New York, 2008): 29–54.
Robertson, Iain, 'The Art Market in Transition, the Global Economic Crisis and the Rise of Asia,' in Harris, Jonathan (ed.), *Globalization and Contemporary Art* (Wiley-Blackwell: Oxford, 2011): 449–463.
Rosenberg, Harold, *The Tradition of the New* (Horizon Press: New York, 1959).
Rother, Rainer, *Leni Riefenstahl: The Seduction of Genius* (Bloomsbury: London, 2003).
Ryan, Janette (ed.), *China's Higher Education Reform and Internationalisation* (Routledge: Abingdon, 2011).
Sadek, Walid, 'Peddling Time When Standing Still: Art Remains in Lebanon and the Globalization that Was,' in Harris (ed.) *Globalization and Contemporary Art* (Wiley-Blackwell: Oxford, 2011): 43–55.

Said, Edward, *The End of the Peace Process: Oslo and After* (Granta: London, 2003).

Salmon, Andrew, *Modern Korea* (John Murray: London, 2014).

Sassen, Saskia, *Territory, Authority, Rights: From Medieval to Global Assemblages* (Princeton University Press: Princeton NJ, 2006).

Saussure, Ferdinand de, *Course in General Linguistics* trans. Roy Harris (Bloomsbury: London, 2013 [1916]).

Seoul Museum of Art, *SeMA Nanji Residency 2013* (Seoul Museum of Art: Seoul, 2013) (catalogue).

Seoul Museum of Art, *Analog Welcome, Digital Archive* (Seoul Museum of Art: Nanji, 2013) (catalogue).

Seoul Museum of Art, *Real DMZ Project 2013* (Samuso: Seoul, 2013) (catalogue).

Seoul Museum of Art, *The 70th Anniversary of Liberation Day: NK Project* (SeMA: Seoul, 2015) (catalogue).

Shah, Svasti P., *Street Corner Secrets: Sex, Work, and Migration in the City of Mumbai* (Duke University Press: Durham, N.C., 2014).

Sharaf, Rawan, 'The Role Played by Palestinian Cultural Institutions in the Formation and Transformation of Palestinian Visual Art/Culture' (unpublished essay: 2014): 6–7.

Silberman, Neil Asher, *Between Past and Present: Archaeology, Ideology and Nationalism in the Modern Middle East* (Holt: New York, 1989).

Silverstein, Michael and Neil Fiske, *Trading Up: The New American Luxury* (Boston Consulting Group, Boston: 2004).

Smith, David, *The Dragon and the Elephant: China, India and the New World Order* (Profile Books: London, 2008).

Smith, Terry Okwui Enwezor, and Nancy Condee (eds.), *Antinomies of Art and Culture: Modernity, Postmodernity, Contemporaneity* (Duke University Press: Durhan NC, 2008).

Smith, Terry, *What is Contemporary Art?* (University of Chicago Press: Chicago, 2009).

Smith, Terry, *Contemporary Art: World Currents* (Laurence King: London, 2011).

Soyoung Kim, 'How Films in the 21st Century Respond and Adopt to the Digital Era: *Two Doors* – a Transmedia Documentary,' in Jinsuk Suh (ed.), *Moving On Asia* (Alt. Space Loop: Seoul, 2013): 346–9.

Sreekumar, Hemant, 'DDA to DLF,' in Robert E. D'Souza (ed.), *Outside In: Dialogues and Documents of Art and Social Change* (W + K Publishing: New Delhi, 2012): 24–31.

Stallabrass, Julian, *High Art Lite: The Rise and Fall Young British Art* (Verso: London, 2006).

Stanley, Phiona, 'The hidden curriculum: A critical analysis of tertiary English teaching in China,' in Janette Ryan (ed.), *China's Higher Education Reform and Internationalisation* (Routledge: Abingdon, 2011):193–210.

Suchitra Balasubrahmanyan, 'The India Report: The Search for Culturally Relevant Roots. Towards a History of Design in India,' TAKE (vol. 2, issue 7): 26–28.

Tae-Ho Kim, 'Burning Rice: the economics of the division and rice,' in Seoul Museum of Art, *Real DMZ Project 2013* (Samuso: Seoul, 2013): 89–91 (catalogue).

Taraki, Lisa, 'Urban Modernity on the Periphery: A New Middle Class Reinvents the Palestinian City,' *Social Text* 95 (vol. 26, no. 2: Summer 2008): 61–81.

Taraki, Lisa, 'Enclave Micropolis: The Paradoxical Case of Ramallah/Al-Bireh,'*Journal of Palestine Studies* (vol. XXXVII, no. 4; Summer 2008): 6–20.

Taylor, Astra, *The People's Platform: Taking Back Power and Culture in the Digital Age* (Fourth Estate: London, 2014).

Terrill, Robert, *The New Chinese Empire and What it Means for the United States* (Basic Books: New York, 2003).

Tharakan, Hormis, 'Kochi and Venice: A Tale of Two Cities,' *Biennale Leaf* (vol. 1, no. 1, 21 November 2012): 6.

Thompson, Don, *The Supermodel and the Brillo Box: Back Stories and Peculiar Economics from the World of Contemporary Art* (Palgrave Macmillan: New York, 2014).

Thoughtshop Foundation, 'A for Amitabh: Games and Tools for Empowerment,' TAKE (vol. 2, issue 7):22–25.

Tickner, Lisa, *Hornsey 1968: The Art School Revolution* (Frances Lincoln: London, 2008).

Tobin, Sarah, *The Syrian Refugee Crisis and Lessons from the Iraqi Refugee Experience* (Institute for Iraqi Studies: Boston, 2013).

Tribe, Mark and Reena Jana, 'Art in the age of digital distribution,' in Uta Grosenick (ed.), *New Media Art* (Taschen: Hong Kong, 2009): 6–25.

Trotsky, Leon, *The Revolution Betrayed: What is the Soviet Union and Where is it Going?* (Pathfinder: New York, 2007 [1937]).

Tsinghua University, *Academy of Arts & Design, Tsinghua University* (information brochure, nd).

Tsinghua University, *2011: Collection of Graduate Works* (Academy of Arts & Design, Tsinghua University, 2011).

UN Office for the Coordination of Humanitarian Affairs, *Restricting Space: The Planning Regime Applied by Israel in Area C of the West Bank* (OCHA, 2009).

Valiavicharska, Zhivka, 'Culture, Neoliberal Development, and the Future of Progressive Politics in Southeastern Europe,' in Jonathan Harris (ed.), *Globalization and Contemporary Art* (Wiley-Blackwell: Oxford, 2011): 496–509.

Vanderlinden, Barbara, and Elena Filipovic (eds.), *The Manifesta Decade: debates on contemporary art exhibitions and biennials in postwar Europe* (MIT Press: Cambridge, Mass, 2005).

Varoufakis, Yanis, *The Global Minataur: America, Europe and the Future of the Global Economy* (Zed Books: London, 2015).

Vasudev, Aruna and Wong Tuck-Cheong, 'The Conference,' *2010: Imagining Asia*: (Netpac in association with Goethe Institut, Max Mueller Bhavan: Delhi, 2010):43.

Veg, Sebastian, 'Legalistic and Utopian: Hong Kong's Umbrella Movement,' *New Left Review* 92 (March–April 2015): 55–73.

Veracini, Lorenzo, *Settler Colonialism: A Theoretical Overview* (Palgrave Macmillian: Basingstoke, 2010).

Videotage, *One World Exposition*, presented by Videotage at Hong Kong oneworldexpo 8 December 2011–8 January 2012.

Wang Chaohua, 'The Party and its Success Story,' *New Left Review* 91 (Jan–Feb 2015): 5–37.

Weibel, Peter, and Andrea Buddensieg (eds.), *Contemporary Art and the Museum: A Global Perspective* (Hatje Cantz/ZKM: Ostfildern, 2007).

Weizman, Eyal, *Hollow Land: Israel's Architecture of Occupation* (Verso: London, 2007).

Williams, Michael Hue, 'The auction houses are distorting our understanding of Chinese art,' *The Art Newspaper* (25 January 2008): 24.

Williams, Raymond, *The Long Revolution* (Parthian: Cardigan, 2011 [1961]).

Williams, Raymond, *Marxism and Literature* (Oxford University Press: Oxford, 1977).

Williams, Raymond, *Problems in Materialism and Culture* (Verso: London, 1980).

Williams, Raymond, *Culture* (Fontana: Glasgow, 1981).

Williams, Raymond, *The Politics of Modernism: Against the New Conformists* (Verso: London, 1989).

Williams, Patrick and Laura Chrisman (eds.), *Colonial Discourse and Post-Colonial Theory: A Reader* (Pearson: London, 1993).

Wong, Joshua, 'Scholars on the March,' *New Left Review* 92 (March–April 2015): 43–52.

Wu Guanzhong, 'Formalist Aesthetics in Painting' (1979), reprinted in Wu Hung (ed.), *Contemporary Chinese Art: Primary Documents* (MOMA: New York, 2010): 14–17.

Wu Hung, 'Imagining Asia: A Genealogical Analysis,' in Chiu and Genocchio (eds.), *Contemporary Art in Asia* (MIT Press: Cambridge MA, 2011):87–106.

Wu Hung (ed.), *Contemporary Chinese Art: Primary Documents* (MOMA: New York, 2010).

Xiaoyan, Guo, 'How to Self-Construct: The Primary Facts and Narration about Moving Image in China,' in Jinsuk Suh (ed.), *Moving On Asia* (Alt. Space Loop: Seoul, 2013):394–407.

Yau-Chung, Robert Ho, 'Nurturing Through the Arts,' in *Leap: The International Arts Magazine of Contemporary China* 23/5/2013–26/5/2013 (Art Basel Hong Kong special edition): 32–35.

Yeunho Kim Jang, 'Towards a Social Role for Korean Moving Image: A Proposal towards a Political and Aesthetic Korean Alternative Visual Culture,' in Jinsuk Suh (ed.), *Moving on Asia* (Alt. Space Loop: Seoul, 2013): 350–7.

You-tien Hsing, *The Great Urban Transformation: Politics of Land and Prosperity in China* (Oxford University Press: Oxford, 2016).

Yudice, George, *The Expediency of Culture: Uses of Culture in the Global Era* (Duke University Press: Durham SC, 2005).

Yueh, Linda, *China's Growth: The Making of an Economic Superpower* (Oxford University Press: Oxford, 2013).

Index

The Global Contemporary Art World, First Edition. Jonathan Harris.
© 2017 John Wiley & Sons, Inc. Published 2017 by John Wiley & Sons, Inc.

b

d

n

q

t